OFFENDER PROFILING SERIES: Vol II

PROFILING IN POLICY
AND PRACTICE

D0618580

OFFENDER PROFILING SERIES: Vol II
PROFILING IN POLICY AND PRACTICE

Edited by

DAVID CANTER and LAURENCE ALISON
Centre for Investigative Psychology
University of Liverpool

Ashgate

DARTMOUTH

Aldershot • Brookfield USA • Singapore • Sydney

Published by
Dartmouth Publishing Company Limited
Ashgate Publishing Limited
Gower House
Croft Road
Aldershot
Hants GU11 3HR
England

Ashgate Publishing Company
Old Post Road
Brookfield
Vermont 05036
USA

Ashgate Publishing Company
Suite 420
101 Cherry Street
Burlington, VT 05401-4405
USA

Ashgate website: http://www.ashgate.com

British Library Cataloguing in Publication Data
Profiling in policy and practice. - (Offender profiling series ; v. 2)
1.Criminal psychology 2.Psychology, Pathological
I.Canter, David, 1944- II.Alison, Laurence J.
364.3

Library of Congress Catalog Card Number: 98-74579

Reprinted 2005

ISBN 1 84014 779 2 (Hbk)
ISBN 1 84014 782 2 (Pbk)

Printed in Great Britain by Antony Rowe Ltd, Chippenham, Wiltshire

Contents

Series Preface

'Offender Profiling' has become part of public consciousness even though many people are not really sure what it is and the great majority of people have no idea at all of how it is done. This ignorance is just as prevalent in professional circles as amongst the lay public. Psychologists, psychiatrists, probation officers and social workers all have an interest in how their disciplines can contribute to police investigations, but few practitioners are aware of exactly what the possibilities for such contributions are. Others, such as police officers and lawyers, who seek advice from 'profilers' often also have only the vaguest ideas as to what 'profiling' consists of or what scientific principles it may be based on. The army of students who aspire to emulate the fictional activities of psychologists who solve crimes is yet another group who desperately need a systematic account of what 'offender profiling' is and what the real prospects for its development are.

The public fascination with the little understood activity of 'profiling' has meant that no fictional account of crime, whether it be heavy drama or black comedy, seems to be complete without at least one of the protagonists offering as a 'profile' their opinion on the characteristics of the perpetrator of the crime(s) around which the narrative is built. This popular interest combined with widespread ignorance has generated its own corpus of urban myths: such mythical 'profilers' produce uncannily accurate descriptions of unknown killers, solve cases that had baffled the police and seem to know before the criminal where he would strike next.

Sadly, like all myths not only do they only have a very loose connection with reality but they also distract attention away from a range of other significant and more intellectually challenging questions. These are the important questions that are inherent in the processes of criminal behaviour and its investigation. Such considerations include assessments of the quality and validity of the information on which police base their decisions and subsequent actions. This also involves assessing the possibilities for detecting deception. There also exist questions about the consistencies of a criminal's behaviour and what the crucial differences are between one offender and another.

Group processes of criminals raise other questions, which surprisingly are seldom touched upon by 'profilers' in fact or fiction. These ask about the form such groups take and the influence they have on the actions of the criminals, the role of leaders in crimes or the socio-cultural processes of which they are a part. There are also important issues about the implications and use of any answers that may emerge from scientific studies of crimes and their investigation

These and many other questions are raised by the mere possibility of psychology being of value to police investigations. To answer them it is essential to go beyond urban myth, fiction and the self-aggrandising autobiographies of self-professed 'experts'. A truly scientific stance is necessary that draws on a wide range of social and psychological disciplines

Many of these questions relate to others that are central to any psychological considerations of human actions, such as the nature of human memory, the processes of personality construction, group dynamics and interpersonal transactions. Therefore the systematic, scientific study of the issues relevant to 'offender profiling' are recognisably part of a burgeoning field of psychology and related disciplines. In an attempt to make this point and distinguish the steady accretion of knowledge in this area from the mythology, hyperbole and fiction of 'offender profiling' I labelled this field *Investigative Psychology*. This term seems to have taken root and is now evolving rapidly throughout the world.

Yet in the way that labels and terminology have a life of their own 'offender profiling' and its variants will just not lie down and die peacefully from a robust youth and dissolute old age. So we are stuck with it as a somewhat unhelpful shorthand and therefore the term has been kept for the title of this series in the hope that we may gradually re-define profiling as a systematic and scientific endeavour.

The books in this series provide a thorough introduction to and overview of the emerging field of Investigative Psychology. As such they provide a compendium of research and discussion that will place this important field firmly in the social sciences. Each volume takes a different focus on the field so that together they cover the full range of current activity that characterises this energetic area of research and practice.

David Canter
Series Editor

Acknowledgements

We are grateful to Julie Blackwell for the level of organisation, commitment and precision she has brought to pulling these volumes together and to Steve Deprez and Julia Fossi for their help in compiling the volumes.

1 Profiling in Policy and Practice

LAURENCE ALISON AND DAVID CANTER

The term 'profiler' has commonly been applied to the media hungry defintion of a sole individual responsible for solving an offence where others have failed. This chapter extends the meaning to any individual or self professed 'expert' who has attempted to explain the motivations of others and categorise certain details of their backgrounds. This may include clients within therapy, suspects within a police enquiry or assessments of the likely motives and qualities that lie behind different written texts. In expanding the term this chapter explores the extent to which profiling has been abused. Where the area has been redolent with poor policy and practice we attempt to outline an alternative to the scenario of the lonely expert contributing to the enquiry. This involves closer liaison with and education of the individuals relevant to the enquiry and of conceptual and empirically derivable hypotheses appropriate to developing systematic and replicable models of behaviour set within a social science framework.

Laurence John Alison is currently employed as a lecturer at the Centre for Investigative Psychology at the University of Liverpool. Dr Alison is developing models to explain the processes of manipulation, influence and deception that are features of criminal investigations. His research interests focus upon developing rhetorical perspectives in relation to the investigative process and he has presented many lectures both nationally and internationally to a range of academics and police officers on the problems associated with offender profiling. He is currently working on false allegations of sexual assault and false memory. He is affiliated with

*Offender Profiling Series: II - **Profiling in Policy and Practice***
Edited by D. Canter and L. Alison. © 1999 Ashgate Publishing, Aldershot. pp 1-19

The Psychologists at Law Group – a forensic service specialising in providing advice to the courts, legal professions, police service, charities and public bodies.

David Canter is Director of the Centre for Investigative Psychology at the University of Liverpool. He has published widely in Environmental and Investigative Psychology as well as many areas of Applied Social Psychology. His most recent books since his award winning *"Criminal Shadows"* have been *"Psychology in Action"* and with Laurence Alison *"Criminal Detection and the Psychology of Crime"*.

1 Profiling in Policy and Practice

LAURENCE ALISON AND DAVID CANTER[1]

The trouble also is that we as analysts apparently cannot resist the seductiveness of being directly helpful.

Brian Bird (1972, p. 286)

This volume is concerned with the variety of account giving processes within the domain of 'profiling'. This can be in relation to giving an account of the likely characteristics of an offender from an assessment of the crime scene, a therapist's assessment of the root of a client's disorders or the presentation of material in a court of law.

There seems to be reluctance for the media to relinquish fully the notion that psychologists can provide some special insight into the human mind. This is especially true when the actions being examined involve rape and murder. With a morbid fascination reminiscent of the attitudes to freak shows, there appears to be an inability to resist the desire to probe into the darker recesses of the more bizarre features of criminal behaviour. 'Experts' are commonly credited by the press with almost mythical powers of deduction if they appear to have contributed to police investigations and there appears to be a strong relationship between the presumed powers of the expert and the bizarre nature of the offence. Needless to say, scant attention is paid to the process by which these 'deductions' are made, or to the limitations of such offerings.

This volume in the Offender Profiling Series demonstrates that whilst psychologists may be relatively powerless to kerb the media's inappropriate image of the expert, exclusive focus on product over process makes for poor policy decisions and poor practice.

An obsession only with outcome rather than acquiring an understanding of the limitations and processes by which answers were derived is an understandably urgent concern for the police, courts, clients in therapy and for the psychologists themselves: offenders need to be

3

caught, jurors need to make clear decisions, clients want to understand the route of their problems and psychologists need to feel they have helped. However, in such cases these issues are rarely so black and white simply because the questions asked are often complicated and multi faceted.

Consider, for example, the construction of an offender profile. Conditions under which any single offence has been committed often have features relatively unique to that case. Moreover, information is often partial, potentially inaccurate and/or irrelevant and as discussed in Canter and Alison's (1999) 'Interviewing and Deception', errors early on in an enquiry can compound subsequent misguided interpretations. Thus, before reliable assumptions of an individual's background characteristics may be given, the purification of the information collection process must be prioritised. Neither statistically nor clinically produced profiles are immune from the ramifications of such 'muddy' information. Moreover, the interaction between expert and inquiry team is prone to social processes of influence that may degrade or misrepresent the information.

Offender profilers are never produced under closely controlled laboratory experiments. Experts consult with an enquiry team who have their own opinions and agendas. Thus the opinions given regarding the characteristics of the offender may be profoundly shaped by the nature of the interaction between police and psychologist. Even if such material is subject to empirical test subsequent to these interactions there is still room for error because of the nature of the material and because it has not been collected in an unsullied way purely for research purposes.

Similar processes of distortion may arise in a therapist's 'profile' of a client. Although there may be a desire to help the individual find a cause for their problems as soon as possible, during the course of such intense, close knit interactions there is a potential for subtle processes of influence and persuasion to occur. There exists the possibility for the therapist and client jointly to construct increasingly detailed and potentially artificial 'explanations' for depression, eating disorders or drug abuse. Having helped to construct these accounts, subsequent challenges to them may be met with very powerful resistance - particularly if this new found explanatory role satisfies the client's search for a causal explanation for their present state. Thus both in the therapist's interaction with the client and the profiler's interaction with the inquiry there is a strong likelihood that reciprocal persuasion distorts in the joint accounts constructed.

Our concern lies in exploring the fundamental problem for practitioners that arises in cases where there is uncertainty or lack of clarity in understanding the nature of the process by which opinions were given.

Ultimately, these opinions arise in the courtroom, where certainty has to be established beyond reasonable doubt. This volume therefore also serves as a guideline and warning for what might be expected in court if an opinion on the likely characteristics of an offender is offered. As the chapters in this volume illustrate many of the psychological issues that are finding their way into courtrooms concern highly contentious and controversial issues that psychologists simply cannot be certain of and in many of these cases the explanations for their opinions are less than satisfactory. These accounts include whether to accept the testimony of an individual who has recovered memories of sexual abuse, whether an offender profile might ever be used by the prosecution or the defence to implicate or exonerate a suspect and whether strategies of interviewing inappropriately influenced the discourse of a witness/suspect. In relation to these issues, the volume examines the nexus of contacts between psychologists and police officers, the clients under psychologists' care as well as the relationship that psychologists have with the courts when they must disclose the details of these interactions within the witness box as an expert witness.

The Absence of Psychology in Psychological Profiling

'Offender Profiling' is commonly associated with inferring characteristics of an offender from the actions at a crime scene. However, we employ the term more loosely in this volume to refer to those instances where characteristics of the offence and offender may be inferred from other sorts of information. For example, a psychologist may accuse a client's parents of abuse based on information that the client revealed in therapy; a murderous motive may be inferred from what otherwise might have been presumed a suicide in the case of an equivocal death, or inferences about the likely characteristics of an extortionist may be based upon a letter known to be made by the offender. In each case, the psychologist is reconstructing information about the likely sequence of events and characteristics of the person presumed to be involved in that offence from a wide array of information (accounts from a client, witness details surrounding a death, various linguistic features of extortion letters). Our concern throughout the volume lies within the legitimacy of making those inferences based on an examination of the processes by which they are made. As the other authors and we illustrate many of these processes, whilst presented with great conviction are, at the moment, highly contentious. They are often little more than, at best, subjective opinion, common sense or ignorance or at worst, deliberate deception.

Offender Profilers

Although, as stated, the advice that profilers give comes in many forms, the most popularly promulgated 'success' stories of these experts concerns their power to infer characteristics of offenders from an analysis of crime scene behaviours. As pointed out in chapter one, despite evidence to suggest that current profiling methods are little more than subjective opinion (albeit informed by experience), the notion of an expert profiler, who is able to succeed where the police have failed appears to be a myth that our culture is unable to shake off.

Many of the individuals who are considered the 'old masters' of profiling have produced accounts of their successes in the form of autobiographies. Whilst we do not deny their considerable experience of working on such cases, and the possibility that the sheer number of cases they have worked on may stand them in good stead to give an informed opinion, a careful examination of the content of their profiles reveals a severe lack in the accounts of any systematic procedures or any substantive, theoretical models of behaviour. There is no reference to any commonly accepted psychological principles - pathological or social. Why is there such an absence of any principles of psychology in these accounts? Of course, it is possible that individuals wish to avoid such dry academic references in order to appeal to popular audiences, but the promotion of such an intuitive and yet allegedly successful outlook on profiling is misleading both for students who wish to study the psychology of criminal behaviour, for law enforcement officers and for other professionals who may harbour unrealistic expectations. The gross misrepresentation of psychology portrayed in these accounts should be of particular concern for any professional psychologist. Such misrepresentation is an ethical concern. In the Codes of Conduct, Ethical

Principles and Guidelines of the British Psychological Society, the Code states in section 3.3 'Obtaining consent' that psychologists must:

refrain from making exaggerated, sensational and unjustifiable claims for the effectiveness of their methods and products, from advertising services or products in a way likely to encourage unrealistic expectations about the effectiveness of the services or products offered, or from misleading those to whom services are offered about the nature and likely consequences of any interventions to be undertaken.

It is rare for an individual who has published their memoir's to outline inaccurate and unsuccessful profiles. Are we to assume that these individuals are immune from error? That their atheoretical accounts that ignore any psychological model, paradigm, theory or approach to social science are a product of their own unique powers? Certainly the picture that they present presumes such infallibility. Their accounts invariably involve cases that the author can refer to in a favourable light and in protean fashion they can deftly cover up any inconsistencies by the interpretation of events and their own successes that they present. An example is the profiler who, on realising that he underestimated the age of the offender by over ten years re-interpreted this inaccuracy as a result of the offender's incarceration for 8 years. The profiler re-interpreted this inaccuracy by stating that the offender was socially stunted by ten years.

The style of such accounts are often engaging, almost evangelical in tone with references to the ways in which the profiler, wandering around the crime scene can proselytise hardened Detectives into the conviction in the expert's ability to 'get inside' the offender's mind. The profiler's experiential acumen elevates him above any 'normal' Detective and any approach that deviates from this 'gut feeling' is perceived as inferior and unlikely to bear fruit. For example, in Douglas' (1997) account of a murder in which he correctly insisted the offender must be white despite a Negroid hair being found at the crime scene, he replied when asked how he could account for his conviction, "I couldn't, but I was right to stand by it". These accounts bear some striking similarities to the advice psychics might give to an enquiry team. Both are based on nothing but feelings - systematic observations and procedures are discouraged in favour of instinct and intuition. By his own admission Douglas admits that a Detective stated, "We had a psychic in here a couple of weeks ago and she said just about the same things".

A closer examination of Douglas' profiles, with all the rhetoric surrounding the account stripped away, reveals startling simplicity to many of the conclusions. In the majority of cases what one might refer to as a 'basic' profile is laid down that includes elements very likely to represent the general characteristics of offenders convicted for serious crimes of violence - namely 'has problems with women', 'lives in area of the crime', 'has few close relationships' and 'has previous convictions'. Douglas occasionally makes assertions regarding characteristics that he feels are *unlikely* to be present. These 'accurate non occurrences' are often *low* base rate characteristics that are very likely *not* going to be a feature in such populations - i.e. no military experience. Thus Douglas thinks he is gaining additional points by telling us what is not going to appear as a characteristic. Added to this are characteristics that are very difficult or impossible to test directly: 'low frustration level', 'unable to accept defeat', 'unsure of himself'. Occasionally, seemingly startlingly specific and accurate assessments are added - for example that the offender would have a speech impediment. Of course, we are not told whether any other very specific characteristics given were ever incorrect.

Similar features are present in Britton's (1997) 'The Jigsaw Man'. Britton uses an additional device to help convince the audience of his profiling expertise - he presents points as separate though they are clearly related. For example in stating that an individual is sexually immature also implies he has few if any previous girlfriends. However, Britton is able to give the impression that these are two separate points merely by separating them by another point in a list of characteristics. It is perhaps more surprising, given that Britton has had some training in forensic psychology, that nowhere in Britton's account are there any references to psychological principles or any indication of a process by which he has come to his conclusions. Thus despite an advert for Britton's book that boasts, 'If you did it he'll get you' we are no clearer by the end of the book of *how* 'he will get you'.

Whether one advocates such intuitive personal opinion or not it is certainly the case that such types of advice have not progressed our knowledge of offender behaviour in over one hundred years. As Canter pointed out a number of years ago (Canter 1994) and we develop in chapter two such opinions have barely moved forward from the days of

Dr. Thomas Bond who in 1888 provided a profile of Jack the Ripper. Indeed, Dr. Bond's profile may be said to include more psychological references than current examples since he refers to diagnostic terms that were held at the time to be pathological variants of behaviour. This is at least an approach to a process of giving advice:

> *The character of the mutilations indicate that the man may be in a condition sexually that may be called Satyriasis.*
> (Fr. Donald Rumbelow, The Complete Jack the Ripper 1987, p. 140-141)

One must seriously question then whether psychologists wish to portray themselves as individuals with special knowledge, not borne of education or of learning but merely of flair and intuition. Perhaps some individuals have a feeling for issues within psychology and may be more creative in their generation of competing hypotheses. They may also have ability more readily to anticipate what might be at the heart of a problem. However, even if there are such gifted individuals should they be at liberty to ignore the parameters of the scientific framework within which they work? Flair alone is not sufficient when judgements are likely to influence serious decisions across an investigation and within a court of law. We have to ask whether we would prefer a poet or a scientist to represent us in court.

The second chapter therefore explores the issues associated with working within a scientific framework and the benefits that this can afford. We outline that investigative psychology is not a new discipline at all, or a model of offender behaviour, but that there is a wealth of psychological literature that can be drawn upon to aid in the contribution to the psychology of investigations. This may be drawn from social psychological principles, clinical models, and the psychology of organisational behaviour, decision-making and so on. The argument revolves around processes of best practice as aided by recourse to scientific principles of hypothesis generation, testing and deconstruction. Moreover, we highlight how too heavy a reliance on intuition and experience can encounter difficulties because of the frailties of human decision making. We comment on how endemic the myth of the expert is and how destructive this can be to an enquiry. Finally, chapter two notes how important the knowledge of ethical concerns is if an individual is to give advice to an investigative team. Chapter two is therefore a caveat to anyone wishing to construct a profile of an offender by crime scene analysis. This is not to dissuade liaisons between police and psychologists - indeed some of our closest colleagues are police officers. Rather our concern lies in challenging the reliance on bringing experts in at a stage when all else has failed.

The Research Framework and the Police Service

Hypothesis building may look 'academic' and not quite fitting into the police culture, yet it may prove to be the most parsimonious way of tackling complicated organised crime puzzles.

Petrus van Duyne (see Chapter Three - this volume)

Chapter three clearly illustrates the benefits of more professional relationships between psychologists and the police force. As van Duyne notes, police attitudes in the Netherlands are looking at alternative perspectives: "in daily police practise the psychologist or sociologist is kept at the back door, to be consulted when the 'men of action' have a problem for which they need a specialist... However in the Netherlands the attitude of the higher police officers is changing". Whilst he refers specifically to issues associated with organised crime there are clear benefits for other types of investigations. In particular Van Duyne refers to a number of specific strands of policing within which psychologists and police officers may work together: hypothesis construction, target profiling, recruitment and education and training. Van Duyne's more considered approach to these professional issues is highlighted within the terms of reference and systems by which he considers such procedures may be effectively dealt with. For example, his term for 'offender profiling' is encapsulated within the more generic term of hypothesis testing. Moreover, he is well aware of the need not to focus merely on individual characteristics of likely offenders but on what he refers to as the social or entrepreneurial landscape within which they are operating. Thus, rather than focusing upon intuition and gut feeling to give an opinion where police officers may be faltering, Van Duyne advocates employment to empower the investigative team themselves in working within a scientific framework.

In outlining a very different relationship between psychologist and police officer van Duyne's chapter points to a major gap in the research into police decision making and the organisational features of inquiry teams that may facilitate or impede the successful resolution of enquiries. With the fervour associated with offender profiling an important area of research has been left virtually untouched. Many of the issues are associated with the progression of the decisions made across the enquiry and are likely to gain from an outlook that incorporates knowledge from the domains of decision making and occupational psychology as well as more general issues associated with the social psychology of influence, persuasion and leadership. Van Duyne touches on many of these and highlights in particular the need for psychologists' expertise in psychological screening of applicants, of training and of assessing teams' interactions. As he points out these are not compartmentalised domains that the psychologist may occasionally 'chip' into. Instead, they are related processes in which the psychologist must develop a more general picture of the investigation rather than focusing solely on the more bizarre features of offence behaviour that police officers very rarely have to deal with. Chapter two therefore centres on issues associated with social scientists' perspectives and utilisation within the investigative framework.

Fielding, in chapter four pursues this line - with particular reference to investigative interviews. He highlights a number of problems for the social scientist in examining the qualities of police interviewing. These involve sacrifices of reliability for validity and vice versa. In other words, maintaining strict laboratory control over conditions through mock interviews removes many of the intense qualities of police interviews. On the other hand, exploring cases as they occur can prevent reliable assertions from being made. Fielding notes the strengths and weaknesses of a variety of approaches to such issues - from ethnographic studies to controlled replications. A fundamental concern in his chapter centres on limitations for social scientists. These include the limitations on the extent to which the social scientist can manipulate independent and dependent variables. Because of such restrictions conclusions are unlikely to be unequivocal. Thus a stiff resoluteness of opinion may be a warning sign that the expert has not truly examined the limitations of the material or considered very deeply the processes by which s/he came to her/his conclusions.

Because much of the information collected for the investigation of an offence is not collected for research purposes there are limits upon what can be ascertained from the material provided and the confidence with which any opinion can be given. An example would include an assessment of whether a confession was given voluntarily or not. As Fielding notes, it is exceptionally difficult to discriminate between voluntary and involuntary confessions not least because there are no criteria for establishing at what point an interview has become coercive or for establishing what constitutes 'voluntariness' (see also Sear and Williamson 1999). Therefore, as Fielding points out whilst the drive towards a consistent set of rules for all interviewing contexts is a virtuous aim, the nuances and subtleties of interviews make a totally inflexible set of specific guidelines all but impossible to adhere to.

There are many examples of this - especially in reference to interviews with children where the children themselves make it very difficult for interviewers to stick to entirely neutral interviewing strategies. However, this does not rule out the possibility that the interviewer may be promoting, encouraging or influencing the discourse of the child. These are simply features of human behaviour -influence is a natural product of interaction, but the point at which influence becomes coercion is less clear. However, to eschew the issue by reducing the interview to a totally non-directive dynamic is unrealistic. Researchers have encountered considerable difficulty in verbal conditioning because of the problems associated with maintaining a laboratory level of control with the participants in the study (Azrin 1961). That these problems exist is reason to explore the potential for influence and persuasion that occur as a product of interaction. As stated earlier, these social processes are also of crucial importance in pointing to the possibility for distortion in practitioners' opinions of likely characteristics of offenders. They may well be influenced by the investigating officers who are directly involved in the enquiry.

Profiling Processes in Assessing Clients

Therapists wield enormous power, whether or not they seek it. Imbalance in power rarely leads to compassionate behaviour.

Jeffrey Masson, p.298

Processes of social influence are likely to be of considerable concern within a therapeutic environment where individuals in therapy are potentially already vulnerable. As Aldridge-Morris' review in chapter five reveals the number of false allegations of child sexual abuse shows how far some processes of persuasion may go. He discusses the claims of Smith and Pazder (1980) and Bass and Davies (1988) that cases of ritual serial sexual abuse are frequent occurrences, that memories of such abuse are repressed, only to be elicited under therapy. He takes issue with these claims and the appalling consequences that the people suspected of such atrocities endure. Despite a complete lack of any evidence to support the allegations against them, individuals have been incarcerated, never to be allowed to see their children again. Thus despite the wealth of evidence to support the notion that memory is a reconstruction open to processes of influence and the lack of scientific support for the process of repression, it has still been argued that cases of serial sexual satanic abuse are not the result of a gradual re-shaping of memory under therapy but the sudden recall of distant, repressed accounts of abuse.

As the chapters in this volume reveal, some of the accounts that are constructed in therapists' consulting rooms share some similarities to processes of offender profiling. Where therapists are ignorant of the controversies surrounding issues such as repression, influence and the reconstruction of memory they may also ignore the possibilities that their patients may come to create increasingly artificial accounts of abuse to legitimise their current problems. There may be many routes that lead to artificial memories of abuse. The therapist may elicit them, the client may promote them and manipulate the therapist into believing them, or both may be instrumental in feeding off of each other. It should also be pointed out that such accounts are not always a product of therapeutic intervention - in a small proportion of such cases individuals claiming bizarre accounts of abuse have never been in therapy (Gudjonsson 1997). It is clear then that false memory 'syndrome' is not a unitary phenomena or diagnostic illness that an individual catches like influenza, but rather a multivariate social process.

As with profilers, therapists need to be aware of two related issues. The first is a clear and systematic rationale for their particular approach to therapy - how it operates, what features of the client it operates upon and what are the likely outcomes of therapeutic intervention. Obviously, within a scientific framework, each of these issues requires empirical support and a theoretical frame of reference. The second issue relates to the likely problems that therapeutic intervention may present. These, as we have suggested most likely relate to the processes of imaginative reconstruction and the social processes of influence. As the practitioner develops a well-rounded picture of the likely problems s/he may catch them early and take steps to avoid them. An obvious problem with many therapies is that not only is it unclear whether they work it is unclear *how* they work. Assumptions about an individual in therapy based on personal opinion; intuition, gut feeling and lack of empirical support can be highly destructive. This is not to suggest that any therapy that is based on an empirically supported footing or that has proven merits will never result in failure. Just as a knowledge of anatomy and of the appropriate surgical interventions in, for example, hip replacement has a history of scientific research there is no guarantee that any given operation will be successful. But, at least in such cases we have a greater level of assurance of how the procedure works, what the likelihood of success is and what the results of a bad outcome are likely to be. An understanding of the anatomy of behaviour is a prerequisite for dealing with it in a therapeutic context and where there is uncertainty there should be considerable effort not present assumptions as if they were facts.

Assumptions are equally dangerous when it comes to assessments of suspicious deaths. The investigation of equivocal deaths, as Canter points out in chapter six is similarly fraught with problems associated with lack of theory, too heavy a reliance on techniques that are merely at an embryonic stage of development and over exaggerated claims of assurance in establishing whether an individual committed suicide or not. Canter points out his own difficulties in making an assessment of a case (and in particular the examination of a questionable suicide note) in which there was precious little systematic research to draw upon. As Gregory (see Canter and Alison 1999) points out many of the early studies of suicide notes were atheoretical and based solely on counting frequencies of various features of genuine vs. artificial suicide notes. Despite Gregory's contribution to developing this area he too is cautious of over interpretation and too ready a willingness to rely on the sketches of early studies.

Each of these areas presents the practitioner with some considerations that are relevant generally and others that are peculiar to their particular field of expertise. In the case of a therapist there are professional and ethical obligations to the client but in a psychological autopsy who is the main recipient of the psychologist's expertise? The deceased? The deceased's family? Issues of consent, duty of care, accountability and confidentiality all become considerably more problematic in such cases. The same is true of offender profiling. For example there is nothing in the BPS guidelines to prevent a profiler from directly implicating a particular suspect in a murder inquiry. Because the suspect is not a client of the psychologist there is no duty of care. Similarly, if the suspect is unaware of being assessed by the psychologist there is no clause to prevent the psychologist from indulging in a variety of forms of deception and manipulation. Furthermore, in such cases there is no requirement to debrief the suspect. Therefore, potentially, a psychologist could set up conditions under which he could influence an individual's behaviour to certain pre-defined criteria and could profoundly effect the suspect emotionally, but would be unlikely to debrief the suspect. Similarly a profiler could implicate an individual with a particular offence through totally unreliable and untested methods with little in the way of recompense for the suspect after the error was made clear. Because such an individual is not a willing participant in the study there are no restrictions on how s/he may be dealt with.

We have tried to outline some possibilities for developing guidelines specifically for psychologists in the second chapter of this volume but further debate would be most welcome - particularly from the members of the British Psychological Society. Clearly, the free reign that psychologists have at the moment to indulge in profiling activities that are devoid of any ethical or professional parameters is of considerable concern. Whilst the British Home Office is drawing up accreditation lists of 'profilers' there exists no agreement generally of what the relevant psychological expertise is in relation to making such judgements and what the main criteria ought to be. What the appropriate balance of knowledge, skills and professional ethical constraints ought to be has never been specified. Even more importantly is the absence of any debate over the processes by which advice is given. Most attention is given to outcome and the number of accurate 'hits' in a profile. There is little consideration of the problems associated with measuring 'profiling accuracy'. It is perhaps a misguided assumption that such comparisons can be made as Ormerod points out in the final chapter.

Profiling in Court

> *The notion that a psychological profile is in any circumstances admissible in proof of identity is to my mind redolent with considerable danger.*
> Mr Justice Ognall Fr. Judges summing up, Regina v Stagg

Many of the controversies over process, policy and practise do not emerge until they become part of the legal process. When they are first considered in the courtroom much of the damage has already been done. Although the use of offender profiling in court is thankfully rare, there are many examples where 'profilers' have indicated who may be likely offenders or have provided guidelines that has helped implicate innocent individuals. Many of the techniques promoted by these 'profilers' are atheoretical, relatively untested and therefore highly controversial. Although not conventionally considered 'profilers' many of these issues extend to the use of expert witnesses giving opinions on the likely characteristics or origins of written texts. Aked et al, for example, in chapter seven, note that many of the judgements made upon linguistic material are devoid of theory yet they have been used to suggest that contemporaneous notes taken by police officers were meddled with by an inquiry team, that particular individuals were responsible for extortion letters or abusive and that written confessions were fabricated by police officers. However, it is not even certain if individuals consistently differ from each other in the style of their speech or writing let alone why they might do so. Many of the underlying 'principles' of linguistic variation are therefore based upon assumption rather than substantive theory or empirical proof. In chapter seven Aked et al criticise one of the most popularly promoted devices for discriminating between individual techniques - Morton's "cusum analysis". They assert that the use of such techniques are redolent with danger because of the lack of empirical proof and the problems associated with the process employed to carry out the analysis. The advocating of linguistic analysis to discriminate authorship has its critics within the literary field and equally vociferous challenges must be considered where authorship identification is promoted in the courts.

In the penultimate chapter Cox illustrates the growth in the possibilities for expert influence on legal proceedings. She describes how psychologists, who are increasingly being called in as expert witnesses, are involved at the utilisation stage of investigative information processing. Reassuringly, she notes that whilst traditionally experience has been seen as paramount, there is an expansion of recognition of the value of scientific knowledge and expertise. This can be seen in the attempts to professionalise registers of experts (for example the Academy of expert witnesses, The Institute of expert witnesses, the UK Register of Expert Witnesses).

Whilst we welcome such systems, the employment of psychologists within the legal profession (and for that matter within investigations as a whole) is still fraught with many very serious problems. Cox points out that these experts are, "visitors to another system which they did not devise, do not fully understand and in which they can exercise limited power". The same is certainly true within the context of the investigative process. There are many cases where failed enquiries have not simply been the blundering of the investigative team, but rather are helped along in compounding errors by the employment of an 'expert'. These individuals often admit that they are unfamiliar with the process, demands and level of rigour required to allow the advice given to stand up in court. In such cases, the actual refining and filtering process of the collection of information is made more muddy by the involvement of an 'expert' - not less so. In the concluding chapter by Ormerod this point is driven home in reference to his comments regarding *R v Stagg*. Ormerod's chapter focuses on the number of legal hurdles that any psychologist will have to overcome if s/he is called in to act as an expert profiler in a court of law. Ormerod warns that, following the negative judicial attitude towards the Stagg case, 'profilers' should be prepared as far as possible for any attempts to rely on their work in court. In other words, profilers must exercise considerable caution in generating and testing their hypotheses because the less professional inquiry teams may be relying heavily on 'profiling' evidence in lieu of more robust evidential material. Because of the many legal obstacles that present themselves to the profiler, opinions given must be of considerable empirical resilience to counter these criticisms in court.

Although Ormerod's chapter is most welcome in highlighting these concerns it reflects a sorry state for those psychologists who should have been aware of the limits of their contributions. We would go further and note that more detailed concern with the processes by which such advice is given and greater attention to the methods by which opinions are realised could have avoided such courtroom embarrassments. A fundamental question that psychologists must ask themselves is to what extent do they wish to make contributions based on their personal opinion to any given inquiry? Though the temptation to help may be seductive, the ramifications of emotional involvement are potentially very destructive, both for the recipients of the advice and for the psychologist him/herself. Indeed, psychologists have not explored how contributing to enquiries can affect practitioners in terms of the perceived financial, ego fulfilling and emotional pay offs. Again, this problem arose in the Stagg case, where the undercover officer recently underwent considerable psychological stress and left the force.

Given the increasing numbers of students who apply for courses in criminal psychology, forensic behavioural psychology and investigative psychology it must be the case that the area is becoming increasingly enticing. Resisting the temptation to potentially 'make' a difference when there is insufficient evidence to help support the processes that are being employed may be extremely difficult and there may well be a genuine desire to help. Outlining more carefully the parameters within which psychologists must work to help avoid over involvement, bias and distortions is one way to help avoid subsequent profiling disasters. However, each individual must make the decision as to which camp they belong to - those that accept the more prosaic approach of science or those that wish to take greater risks by relying on intuition. As Aldridge-Morris notes many of the concerns in this area exist as a function of the continuing debate between what McHugh (1994) defines as the empiricists vs. the romanticists. The latter rely on intuition and the slippery notion of 'expertise' rather than a cumulative wealth of knowledge and techniques for reducing bias. The empiricist is often seen as the frosty killjoy, waiting to spoil the more engaging performance of the romantic - who has the 'real heart' of the case.

Certainly science requires a greater degree of self-discipline. However, even with scientific developments caution must be observed - whilst aspects of the scientific framework may make for progress even there its effectiveness should be not overestimated. An analogy drawn from Greek mythology serves to illustrate the point: Although Daedalus was able to craft wings made from wood, wax and feathers to fly from Crete to Italy, the fall of his son Icarus was a result of ignorance as to the limitations of his Father's craftsmanship. Icarus' desire to fly ever higher and his subsequent fall is a useful allegory of how newer generations of 'profilers' may misunderstand the craft of their progenitors and court disaster by flying to near the legal sun.

References

Bass, E. and Davies L. (1988). *The Courage to Heal: A Guide for the Women Survivors of Child Sexual Abuse.* New York: Harper & Row.

Bird, B. (1972). Notes on Transference: Universal Phenomenon and Hardest Part of Analysis. *Journal of the Amercian Psychoanalytic Association,* 20, 267-301.

BPS (1991). *Codes of Conduct, Ethical Principles and Guideline.* Leicester: BPS.

Canter, D.V. (1994). *Criminal Shadows.* London: Harper Collins.

Canter, D.V. and Alison, L.J. (1999). *Interviewing and Deception.* Aldershot: Dartmouth.

Britton, P. (1997). The Jigsaw Man. London: Bantam Press.

Douglas, J. and Olshaker, M. (1997). *Mindhunter: Inside the FBI Elite Serial Crime Unit.* London: Mandarin Paperbacks.

Gregory, A. (1999). The Decision to Die: The Psychology of the Suicide Note. in D.V.Canter and L.J.Alison (eds) *Interviewing and deception.* Aldershot: Dartmouth.

Gudjonnson, G. (1997). Accusations by adults of childhood sexual abuse: a survey of the members of the British false Memory Society (BFMS) *Applied Cognitive Psychology,* 11, 3-18.

McHugh, P.R. (1994). Psychotherapy Awry. *The American Scholar,* 63, 17-30.

Rumbelow, D. (1987). *The Complete Jack the Ripper.* London: Star Books.

Sear, L. and Williamson, T. (1999). British and American Interrogation Strategies. in D.V. Canter and L.J. Alison (eds) *Interviewing and Deception.* Aldershot: Dartmouth.

Smith, M. and Pazder, L. (1980). *Michelle Remembers.* New York: Congdon and Lattes.

---

[1] The authors are grateful to Claire Brennan for all her work on the assessments of Paul Britton's 'The Jigsaw Man' and John Douglas' 'Mindhunter'.

2 Professional, Legal and Ethical Issues in Offender Profiling

LAURENCE ALISON AND DAVID CANTER

This chapter addresses a neglected area of offender profiling, namely ethical and professional issues. Through a consideration of the general standards of practice deemed appropriate by the British Psychological Society we outline how many profiling standards fall short of these recommendations. In doing so we highlight the importance of processes over outcome and note how endemic unprofessional and unethical practices are maintained by the failing to consider appropriate procedures. We do not promote this as the definitive set of regulations but rather wish to open up debate about standards where, previously, such discussion has been entirely absent.

Laurence John Alison is currently employed as a lecturer at the Centre for Investigative Psychology at the University of Liverpool. Dr Alison is developing models to explain the processes of manipulation, influence and deception that are features of criminal investigations. His research interests focus upon developing rhetorical perspectives in relation to the investigative process and he has presented many lectures both nationally and internationally to a range of academics and police officers on the problems associated with offender profiling. He is currently working on false allegations of sexual assault and false memory. He is affiliated with The Psychologists at Law Group - a forensic service specialising in providing advice to the courts, legal professions, police service, charities and public bodies.

Offender Profiling Series: II - Profiling in Policy and Practice
Edited by D. Canter and L. Alison. © 1999 Ashgate Publishing, Aldershot. pp 21-54

David Canter is Director of the Centre for Investigative Psychology at the University of Liverpool. He has published widely in Environmental and Investigative Psychology as well as many areas of Applied Social Psychology. His most recent books since his award winning *"Criminal Shadows"* have been *"Psychology in Action"* and with Laurence Alison *"Criminal Detection and the Psychology of Crime"*.

2 Professional, Legal and Ethical Issues in Offender Profiling

LAURENCE ALISON AND DAVID CANTER

"I am afraid that this behaviour betrays not merely an excess of zeal but a substantial attempt to incriminate a suspect by positive and deceptive conduct of the grossest kind."

The Honourable Mr Justice Ognall from Regina v Colin Stagg

Although the data is not clear there is some evidence that contributions from psychologists to police investigations have been steadily increasing (Copson 1995). Commonly, this has been for the defence (Haward 1985) but more recently psychology has been used to provide advice to investigators by drawing up 'psychological profiles' of offenders in order to narrow the parameters of a suspect search (Canter 1989, Canter and Alison 1997). Despite concerns about the use of experts outside the police to guide enquiries that date back to the 1920s' Royal Commission reports, it has only been recently, and in a select few fields, that ethical and professional guidelines for these activities have been considered by psychologists.

For example, contributions have been made to interviewing strategies for many years from the study of memory recall (Fisher and Geiselman 1987); deception (Ekman 1991, Kohnken 1987) and the psychology of suggestibility (Gudjonsson 1992) but Shepherd (1991) is one of the few people to propose ethical guidelines. In the relatively new area of 'offender profiling', psychologists have remained silent.

The purpose of this chapter is to break that silence by outlining some of the professional, legal and ethical issues associated with profiling and, in particular, the implications of expert opinion in investigations and in the courtroom.

Offender Profiling and Psychology

Origins of Profiling

> *Let me have men about me that are fat; Sleek headed men and such as sleep o'*
> *nights; Yond Cassius has a lean and hungry look; He thinks too much: such*
> *men are dangerous.*
>
> Shakespeare (from Julius Caesar)

Associating idiosyncratic features with particular forms of behaviour has been a common theme throughout history and literature. Whilst the FBI have staked a claim to the genesis of 'offender profiling', the notion of inferring offender characteristics from actions has its origins as far back as Biblical references (Canter and Alison 1997).

For many years, a variety of different sorts of people, with many different types of experience to draw upon, have always been prepared to give advice to the police about the type of person who has committed an unsolved crime. Over one hundred year ago, for example, Dr Thomas Bond described the characteristics of 'Jack the Ripper' by using his clinical experience to make inferences from the ways in which the Ripper's victims had been killed. During World War II, William Langer, a psychiatrist, was commissioned by the United States Office of Strategic Services to provide a profile of Adolf Hitler. Langer was correct about Hitler's determination to fight to the end, his worsening mental condition and, ultimately, his suicide.

The technique rose to prominence after James A. Brussel's profile of the 'Mad Bomber of New York' and in particular during the 1960s and 1970s with the increasing trend in serial killing which led to the development of a 'profiling' unit at the FBI Academy at Quantico in Virginia who defined the process of profiling as one of:

> *Identifying the gross psychological characteristics of an individual based*
> *upon an analysis of the crimes he or she committed and providing a general*
> *description of that person.*
>
> Ressler, Burgess and Depue 1985

Since the FBI gave publicity to profiling a number of people around the world have come forward to offer opinions based on their own personal experience, typically of offenders in therapy. The claims of these individuals have often been little more than anecdotal accounts, on par with the claims of psychics and astrologers (although not usually so clearly based on any specific process!). There have been, and still are, a variety of people and a variety of methods employed to give advice to investigations. This situation is likely to remain so long as there are people prepared to give advice and there are investigators who are prepared to listen.

Approaches to Profiling

I knew how this killer functioned; I knew what drove him, because I had seen the same impulse in other people I'd interviewed and treated over the years.
Paul Britton (from 'Inside the mind of Rachel's killer - *The Mail on Sunday,* December 1, 1996)

Consider one example of the need for research: the seemingly obvious conclusion that Duffy was out of a job because he attacked during working hours. A general analysis of solved cases to see if offenders with jobs tend to attack at different times from those without would be one step in testing the robustness of even such an 'obvious' inference. That type of test is the cornerstone of turning profiling into a science.
David Canter (p. 90, from 'Criminal Shadows' 1994)

In terms of processes of generating profiles, the procedure of Offender Profiling has taken on two rather different meanings. One is as the presentation of the personal opinion of an individual who has some experience of criminals through interviewing them as part of his or her professional activity. The second is as the development of the area of applied, scientific psychology known as 'Investigative Psychology'.

It has only been in the last few years that any attempts have been made to set up a structured, systematic approach directly to explore psychological contributions to the investigation of crime. Even those adopting the clinical approach have recently come to the conclusion that a systematic framework is important for contributing to enquiries (Britton 1997) though for many years this has not been the case. Indeed, the FBI conceded in relation to their own work that:

...At present there have been no systematic efforts to validate these profile derived classifications.

Ressler, Douglas, Burgess and Burgess (1993)

However, David Canter has coined the term 'Investigative Psychology' to summarise a growing discipline that examines broadly three areas - (i) criminal behaviour, (ii) information and evidence and (iii) investigative decision making (Canter and Alison, 1997). These areas are seen as closely intertwined components of the investigative process. However, he and his colleagues at the University of Liverpool are well aware that such a discipline must draw upon established principles and the methods that have been the backbone of scientific research in the development of psychological understanding of human behaviour in other areas. In this respect Investigative Psychology is not a new discipline at all but rather a term that encapsulates and focuses upon those areas of psychological research that connect directly with processes in investigations. Investigative psychology is not a new approach or an 'angle' on examining criminal behaviour but rather a term that encapsulates a wide range of procedures centring around a scientific framework.

In a recent edited review of psychological examinations of aspects of investigation Canter and Alison (1997) have made this clear by drawing upon a number of texts of historical scientific interest - many of which illustrate that the process of inferring general characteristics of offenders is not new. For example, Bowlby (1949) compared the characteristics of 44 serious juvenile offenders with a group referred to a Child Guidance Clinic who did not steal. He established that children given less affection at an early age were significantly more delinquent than the control group, were more likely to have mentally disordered parents or were separated from their parents or they had parents that openly displayed their hostility. Burt, in the same year, provided similar explanations of delinquency:

Judged by the coefficients, the following proves to be the order of importance of the various conditions we have reviewed:
(1) Defective discipline (2) specific instinct (3) general emotional instability (4) morbid emotional conditions, mild rather than grave, generating or generated by so called complexes (5) a family history of vice or crime (6) intellectual disabilities such as backwardness or dullness (7) detrimental interests such as passion for adventure...

These conclusions by Burt and Bowlby could be used as 'profiles' of the typical delinquents of their day and could certainly have been used to focus a police enquiry.

The common ground between the two pieces of research was that they were attempts to set conclusions and processes of investigation within the context of a scientific approach. The defining components of such a discipline involve the making of observations (empirical/factual component) and the systematic attempt to explain these facts (theoretical component). Early on in the observation phase of a given domain, hypotheses are necessarily quite general. With increasing knowledge of the area such hypotheses can be developed and refined. Hypotheses are devices used by scientists to force between selections in the hope of generating increasingly precise explanations for behaviour - those that survive the rigours of scientific debate become 'laws' - those that are rejected on the basis of discoveries are abandoned.

According to Hull (1943) the core of the scientific method is the generation of a theory to help explain a given area of observable interest:

A theory is a systematic deductive derivation of the secondary principles of observable phenomena from a relatively small number of primary principles or postulates, much as the secondary principles or theorems of geometry are all ultimately derived as a logical hierarchy from a few original definitions and primary principles called axioms. In science an observed event is said to be explained when the proposition expressing it has been logically derived from a set of definitions and postulates coupled with certain observed conditions antecedent to the event. This, in brief is the nature of scientific theory.

C. L. Hull (1943)

Thus the starting point for the scientific method is a definition of the given domain of interest followed by a theoretical stance on explaining the phenomenon and finally the empirical testing of this theoretical standpoint.

Curiously, offender profiling has developed the tendency for these principles to be ignored in favour of quick answers based on experience rather than any systematic cumulative study. In part, this may have been influenced by expectations based on unrealistic, fictional media portrayals (Gerbner, Gross, Morgan and Signorielli 1994). If a senior investigator has such an unrealistic perspective s/he may ask for advice from a psychologist that cannot be scientifically provided and is only speculative opinion. At the moment, there is no professional qualification of 'offender profiler'. As stated, there are different approaches used by a variety of different individuals. Outlined below are a number of concerns related to this lack of formalisation of 'advice giving' and in particular a number of concerns in relation to the lack of a systematic scientific procedure. The general tenet, then, is that profiling as an art form or 'craft' is not ethically or professionally acceptable.

Training and Credentials in Offender Profiling

It would be intriguing to know why demands made upon occupational and clinical psychologists in terms of specific training in these areas are not similarly applied to individuals giving a consultancy service as an offender profiler to police investigations - an area in which there has been hardly any special training. It is doubtful that a senior officer would neglect to examine the credentials and training of a financial advisor and yet it does not appear to be the case that similar considerations are given to the background and training of an individual who claims to have special expertise in offender profiling. By definition there cannot have been any special consideration because, as stated, there *is* very little training in offender profiling.

The Crime Faculty based at the police staff training college has drawn up a list of people who may act as 'profilers' to police investigations. But that list was not based on any professionally agreed criteria, but on police assessment of the self-reports of people who wished to be on the list.

Whilst the FBI had a behavioural science unit the qualifications it gave were provided as credits to the local university. People who completed a course of study at Quantico were still required to keep in touch with the 'masters' at the BSU until it was felt they had amassed enough experience to go it alone. Thus, despite the possibility that such individuals may have developed experiential skills as profilers, with the retirement of these masters it is unclear how future generations can gain recognised accreditation.

Similarly, although The Investigative Psychology Unit at Liverpool University runs a variety of courses in psychological contributions to police investigations, including a one year MSc course and PhD related training in specific areas of research including homicide, arson and rape, the focus on profiling is minimal and is seen as a small part of a much broader perspective on understanding, exploring, explaining and aiding police enquiries. In other words the course does not advocate the use of or seek to 'produce' profilers. In fact, 'profiling' is seen as a somewhat redundant area of activity that is more of a media promoted anachronism than a developing field. More fundamental concerns such as systematising information in a format that can be used as data, in developing prioritisation systems, in aiding police interviewing and in examining detective decision making are seen as priorities. Thus profiling plays a relatively minor role in the academic syllabus.

The Frailties of Human Thinking

Without recourse to a cumulative systematic research based approach, inferences made on the basis of experience and opinion are subject to a number of distortions, biases and shortcomings that are associated with the frailties of human decision making.

The phenomenon known as 'hindsight bias' (Fischhoff 1975) is a particularly apposite example - where an individual underestimates how much they have learned, claiming that they knew all along the outcome of a situation. For example, Wiseman, West and Stemman (1996) established that where psychics had contributed to police enquiries the psychics and the police they advised were only likely to remember those aspects of the case they were correct about and forgot a considerable number of assertions that were totally incorrect. Similarly, Rowe (1993) noted the fact that vague predictions were later made to fit the facts of the case. If psychics are able to convince themselves and police officers that they made successful contributions (as Wiseman et al 1996 show) then similar processes may lead to apparently convincing contributions from 'expert' profilers.

Canter (1994) takes this comparison head on:

> *For some detectives the idea of approaching a psychologist for help hardly*
> *differs from approaching a psychic or astrologer. It might work so where's the*
> *harm in trying? To my mind, the harm comes if there is no accumulation of*
> *tested and proven logic.*
>
> From 'Criminal Shadows' (p. 79)

Thus the approach does not rely on intuition or experience. 'Success' is not measured on the basis of how many 'correct hits' have apparently been made but rather on developing, in accordance with the scientific process, appropriate strategies for researching criminal actions and the characteristics associated with those actions. Concern lies within the slow, steady accumulation of knowledge based on the foundations of psychology and the scientific process. It is to the professional, legal and ethical considerations associated with this approach that we now turn.

Professional Issues

A psychological approach to aiding criminal investigations represents an example of a scientific mode of thinking set against and tested by a variety of statistical procedures. Such a mode of thinking involves the testing of hypotheses where evidence comes from scientific observation.

As with all modes of thinking (such as diagnosis, insight, and reflection) good thinking is represented by a thorough search for alternatives without favouring what one already has in mind. Poor thinking involves missing something in the search and/or seeking evidence that prevents the scientist from choosing between alternatives.

Avoiding Bias

A powerful argument for relying heavily on the scientific mode of thinking is to counter the frailties of poor thinking. For example, explorations of accuracy of probability judgements show that there is a normal human tendency to underestimate high frequencies and overestimate very low ones. This inappropriate heuristic could be counteracted through statistical observations but is potentially dangerous if a profiler is relying on experience to compare similar cases. Moreover, if bound by normal human reasoning the profiler is likely to be overconfident in his predictions because as Fischhoff, Slovic and Lichtenstein (1977) have suggested it is not usual for people to have a clear perception of what probability means. For example whilst degrees of certainty are often used in everyday language they are rarely expressed numerically. Employing statistical procedures can help to prevent such errors. Thus when a person offers the opinion that there is a high probability that the offender is white it may be assumed by many police officers that the offender must be white, although the statistical probability may be only 65%.

For example, in reference to the profile in the Wimbeldon Common enquiry the comment by Britton that the probability of the offender having particular characteristics was 'vanishingly' rare is an indication of a confused view of the probabilities involved - particularly given that in reference to the features of the profile that Britton mentions, some studies indicate the alleged characteristics are prevalent in at least 10% of the population (Comfort 1987, Leitenberg and Henning 1995; Alison and Lee 1999).

Inappropriate Heuristics

As well as problems associated with estimating probabilities, it is part of human nature to use inappropriate heuristics in decision making. Tversky and Kahneman (1982) have highlighted a number of these.

Perhaps the most relevant to this area is the availability heuristic (Tversky and Kahneman 1973) where the individual makes judgements on a probability by thinking of examples that are easily accessible to memory whilst less salient counter examples are forgotten. Individuals are more likely to remember their own point of view more vividly thus resulting in a bias in the recall of information. Ross and Silcoly (1979) for example established that in asking husbands and wives their share of responsibilities they were only likely to be able to recall their own share rather than that of their partner - they were also more likely to remember instances when they had shirked their responsibility than similar instances when their partner had done so. Thus a profiler may remember more clearly offenders that had a significant impact on him than those, that for whatever multitude of reasons, are not so accessible to memory.

Anchoring and Adjustment

Further biases include anchoring and adjustment (Tversky and Kahneman 1974) where individuals will base a decision on what they have already been told - even if what they have been told is irrelevant to making an accurate assessment. For example, simply spinning a wheel with probabilities ranging from 1-100% will result in a probabilistic prediction being biased by the position the arrow lands on. So, for example, if asked the probability of rain, individuals will be influenced in their decision by a random probabilistic guess - i.e. given a prior random probability of 95% as opposed to 20% will result in the individual making a higher prediction of rain. In simple terms we tend to be biased by our 'starting point' beliefs - even if they are irrelevant to the case at hand. So if investigators mention a possible culprit to the profiler this may bias his approach to the case even if the suspect is later excluded from the investigations.

The frequently reported police assumption that a suspect is lying is also a good illustration of the anchor belief of the person being a suspect having a biasing influence.

Hypothesis Testing

Search inference processes in hypothesis testing are also prone to these type of problems. The simplest form of hypothesis testing is to imagine some result that would be definitely obtained if the hypothesis is true and then look for that result. An obvious danger with this is that there may be alternative explanations, which have not been considered. A second danger is that a hypothesis will be falsely rejected because of poor experimentation. The tendency to look for confirmation of a hypothesis is demonstrated by Wason's (1960) experiment of asking subjects to find the rule behind the sequence 2, 4, 6. If individuals first 'rule' to test this sequence was, "increase the digits by two" then they would not search for an alternative hypothesis - such as the more parsimonious alternative, "increase the number" - i.e. 2, 4, 6, 9, 167, 2204. This is an elegant example of confirmation bias - the tendency to look for information to support a theory rather than discount it. This process can explain a number of miscarriages of justice. Having decided who was guilty evidence was sought to support that and contradictory evidence was re-interpreted.

Illusory Correlation

Another curious feature of human thinking is to find associations between variables where there are none. Smedslund (1963) for example presented nurses with a random correlation between a symptom and disease. Despite no association 85% of nurses said there was a relationship. This is probably because individuals are more likely to examine present/present cells of a contingency table than absent / present and absent / absent cells. In this case the nurses only examined cases where the disease and the symptoms were present. Illusory correlation is also influenced by prior beliefs. For example, Chapman (1967) questioned why clinicians used 'Draw-a-person' tests even though they proved diagnostically useless. The reason it seemed was that the clinicians had already convinced them that there must be some evidence of usefulness in the test despite evidence proving otherwise. The clinicians were also likely to have only been attending to cases where results did tie in with characteristics. This effect of attention bias can be increased by prior belief - when prior belief is present one tends to focus on evidence that supports it and ignore evidence against it.

Illusory correlation and attention bias distort perceptions of the evidence available. It appears to be human nature to think that evidence weighs more heavily on the side of beliefs we already hold than it actually does.

In a criminal investigation many processes, including what the media give emphasis to may feed such illusory correlations. So it may be assumed that many violent offenders are insane, even though people diagnosed as mentally ill are no more likely to commit violent crimes than anyone else. A profiler brought in because he has treated mentally ill people may be especially prone to such an illusion, supported by an attention bias.

Irrelevant Information and Belief Persistence

Other seemingly innocuous and irrelevant factors can also effect judgements. An example would include the 'ordering effect' - i.e. when the order in which information is gained is not relevant the order should not be considered as significant. An example of a primacy ordering effect would be Asch's (1946) use of reordering adjectives to describe a person. When the first adjective used to describe a person was negative (for example 'mean') this tended to colour perceptions of more positive adjectives that came later in the list. However, if the order was reversed and the negative came at the end of the description the more positive adjectives were not tainted by the negative starting point. In simple terms such distortions occur because of an initial commitment to a prior belief. Dailey (1952) for example, found that subjects were less sensitive to new information when they answered inferential questions after receiving early evidence in an impression formation task. Similar processes occur even in perceptual experiments - Bruner and Potter (1964) discovered that the initial hypothesis in identifying an out of focus image inhibited recognition when the picture came into focus.

A case where a particular type of individual or a specific individual has been focused on may represent an example where the profiler could be prone to look for confirmation of the assertion rather than evidence to challenge it. This is a common phenomenon, examples of which are exemplified by 'Ripperologists' (individuals who have theories as to the identity of Jack the Ripper). Ripperologists tend to cite a specific individual as a possibility for the crimes and then seek out evidence to support their claim rather than seeking to disconfirm their evidence through a search for alternatives.

As well as the inappropriateness of adhering to an initial incorrect belief after contrary evidence there is a tendency for individuals to strengthen their beliefs with neutral information - i.e. information that is consistent with the belief and its converse. Lord, Ross and Leper (1979) selected people on the basis of whether they were for or against capital punishment. Each person was then presented with mixed evidence on the effectiveness of capital punishment. People more easily found flaws in the reports that went against their belief whilst using pro-belief neutral evidence in a far more glowing light than it should have been given credit for. This phenomena is particularly pernicious in unscientific profiling because much of the material drawn upon will have no known validity and is likely, in effect, to be neutral with regard to the offence. For example, a suspect may have had a minor conviction as a teenager for indecent exposure because someone complained that he urinated on their fence. This could then be treated as if it were a chronic history of sexually related offending that is in accord with the putative profile.

Furnham and Alison (1994) have established that there are a number of beliefs that police officers may hold in relation to juror bias. Bias in this context was measured by a Juror Bias Scale (Kassin and Wrightsman 1983) which measures the degree to which an individual is biased towards a prosecution or defence standpoint in the face of neutral evidence. Furnham and Alison found that the police were more likely than a control group to believe a suspect is guilty on the basis of neutral information. According to theories of irrational belief persistence, given this biased view, officers would be more inclined to look for examples to support presumed guilt, be less able to search for evidence to counter these beliefs and to view neutral information as proof of guilt. As Furnham and Alison suggested it may be that one's role has some influence on the information to which one attends. In the case of a police officer one may reasonably assume that the number of cases on which individuals are not tried and convicted for crimes, where the officer was convinced of guilt, would become more salient than those where the individual was correctly convicted.

Cultural and Group Effects

In terms of the promulgation of poor thinking through cultural norms, institutions where defence of one's beliefs is a virtue and questioning a vice are the ones most likely to overcome challenges from the outside. However this does not necessarily make for good decision making. It is possible that the strong cultural identity of the police force to some extent condones such a way of thinking and so may be particularly susceptible to biases. Furthermore, when such beliefs are challenged the first instinct is to bolster them (Janis and Mann 1977). Accompanying factors such as stress, where excessive levels can lead to hypervigilance in which the decision maker considers one option after another with little search for evidence (Keinan 1987) creates a decision context fertile for distortions if not closely monitored.

Finally, there are group effects that could contribute to ineffective decisions. Studies carried out extensively by Janis (1982) identified the following major causes of inappropriate decisions on the basis of inefficient group processes. Many of these bear similarities to problems known to exist within management circles and organisations (Blau and Scott 1963).

Overestimation of the group This involves what Janis has termed 'The Illusion of invulnerability' - often fostered by past success where there is a belief in the inherent morality of the group - in which immoral means are used to obtain supposedly moral ends. This is a similar process to the identification of 'Bottom line mentality' in organisations where a financial success is believed to be the only value worthy of consideration even at the expense of long-term finances.

Closed mindedness Involves collective rationalisation - where members convince themselves and others that they do not have to consider other information or alternatives.

Stereotypes of out groups The tendency to believe that the group's opponents are weak, foolish and immoral - therefore underestimating them. Again a similar process - 'Exploitative mentality' has been examined in organisations and concerns the promotion of stereotypes thereby undermining empathy.

Pressures towards uniformity The use of self censorship where members hold back from expressing inconsistent views in order to conform.

Illusion of unanimity Related to the above the use of self-censorship is reinforcing because it creates an illusion of unanimity.

Direct pressure on dissenters Occurs where 'self-appointed mind guards' in the group take it upon themselves to keep others in line with the supposed consensus viewpoints. 'Madison Avenue Mentality' conforms to such a process where the group is happy with the belief that anything is right if the public can be made to believe so. Such a belief system, as well as being ethically unsound, are professionally inefficient and, therefore, very rarely financially beneficial in the long run.

Thus, a fundamental proposition is that without recourse to a scientific mode of thinking and the establishment of an approach based on cumulative knowledge which can be challenged and reworked, investigative 'expertise' is subject to all the frailties of human thinking whether the individual is a profiler or an experienced Detective.

The Influence of the Expert

The profiler, however, may present a danger that is more invidious than an experienced detective if he or she is considered to be an informed 'expert'. Much of the literature on persuasion demonstrates that the perceived authority of the information source is crucial in determining the impact of the opinion offered (Milgram 1974, Arendt 1963, Comfort 1950). The notorious Milgram experiments also serve to illustrate how much power apparently neutral 'scientists' can wield. The proneness of experienced investigators to these influences has certainly been demonstrated both in the Yorkshire Ripper enquiry and in the enquiry into the murder of Rachel Nickell. The danger then is that the profiler brings in many biases that are masked by the belief in his/her neutral expertise and that these are further confused by the investigating officer's own biases. The consequence, clearly demonstrated with 'psychic Detectives' (Wiseman et al 1997) is that both the police and the advisors believe their interaction is much more fruitful than it actually is. The profiler mistakenly believes he/she has made a real contribution, the investigating officers' believing the profiler has strengthened the views they had already formulated. Indeed the prevalence of this process is strongly supported by the findings of Copson's (1995) survey of police officers' opinions of the profiling services they had obtained.

Legal Issues

The notion that a psychological profile is in any circumstances admissible in proof of identity is to my mind redolent with considerable danger.
The Honourable Mr Justice Ognall (1994) from Regina v Colin Stagg

Definitional Problems

Despite the FBI's broad classification (noted under the section 'Origins of Profiling') there is no commonly agreed definition of what constitutes a profile or how one may be constructed. Lack of clear definition regarding the contents or process of constructing a profile is therefore the first stumbling block in terms of its relevance (or irrelevance) in the courts.

One generally agreed principle is that it involves inferring *characteristics* of the offender from *actions* at the scene of the crime. The definitional problem lies in what constitutes an action or characteristic and how best the process of associating one with the other may be carried out.

Because there is at present no established discipline of profiling or widely published scientific literature, each person who provides a profile does so by drawing upon his or her own particular predilections. Some, for example, may give emphasis to the criminal background, whilst others may give special emphasis to the thoughts and wishes (sometimes called 'fantasies') of the offender. Thus, as well as differentiation amongst profilers in their use of different criminal actions to analyse (varying from crime scene reports to witness statements) their generation of criminal characteristics can also vary - from demographic features such as the age or approximate residential location of the offender to the nature of his sexual fantasies.

The Myth of the Expert

Aside from the number of concerns highlighted, there is the question of what an offender profiler's field of expertise actually is and how this relates to the problem of interpreting characteristics from actions. In other words, what special credentials does an offender profiler claim to have over, for example, a police officer in the interpretation of criminal actions?

There is no evidence to suggest that clinicians or experienced detectives have any special skills in constructing offender profiles. In fact, the limited research that does exist suggests that there is little difference between 'professional' profilers, detectives, psychologists and college students (Pinizotto and Finkel 1990). Indeed, there are some studies on other fields where there may be a presumed correlation between experience and expertise that in issues of detecting deception police officers can actually perform more poorly than other groups (Kohnken 1987). Furthermore, the studies by Wilson et al (1997) on the ability of police officers to link rapes validly to a common offender found that experienced rape investigators were no better than inexperienced ones. Clearly, we are not suggesting that experience is a handicap in generating possible suspect characteristics. Indeed, the Investigative Psychology Unit strongly promotes links with the police force precisely for the wealth of investigative acumen that they possess regarding previous cases. We are merely pointing out that one must check and treat with caution all opinions and not simply assume that because it is said with great conviction by someone with experience that it must be true.

There is also of course a fundamental problem of whether a 'profiler' can ever be objectively evaluated anyway. As Ormerod (1996) has pointed out claims to success rates in profiling are

> *...open to attack given the impossibility of an objective assessment of reliability. Given the nature of the exercise, a controlled experiment is out of the question. Similarly, practical difficulties would be encountered in any retrospective evaluation of trial outcomes. It would simply not be possible to disentangle from the ultimate profile what information came from guesswork, what was 'forensic' input, etc.*
>
> p. 870

There must therefore be real doubt as to whether investigating officers are necessarily the best judges of what is useful to their enquiry in terms of profiles or profilers. They may be unaware of what constitutes the scientific rationale behind a profile, unable to implement or put to use any of the statements made within it and unable to question certain aspects of accuracy or process. If they cannot evaluate 'profiles' and there is unlikely to be any in depth objective assessment of them, in what sense can they be regarded as a product of expertise?

Profiling as a Discrete Discipline?

Poythress, Otto, Darkes and Starr (1993) examined the FBI agents' use of psychological autopsy produced to explain the explosion on USS Iowa. These agents formed the opinion that based on their experience in criminal investigation that the explosion was the result of a suicide. After the American Psychological Association examined the case more thoroughly they established that the FBI's analysis was invalid and further evidence came to light that suggested the explosion was the result of an accident.

Poythress et al point out that though it may be tempting to make inferences from crime scene details on the basis of experience there are a number of considerations that may bias and distort these conclusions - not least of which is the nature of the information itself. In other words, if the collection process and the type of information is impoverished then what Poythress et al call "reconstructive evaluations" (by which they mean offender profiles and psychological autopsies) are going to be similarly impoverished, unreliable and invalid. Therefore, a number of research groups around the world (including units set up within police forces) are now following the lead of the IPU research aimed at building up a cumulative scientific discipline that may be drawn upon by the police themselves rather than emphasising 'hands on' advice to ongoing enquiries. Obviously of central concern is the information collection process - distortions in which present similar problems for any scientifically based study. Thus if the information employed to construct hypotheses is distorted the results and conclusions are likely to suffer from such misrepresentative material. An early concern of the investigative psychology approach concerns improving these early stages of information collection.

The fact that the IPU is sceptical of 'profiling expertise' is backed up by other areas of research. Even in more 'conventional' investigative domains both Ekman's (1991) and Kohnken's work (1987) suggests that there is nothing 'special' about Detective or clinical expertise. As mentioned, in detecting deception both studies point to the same conclusion - i.e. that experience is *not* associated with better performance. In fact in Kohnken's study it was found that accuracy was *negatively* correlated with length of on-the-job experience. There is no reason to assume that offender profiling is an exceptional field where experience is associated with increased accuracy. In mind of these early warning signals, the investigator should seriously consider exactly why s/he needs to employ the use of an 'expert' external to the enquiry and if so in what ways can they justifiably, professionally and ethically be employed.

Profiling in Investigations and Profiling in Court

A number of individuals, from a variety of professions have proposed that there is little problem associated with viewing profiling as an investigative tool. For example as Ormerod, Ognall and Canter state:

Statistics show that the police have used psychological profiling to focus their investigations, identify and locate possible suspects, and to assist in prosecution.

Ormerod (1996) p. 866

Nobody questions that in certain cases the assistance of a psychologist of that kind can prove a very useful investigative tool.

The Honourable Mr Justice Ognall (1994) from Regina v Colin Stagg

Changes in the demands made on police forces around the world mean that they are increasingly in need of such help. The lone detective, so popular in fiction, has given way to organized teams which require systematic guidance.

Canter (1994) from Criminal Shadows (p. 4)

However, the dangers to the investigation are greatly magnified when attempts are made to use profiles to single out individuals as probative proof of identity in the courtroom. For example Boon and Davies have highlighted potential problems with the technique:

...it should never be forgotten that its [profiling] contribution to any investigation can only be supportive rather than substantive. Furthermore, it must also be borne in mind that no matter how much research is conducted profiles can be inaccurate and that this can have seriously misleading effects upon an enquiry.

Boon and Davies (1991)

This viewpoint is further extended by Ormerod (1996) in a discussion of the evidential implications of profiling:

...it has been acknowledged that some profiles are 'so vague as to point to practically anyone' and can 'severely hamper an investigation by sending the police off in the wrong direction'.

Ormerod (1996)

Thus, whilst some cases have raised the prestige of profiling (cf. Ormerod 1996) others which have failed have resulted in doubts and scepticism. Not all profiling attempts have been as impressive as those of Langer and Brussel and even those appeared to have no influence at all on the actual police investigation. There are some very clear examples of profiles being outstandingly incorrect:

In one case, for example, a profile on a criminal suspect told investigators that the man they were looking for came from a broken home, was a high school drop out, held a marginal job, hung out in 'honky tonk' bars and lived far from the scene of the crime. When the attacker was finally caught, it was learned that the psychological assessment was 100% wrong. He had not come from a broken home, he had a college degree, held an executive position with a respected financial institution, did not use alcohol and lived near the scene of the crime.

Goodroe (1987)

The authors also have experience of providing totally incorrect profiles. For example, in one of the earliest profiles from the Unit, in the brutal slaying of a teenager the profile suggested a white male between 20 and 30 years old - based purely on the statistical probablity of such offences as carried out in previous similar crimes. The offender was, in fact, a 12 year old black girl. Thus in terms of the actual content of a profile (regardless of the appropriateness or otherwise of the means by which it was constructed), evaluation and the use of the profile can be seriously misleading. In the cases mentioned above, for example, the means by which the profile was obtained may have been scientifically sound but the actual case statistically anomalous. Therefore, even casting aside difficulties of evaluation it is still possible for profiles to present problems for an enquiry team unless they are very carefully considered.

It is hardly surprising then that profiling has never been used in a British court of law. For example, from the concerns highlighted so far - which include (i) definitional problems, (ii) lack of evidence to suggest expertise, (iii) the question of whether profiling is in fact a systematic discipline and (iv) the agreement by a variety of professionals as to its lack of usefulness in identifying and individual it is evident that the use of a profile in court is redolent with danger. Aside from these important issues there are two major hurdles that would have to be overcome by the party relying on the profile. These are the concepts of relevance and admissibility (Ormerod 1996). As Sheldon and MacLeod (1991) have noted in relation to 'statistical profiling' (i.e. profiling based on examinations of the offence behaviours of a number of cases):

Normative data ...is of little use to the courts. The courts are concerned to determine the past behaviour of accused individuals, and in carrying out that function, information about the past behaviour of other individuals is wholly irrelevant.

p. 814

The probative guilt of the accused (or probative innocence - profilers have been asked by defence barristers to present information that suggests their client *did not* commit an offence but so far these opinions have not found their way into the courts) cannot be established by such research or opinion based profiles. Because opinions of clinicians are based upon experience of allegedly similar cases and statistical research is based on purportedly relevant data sets neither connects directly with the specific case at hand. The central problem for the courts lies in the potential for extreme prejudice against the defendant who, by definition, being an individual, does not fit the criteria for a system based on generalities - whether they are based on opinion or research.

Furthermore, as Ormerod (1996) argues very cogently, there are strong legal barriers as to the admissibility of profiles both because they would be legally regarded as based on unacceptable hearsay, and because they would introduce prejudice into the evidence. These are high barriers in English law but may not be so strict in other jurisdictions (Canter 1997).

Ethical Issues

In all their work psychologists shall value integrity, impartiality and respect for persons and evidence and shall seek to establish the highest ethical standards in their work.

BPS Codes of Conduct 1991

The above statement comes from the BPS's fundamental and general principle section. It encapsulates rather well the elements of concern to psychologists contributing to police enquiries with the emphasis on integrity, impartiality and respect. To illustrate how these principles may be maintained, a detailed account is given below of how the psychologist may adhere professionally and ethically to the codes of conduct through keeping detailed documents, outlining sources of the inferences, allowing for peer review of work, searching for alternative explanations through an impartial, objective approach and maintaining a concern and respect for the individuals who s/he may influence through his/her input.

Keeping Detailed Documents

It is essential to keep as full an ongoing account of one's work as possible because (a) crucial details may be forgotten or wrongly interpreted with hindsight and (b) so that others may challenge the steps and assertions after the work has been carried out. If these steps are not open to scrutiny they cannot be challenged or explored. Moreover, the psychologist is laying himself open to the challenge that inferences were made *after* the discovery of certain pieces of evidence. For example, if a profile is constructed and no details of it are recorded, it is feasible that the psychologist could have constructed the profile *after* a suspect became the focus of police attention.

The psychologist should therefore have a dated copy of all information given to the police. Word of mouth is not acceptable - nor is it adequate to sketch out ideas or write them on blackboards later to be removed. The investigating team and the psychologist should have duplicates of every piece of information passed between them.

Sources of the Inferences

The psychologist should always be able to cite where possible what the bases are for his/her inferences. For example, if his/her psychological framework is psychoanalytic, cognitive or behavioural this should be explicitly stated with reference to the appropriate literature. Similarly, the psychologist should be able to give an account of what work s/he has drawn upon with respect to the inferences made. This allows the psychologist (a) to be able to give advice on the strength of the inference (i.e. is the work referred to preliminary or well established?) and (b) to be challenged about his/her assertions. Moreover, the psychologist should provide a definitional system for the given domain of interest. For example, the psychologist may on the basis of the pattern of the stab wounds suggest that the offender knew the victim. If this is based on two clinical cases that the psychologist has previously come across then this inference can be made with less certainty than if the psychologist has been working specifically on the analysis of stab wound patterning and established that in the 400 crimes with similar patterning only three did not involve someone who was known to the victim. In both cases the psychologist would need to define precisely what s/he is looking for in the patterns and why this is relevant.

Peer Review

In a scientific context it is expected that any assertions or inferences are open to challenge and review. This commonly involves the following:

Publication of work in journals;

Having internal documents that can be open to scrutiny if required;

In house reviews of material by other colleagues;

Invitations to external reviewers to oversee the work (this may involve the presentation of material at academic conferences).

From the previous 'stab wound' example both psychologists should be able to direct the appropriate authorities to the work that they refer to - the clinical psychologist should have some documentation on the previous two cases that s/he has come across and the psychologist whose area of speciality lies in the analysis of 'stab wounds' should be able to produce the evidence of his/her results (even if this is only an internal document).

In light of this and in relation to the biases mentioned so far there are a number of measures that may help to prevent distortions in the handling and collection of information:

All the facts. The psychologist should inform the investigative team that they should present *all of the facts* known about the case - suspicions, intuitions and 'gut feelings' are not relevant and may bias the research.

Presentation of the facts It may be beneficial for an individual *not* directly involved in the case to present the psychologist with the material - i.e. if possible, someone who has no suspicions about particular suspects. Therefore it may not be necessary and in fact may be detrimental to the inquiry for the most senior individual to present the information.

The irrelevance of suspicions The psychologist should state that under no circumstances should any information be given about a likely suspect. If an offender profile is to be drawn up it should be without the 'benefit' of a possible suspect. It is the Investigative Psychology Unit's experience that both police officers and members of the legal profession are often inappropriately keen to get involved with who the offender may or may not be. This makes it more difficult for the psychologist to approach the problem with an open mind. Indeed, both authors have experienced the process of being unable to avoid picking up certain cues from the investigating officers as to those officers' likely suspicions. This transference is unlikely to be deliberate on the part of the officer but is simply an unavoidable product of having an opinion on the case. Obviously it would be impossible not to have some preferred account of the possible sequence of events and in the case of experienced Detectives these may be well founded. The profiler may, therefore, simply be picking up on and gaining the benefits of that officers' correct assumptions. Similarly, if the officer is wrong then similar incorrect assumptions could be made by the profiler.

Keeping a record It may be useful to tape exchanges between psychologist and investigating team so that any potential for biasing opinions can be examined.

Respect for Persons

> *'Respect': Deferential regard or esteem felt or shown towards another person or thing; the condition or state of being esteemed or honoured; rank standing or station in life.*
>
> The Shorter Oxford English Dictionary 3rd Ed. 1986

As with ethical concerns regarding the laboratory and fieldwork of psychologist's attention should be paid to the possible consequences that psychological input might have to police enquiries.

In such instances psychologists should be concerned in any advice they are giving to undercover operations or interviews with respect both to the possible future implications for the suspect and the officers involved. In other words, the psychologist should not be cajoled into advocating behaviour that may put the suspect (or the officers involved in the operation) at risk psychologically or physically. Therefore, at the *outset* of any advice on undercover operations the psychologist should have full documentation regarding the likely outcomes of the operation - this would include psychological and physical implications both for the suspect and the undercover officer.

Competence

> 'Competence': "A sufficiency of; sufficiency of qualification, capacity, esp. legal capacity; adequacy."
>
> The Shorter Oxford English Dictionary 3rd Ed. 1986

The British Psychological Society's codes of conduct states that psychologists should endeavour to work within their professional limits and to identify factors which restrict it - in particular recognising the boundaries of their competence. Therefore there are questions as to levels of competence in having the sufficient skills and ability to advise on profiles and give guidance to investigations.

As stated, given that there is no evidence to support any special skill in profiling it is questionable whether psychologists should be used in this way without a careful consideration of their credentials and work. However, as well as the competencies involved in the construction of the profile, there should be additional questions when the psychologist is asked to contribute to other areas of the enquiry. For example, whilst a 'profiler' may give information relating to the characteristics of the offender, s/he should not be concerned with aiding in the interview process when a suspect is called in unless s/he is competent to advise on the interviewing process. Similarly, if the suspect were mentally ill, unless the profiler had the relevant skills as a clinician s/he should not advise with respect to dealing with the peculiarities of the suspect's presumed diagnosis. The number of disciplines that may be called in for relevant expert advise may therefore range from interviewing skills to psycholinguistics to diagnoses of neurological damage.

Competence is a particularly difficult issue for psychologists contributing to enquiries as 'profilers' to assess. As stated, there is no formally agreed discipline or profession, exclusively as a profiler. Therefore police investigators should be extremely cautious of an individual who claims a professional status solely as a 'profiler'. Competence can only really be gauged then in reference to other professionally recognised disciplines and even then it is questionable whether these connect sufficiently closely with the profiling domain.

Impartiality

> *Impartiality: "The quality of being impartial; freedom from prejudice orbias; fairness. Impartial - not partial; not favouring one more than another; unprejudiced; unbiased, fair, just, equitable."*
>
> The Shorter Oxford English Dictionary 3rd Ed. 1986

As stated, profilers may be prone to use inappropriate heuristics where there is no scientific rational for making the assertions and where there is no external monitoring of the enquiry. Further, many of the heuristics outlined may distort views and create biases amongst those profilers who base their assertions with total conviction solely on experience. For example, they may make inferences on the basis of only the most salient cases, only generate information consistent with a prior belief, and neglect to look for alternative explanations and be overconfident in their assertions. Moreover, they may be susceptible to some of the features outlined that relate to stress and distortions through group processes.

We realise that the recommendations here are a counsel of perfection that are very difficult to achieve in the far from ideal pressure and haste of police investigations. We are also aware of the attractions (indeed seductions) in giving immediate and confident answers to police officers involved in nationally important cases. But unless serious attempts are made to reach for the ideals then there is a grave risk of the potential for contributions from experts being lost, or worse, actually resulting in miscarriages of justice.

In the Final Analysis

In summary there are some fundamental questions about offender profiling that need to be addressed:

Why use a profiler? The contribution of an outside expert offering opinions to a very select and particular area needs to be reconsidered. It is not appropriate to generate profiles on the basis of inappropriate information. In other words, unless the means of collecting information is adequate the bases on which characteristics are inferred from actions may be unsound. Crime scene reports may not be entirely appropriate for psychologists to work with. But once that information has been more effectively collected it may not need any very specialist knowledge to make inferences from it. In other words, as the process of Investigative psychology becomes more established within police practice there will be less need to bring in an outside expert, as developments in a number of police forces are revealing (see Lee and Alison 1997).

When are psychological contributions inappropriate? Contributions are inappropriate when the individual(s) concerned cannot demonstrate clearly that their area of expertise is relevant to the area under investigation. In the same way that it would be inappropriate for a psychologist whose speciality is the study of optical illusions to be exploring speech impediments, it is also inappropriate for a psychologist whose speciality is the fitness of a patient to plead in court to be giving advice on how to carry out an undercover police operation.

Who is giving the advice and what are their competencies? Related to the last point, the investigative team need to know the boundaries within which their 'expert' can operate. They need documents that outline clearly what the psychologist's field of expertise is, what his/her formal qualifications are, what tests his/her expertise has undergone, what papers he/she has written or presentations he/she has made and what internal documents he/she has produced. As our review of the room for bias has demonstrated accounts of previous cases may not be the best gauge of competence.

Art is not enough The central principle underlying this area, as with any other approach to science, should be one of impartiality. In the case of profiling, a subjective, intuitive, biased or gut feeling is inadequate, unprofessional and ethically and legally unsound. The recommendation is that an objective systematic framework should be drawn up in which the contribution to investigations is through a cumulative scientific approach rather than one based on personal expert opinion.

It is worth emphasising that there are parallels here to the role of clinical experience versus scientific inference in the therapeutic activities of clinical psychologists. Over three decades ago studies demonstrated clearly the power of science (Meehl 1954). It may be that this debate will need to be revisited in this new area of applied psychology.

Thus, whilst we remain optimistic on the contributions that psychology can make to inquiries, caution must be observed. Unless combined with an ongoing concern with the professional, legal and ethical issues, investigators and psychologists will continue to be blessed one minute and cursed the next by the peaks and troughs of individual successes and failures. As Ormerod (1996) has stated, "...just as these successes [in profiling] herald psychological profiling as a powerful new weapon to combat serious crime, cases which have spectacularly failed, such as *Stagg*, generate doubts and concerns". Since profiling and police work constantly attracts media attention it is evident that to secure foundations for a discipline that can genuinely contribute to dealing with crime individuals employed in the area should put professional, legal and ethical concerns at the forefront of its development. The concern should not simply be with profiling criminals. If that is the only consideration then it is the public 'profile' of these professionals that will gradually fall into disrepute and decline. Again, the BPS codes carry a particularly apposite warning:

> *Psychologists shall conduct themselves in their professional activities in a way that does not damage the interest of the recipients of their services or participants in their research and does not undermine public confidence in their ability to carry out professional duties.*
>
> From the BPS Codes of Conduct 1991

Future Research

One final, scientific point is worth emphasising. There have been very few studies of investigative decision making and only a handful of in depth analyses of how police officers incorporate psychologists, or psychological thinking into their detective work. This chapter can therefore be looked on as a research agenda, outlining hypotheses about the cognitive biases and procedural confusions that may be inherent in the complex and difficult task of solving a crime. Indeed, this is a much-neglected area that connects directly with the structural and professional standards of the police environment itself. Caution must be observed if an individual professing to be a 'profiler' seems unconcerned or has neglected to consider these important aspects of the way in which s/he interacts with the chosen profession that s/he has sought to liaise with.

References

Alison, L.J. and Lee, J. (1999). The feasibility of profiling from sexual fantasies. In D. V. Canter and L. J. Alison (1999). *Profiling Rape and Murder.* Offender Profiling. Series III. Aldershot: Dartmouth.

American Psychological Association (1992). Ethical Principles of Psychologists and Code of Conduct *American Psychologist* 47 (12).

Asch, S.E. (1946). Forming impressions of personality. *Journal of Abnormal and Social Psychology,* 41, 258-290.

Baron, J. (1994). *Thinking and Deciding.* Cambridge University Press.

Bowlby, E.J.M. (1949). Forty four juvenile thieves: Their characteristics and home life. conclusions and summary. *Baillere London* 53-55.

British Psychological Society (1991). *Codes of Conduct, Ethical Principles and Guidelines,* Leicester: BPS.

Britton, P. (1997). Inside the mind of Rachel's killer. Extract from *The Mail on Sunday. December 1st* 1997.

Britton, P. (1997). *The Jigsaw Man.* London: Bantam Press.

Bruner, J.S. and Potter, M.C. (1964) Interference in visual recognition. *Science, 144,* p. 424-425.

Burt, C. (1949). *The young delinquent. Conclusion.* University of London Press p. 599-614.

Canter, D.V. (1989). Offender Profiles. In *The Psychologist 2 (1)* 1989, p. 12-16.

Canter, D.V. (1994). *Criminal Shadows.* London: Harper Collins.

Canter, D.V. (1995). The psychology of offender profiling. In T. H. Blau *Psychological Services for Law Enforcement.* John Wiley and Sons, Inc. p. 261-274.

Canter, D.V. (1997). New Forms of Expertise. *Forensic Update.*

Canter, D.V. and Alison, L.J. (1997). *Criminal Detection and the Psychology of Crime.* Aldershot: Dartmouth.

Chapman, L.J. and Chapman, J.P. (1967). Genesis of popular but erroneous psychodiagnostic observations. *Journal of Abnormal Psychology,* 72, p. 193-204.

Copson, G. (1995). Coals to Newcastle? Part 1: A study of offender profiling. Police Research Group. *Special Interest Series: Paper 7.*

Dailey, C.A. (1952). The effects of premature conclusions upon the acquisition of understanding a person. *Journal of Psychology, 33,* p. 133-152.

Ekman, P. (1991). "Who Can Catch a Liar?" *American Psychologist,* 46 (9), p. 913-920.

Fischhoff, B. (1975). Hindsight and foresight: The effect of outcome knowledge on judgement under uncertainty. *Journal of Experimental Psychology: Human Perception and Performance, I,* p. 288-299.

Fischhoff, B. Slovic, P. and Lichenstein, S. (1977). Knowing with certainty: The appropriateness of extreme confidence. *Journal of Experimental Psychology: Human Perception and Performance, 3,* p. 552-564.

Fisher, R.P., Geiselman, R.E., Raymond, D.S., Jurkevich, L.M., and Warhaftig, M.L. (1987). Enhancing eyewitness memory: Refining the cognitive interview. *Journal of Police Science and Administration,* 15 (4), p. 292-297.

Furnham, A. and Alison, L.J. (1994). Theories of crime, attitudes to punishment and juror bias amongst police, offenders and the general public. *Personality and Individual Differences* 17 (1) p. 35-48.

Gerbner, G. Gross, L. Morgan, M. and Signorielli (1985). Growing up with television: The cultivation perspective. In J. Bryant and D. Zillman (eds) *Media Effects: Advances in Theory and Research,* p. 17-41. Hillsdale, N.J.: Lawrence Erlbaum.

Gudjonsson, G. (1992). *The Psychology of Confessions and Testimony.* England: John Wiley and Sons Ltd.

Haward, L. (1985). Forensic Psychology in S. and D.Canter (eds). *Psychology in Practice.* Chichester: Wiley

Hsu B., Kling A., Kessler K. Diefenbach p. and Elias, J. (1994). "Gender Differences in Sexual Fantasy and Behaviour in a College Population: A Ten Year Replication" Journal of Sex and Marital Therapy vol. 20, No 2.

Hull, (1943). *Methods of Observation.* in R. A. King (1961). Readings for an introduction to psychology. New York: McGraw-Hill Book Company, Inc.

Janis, I.L. (1982). *Groupthink: Psychological studies of policy decisions and fiascos* (Revised edition of *Victims of groupthink: A psychological study of foreign-policy decisions and fiascos,* 1972) Boston: Houghton-Mifflin.

Janis, I.L. and Mann, L. (1977). *Decision Making: A psychological analysis of conflict, choice and commitment,* New York: Free Press.

Kassin, S.M. and Wrightsman, L.S. (1983). The construction and validation of a juror bias scale. *Journal of Research in Personality,* 17, p. 423-442.

Keinan, G. (1987). Decision making under stress: Scanning of alternatives under controllable and uncontrollable threats. *Journal of Personality and Social Psychology, 52,* p. 639-644.

Kohnken, G. (1987). Training police officers to detect deceptive eyewitness statements: Does it work?" *Social Behaviour, 2,* p. 1-17.

Lee, J. and Alison, L.J. (1997). Beyond Cracker. *Police Review 19, 16th May.*

Lieberman, D. (1990). *Learning, Behaviour and Cognition.* Wadsworth Publishing Company.

Lombroso, C. (1911). *Crime: Its Causes and Remedies*. Boston: Little, Brown.

Lord, C.G. Ross, L. and Lepper, M.R. (1979). Biased assimilation and attitude polarisation: The effects of prior theories on subsequently considered evidence. *Journal of Personality and Social Psychology*, 37, p. 2098-2109.

Malamuth, N.M. and Check J.V. (1983). Sexual arousal to rape depictions: Individual differences. *Journal of Abnormal Psychology*, 92, (1).

Meehl, P.E. (1954). *Clinical versus statistical prediction: A theoretical analysis and a look at the evidence*. Minneapolis: University of Minnesota Press.

Ormerod, D.C. (1996). The evidential implications of psychological profiling. *Criminal Law Review, 717*. p. 863-877.

Ormerod, D.C. (1996). Psychological profiling. *The Journal of Forensic Psychiatry 7* (2) p. 341-352.

Poythress, N., Otto, R.K., Darkes, J., and Starr, L. (1993). APA's expert panel in the congressional review of the USS Iowa incident. *American Psychologist Jan* p. 8-15.

Pinizzotto, A.J. and Finkel N.J. (1990). Criminal personality profiling: An outcome and process study. *Law and Human Behaviour, 14* (3), p. 215-233.

Rachman S. and Hodgson R. (1968). Experimentally induced 'sexual fetishism: replication and development' *Psychological Record 18*.

Ressler, R.K., Burgess, A.G., Douglas, J.E. and Depue, R.L. (1985). Violent Crime. *FBI Law Enforcement Bulletin, 54*, no.8.

Ressler, R.K., Douglas, J.E., Burgess, A.W. and Burgess A.G. (1993). *Crime Classification Manual: The Standard System for Investigating and Classifying Violent Crimes*. London: Simon and Schuster.

Ross, M. and Silcoly, F. (1979). Egocentric bias in availability and attribution. *Journal of Personality and Social Psychology, 37*, p. 322-336.

Rowe, W.F. (1993). Psychic detectives: A critical examination. *Skeptical Inquirer Vol. 17* (2), p. 159-165.

Royal Commission (1929). *Duties of police in investigation of crimes and offences*. Report of the Royal Commission on Police Powers and Procedures.

Royal Commission on Criminal Justice (1993). Report Cmnd 2263. London: HMSO.

Shepherd, E. (1991). Ethical interviewing: Aspects of police interviewing. *Criminological and Legal Psychology 18* p. 46-59.

Smedslund, J. (1963). The concept of correlation in adults. *Scandanavian Journal of Psychology, 4*, p. 165-173.

Tversky, A. and Kahneman, D. (1973). Availability: A heuristic for judging frequency and probability. *Cognitive Psychology, 5*, p. 207-232.

Tversky, A. and Kahneman, D. (1974). Judgement under uncertainty: Heuristics and biases. *Science, 185*, p. 1124-1131.

Wason, P.C. (1960). On the failure to eliminate hypotheses in a conceptual task. *Quarterly Journal of Experimental Psychology*, 12, p. 129-140.

Wilson, C. and Odell, R. (1991). *The Complete Jack the Ripper*. Penguin Books.
Wiseman, R., West, D. and Stemman, R. (1996). Psychic crime detectives: A new test for measuring their successes and failures. *Skeptical Inquirer Jan* p. 38-40.

3   Mobsters are Human Too

PETRUS VAN DUYNE

This chapter describes a behavioural science approach to the problem of organised crime. It describes the organised criminal as a crime-entrepreneur, who is essentially a risk-entrepreneur. From this perspective the chapter elaborates the potential for a behavioural science contribution to police investigations in this field. It describes the social-psychological profiling of crime-entrepreneurs and their 'landscape', as well as the potential contribution of psychologists to the organised crime squads concerning interviewing, inner group processes, trial preparation and (self) evaluation.

Petrus C. van Duyne, psychologist and jurist, is professor in empirical, penal science at the Tilburg University, Netherlands and advisor in the Dutch Central Intelligence Service. He has done research on decision making by public prosecutors and judges, fraud and organised crime. At the moment he is leading research projects on financial investigation and money-laundering.

*Offender Profiling Series: II - **Profiling in Policy and Practice***
Edited by D. Canter and L. Alison. © 1999 Ashgate Publishing, Aldershot. pp 55-81

3 Mobsters are Human Too
PETRUS VAN DUYNE

Introduction

The author is professor in empirical penal science at Tilburg University. He wrote this paper in close co-operation with a police psychologist, whose name could not be revealed for security reasons The same applies to the police force where the experiment took place.

Behavioural Science and Organised Crime Investigation

There are few topics which have so much potential for arousing an intriguing mixture of concern and curiosity as the organised crime issue. Organised crime has something dramatic which stimulates the imagination, resulting in blood-curdling movies and fiction. However, as is the case with most dramatisation, the underlying reality is human in all its banality, and banal in all its humanity. Despite all the abundant literature about organised crime, the human aspects of the leading actors receive less attention than the grotesque and monstrous dimensions of their heinous deeds. Without pretending to be complete we would like to point to the interesting studies of Ianni (1974), Anderson (1979) Schoenberg (1992), Adler (1985) and Adler (1994). Though this may satisfy our need for a mental balance of big crimes versus big bad criminals, the investigation of organised crime is better served by less drama and more attention to the human, very mundane aspects of organising crime, which is with hindsight constructed as *organised* crime.

There are many definitions of organised crime. We do not intend to engage in a controversy about the right definition. Our perspective is to look at the human aspects of being involved in organised crime and to elaborate on the function that behavioural science may have in organised crime investigations. Therefore we first have to face the nature of organised crime from this point of view. This is a very contradictory and confusing one.

Criminal Entrepreneurship

The phrase 'organised crime' was not coined by scientists, but by journalists in the first quarter of this century. In daily use during the time of the rumrunners for example, most people had the feeling it was clear what these words denoted. Later criminologists and jurists attempted to formulate a precise definition of this undefined concept. It was to no avail: the concept is too vague and too contradictory for a general scientific definition (van Duyne 1996). Moreover, as soon as one engages in drawing up a real operational definition, the resulting operationalisation will have to be adapted to the various forms of criminal enterprises which can be discerned. However, this renders the two words 'organised crime' redundant. The operational question then becomes: 'when do we have a continuous criminal enterprise?' This is one of the essential conditions for organised crime, but is not enough (Malz 1991), because it leaves unanswered what is meant by criminal enterprise. Perhaps the German Bundeskriminalamt definition provides the best analytical approach to the enterprise idea, though also the German authors remain attached to the string of words 'organised crime' (Khster 1991).

'Continuous criminal enterprise' is a dynamic do-concept: organising something to which should be added enduring co-operation. Otherwise one ends up with a one-man criminal shop! The core characteristics are the criminal aspects of the enterprise. At first sight this seems a platitude, though this seeming platitude hides the contradictory element of organised crime. Criminal entrepreneurship is enterprising in an *enduringly hostile* landscape, which means constant jeopardy to the continuity of the crime-enterprise. For the crime-entrepreneurs it means that the daily organisation of their trade is not only focused on money, but at the same time on a highly elaborated risk avoidance. A good crime-entrepreneur is an expert risk manager, facing the two-fold close down by law enforcement as well as by his criminal competitors.

This criminal risk perspective permeates virtually the whole sociology and psychology of organising a crime-enterprise. One of the most important skills which is a *conditio sine qua non* for any crime-entrepreneur is his information skill: risk management is info-management. One of the smarter top hash-smugglers realised that this management is not only important for tactical operations but has a strategic value of its own. So he elaborated his version of a 'criminal intelligence service' and hired outside professionals to carry out surveillance on police detectives and police cars, communication lines and infiltrate the police with 'criminal' informants who worked for him.

Most crime-entrepreneurs do not display such a strategic feeling for information, but they are all aware that in criminal society there is no such thing as a free flow of information. Other behavioural consequences concern the time span of thinking and planning. Who will devote his energy to long term planning and thinking, when he realises that his ships, trucks or other assets of his business can be wrecked or confiscated tomorrow, finding himself empty handed in prison (frequently betrayed by competitors) or, worse, dead and buried? Despite this, the crime-entrepreneur engages in the systematic planning of crimes for profit: not as a once only project but as an on-going business during which precarious interruptions because of law enforcement have to be weighed against the profits and the prospects of remaining in business. Interceptions of contraband may not put the crime-entrepreneur out of business, but may give him much to explain to his (foreign) suspicious partners. In a wholesale . hash trading line this became problematic because of the lack of 'cross-border' information. The Pakistan intermediary had to find newspaper cuttings concerning customs interceptions and police actions in order to convince his partners at home that the cargo had not been confiscated. Without these reports of police activities the whole trading network would have fallen apart much earlier, because of sheer suspicion and revenge. The nature of organised crime in the sense of risk entrepreneurship is psychologically a contradictory one indeed (van Duyne 1995).

So how should we consider organised crime from a behavioural point of . view? Given the above stated premises it is in the first place not likely that we will find many organi*sing* criminals, acting as 'organisation builders', embodying an enduring, future oriented entity which is established intentionally. Crime-entrepreneurs do not ponder on how to establish an organisation. They have other worries: they must see to it that this shipment or that transaction gets through without detection or deceit. These short-term operations require of course an organisation in the sense of planning behaviour. This is accomplished pragmatically, while reacting to the requirements of the nature of the trade, the availability of the 'staff' and the organisational models the crime-entrepreneur has learned from his environment. An organised fraud scheme requires a different organisation than the trafficking of illegal goods. A crime-entrepreneur that operates in a family culture, like the Italian or the Turkish one, will resort to his family for the carrying out of the operations, resulting in extended family crime-enterprises. North-western European crime-entrepreneurs live in a culture without extended families. So they will turn to networks of accomplices who have little liking for authoritarian 'godfathers' and who operate socially more comfortably in flat networks which have very often little hierarchy (Rebscher and Vahlenkamp 1988). When the criminal operations are successful and are being repeated, people form habits and more stable relations, which the police and prosecution tend to equate to 'organisations', which are depicted in impressive organograms, designating specialised 'sections', 'divisions', command structures etc. Few crime-entrepreneurs recognise such juridical 'corporative' reconstructions. William Adler provides a lively comparison of the daily organising crack-entrepreneurs in Detroit and the corporative-like construction of the police (Adler, 1985).

Crime-entrepreneurship may seem confusing and look like a kind of self-tormentation. Nevertheless, this entrepreneur does not deviate from the more legitimate adventurer-entrepreneurial capitalists who stay (just) within the boundaries of the law. They share the common element of what Lyng (1990) called 'edgeworking'. This researcher tried to understand the curious phenomenon of 'voluntary danger seeking': why do people engage in sporting activities that are very dangerous, like free parachuting? On the basis of his interviews and participant observation he concluded that 'edgeworking' is not gambling with fate. Danger-hunters are no gamblers, but act rationally, calculating the risks relative to their skills. They test the edge of the possible, experiencing deep satisfaction in widening their boundaries further and further. They do not look for the excitement of the gambler, putting his fate in the hands of the unpredictable, but for the feeling of mastery of their bodily and mental skills in relation to the 'elements of nature'. Do adventure (crime) capitalists not demonstrate a similar behaviour? As a matter of fact, it is a behaviour which in our materialistic, competitive society is highly valued.

If the general dogma, that it is only profit that is significant holds true, many crime-entrepreneurs should have quit their industry after having amassed a handsome 'retirement fund'. There are few that display such rationality. Most crime-entrepreneurs continue, perhaps more addicted to a lifestyle than to the money they actually make. Part of their lifestyle is determined by their social environment, which consists mainly of like minded flashy risk seekers. Their incentives do not stem from a disciplined, planned calculation of the risks versus the rewards, but from the rough *expectancy* of huge rewards while (over)estimating their skills in beating the system and their competitors. This attitude is often expressed in off the record interviews with detectives: 'I do not care for the big money anymore, I like the excitement of outsmarting you guys', remarked a hash wholesaler. Another boasted that he was the only one the law could never get at (up until now he has proved correct). This theory does not exclude other motives for entering the business of crime and the resultant learning processes, nor social and cultural variations. But we think that it is difficult to understand the human process of organising crime if one tries to explain it exclusively from monetary motives.

Behavioural Scientists and Police Work

In their introduction to their extensive reader Wilson and Petersilia (1995) make clear that behavioural scientists and law enforcement interact more intensively than the 'ivory tower' metaphor suggests. If one compares the present state of the 'police arts' with the situation a few decades ago, one can say that many ideas and conceptions from behavioural studies have become quite common: the witness credibility (Clifford 1979), or the developmental, social and pathological aspects of criminal behaviour (Andrews and Bonta 1994). For a brief overview of the police-research relation in Washington, D.C., see Buchanan and Hankins (1986).

In the Netherlands behavioural scientists are at present frequently engaged as advisors to the management of police forces, though only in a few instances did they become a permanent member of the advisory board of the management. Direct involvement in concrete police work is much less frequent and seems to be restricted to criminal cases, like domestic violence, or sexual offences which require a psychological or psychiatric investigation of the offender and psychological guidance for victim.

But what about serious crime for profit, like organised crime? What has the behavioural scientist to offer, in this domain of 'calculating' criminals, to the crime squads who chase these crime-entrepreneurs for years? In this paper we will examine the contribution of the behavioural sciences more closely: not from a theoretical but from a practical point of view.

The Role of the Behavioural Scientist in Organised Crime Investigations

As mentioned above, in daily police practice the psychologist or sociologist is kept at the back door, to be consulted when the 'men of action' have a problem for which they need a specialist. Even if he or she is working as a member of staff, he or she is still considered an 'outsider-inside'. However, in the Netherlands the attitude of the higher police officers is changing, especially in the field of organised crime policy. The statement of the minister of justice that 'organised crime is a problem that has to be dealt with by the police, (fiscal) administration and science' was not meant to be a pious gesture, nor taken as such. The police forces of Amsterdam, The Hague and Enschede have taken sociologists and psychologists on board, not only to assist the police during specific 'emotional' events, but to assist in the development and execution of a policy against organised crime. The backgrounds of this development were that on the one hand the police forces were ill equipped to handle complex forms of criminal organisations, especially when they were operating in other areas than drugs, while on the other hand the police, the minister of justice and the political parties had declared the fight (they meant 'war') against organised crime to be a top priority. So the time was ripe to go beyond the 'police-only' line.

A psychologist or sociologist can have a broad background task in which he guides the investigation process from his special discipline. Apart from that he can also have a 'front line' task, in which he co-operates closely with the detectives during the day to day investigation. He is then a member of the squad. As both authors are psychologists and have contributed from this discipline to the work of the police in the field of organised crime, we shall describe the task of a behavioural scientist from this perspective. A sociologist may describe his potential distribution from a different angle, though the reader would certainly recognise similar elements. The experience of the authors of this paper is a mixture of close participation in on-going organised crime investigations and advising the management of the police and the ministry of justice

The Background Tasks

In this section we will describe the various aspects of the broader background tasks of a psychologist acting behind 'the front-line' of operational organised crime investigations. These tasks concern hypothesis construction and target profiling, recruitment, education and training.

Hypothesis Construction and Target Profiling

Organised crime investigations start frequently on the basis of suspicions provided by all sorts of (criminal) informants, whose information (in cases in which they are reliable) is mostly sketchy, partly accurate, providing bits of a social-criminal puzzle. These investigative hunches, strengthened by 'police intuition' are put together and translated into a plan. What is frequently lacking in such preparatory exercises is hypothesis building based on an analysis of the bits and pieces of reported and potential criminal behaviour. For example, if the information is; 'Mr. Philips has a contraband yearly turnover of, 100 million', the first hypothesis-deduction is: 'so Mr. Philips should have a large transportation and/or financial infrastructure" and not: 'where will we find Mr. Philips with dope in his hands'. The infrastructure hypothesis implies the availability of financial experts, haulier's etc., in brief, a social infrastructure.

As can be deduced from the above, analysis and hypothesis building implies the drawing of a - hypothetical - profile of the individual target, but it encompasses at the same time social-psychological profiling of the entrepreneurial landscape. For a practical review of profiling see Horn (1988). Unfortunately most profiling concerns sexual and violent offenders of unsolved crimes. Crime-entrepreneurs (who are usually well known) have received less systematic attention. This goes beyond the usual mapping of 'who goes with whom', which is frequently complimented by the already existing knowledge 'in the head' of the veteran detectives of 'their' old acquaintances. Such knowledge from daily practice can be upgraded by fitting it into an analytical framework, which though hypothetical may yield a useful starting point for further preparatory information seeking. This preparation can facilitate and speed up the operational investigation.

This approach is not completely new: many aspects of this approach are to be observed in daily police practice, but are often unsystematic often superseded by investigative 'vacuum cleaning'. This latter method, surveilling and observing as many targets as possible, usually does yield some results in the end, but one runs the risk of dissipating the scarce resources on many unpromising fronts. Hypothesis building may look 'academic' and not quite fitting into the police culture, yet it may prove to be the most parsimonious way of tackling complicated organised crime puzzles.

Recruiting

The above elaborated, analytical approach may have consequences for the staffing of organised crime squads. Psychological screening of applicants is a traditional task of the police psychologist (Brenner 1986; Hiatt 1986). However when the applicant has passed the tests and has been appointed, there is little psychological screening when the officers are assigned to new tasks. For example, recruiting staff for an organised crime squad is usually carried out on the basis of the (implicit) assumption that all detectives should be equally equipped to do all policework: the 'general task' assumption. This does not hold true for such delicate police tasks, as, for example, juvenile cases and sexual offences. The same is true for organised crime investigations. Investigating organised crime has a romantic aura, but as a matter of fact most of these investigations are tedious, require an extensive preparatory analysis, long term planning with more patience than action and a painstaking building up of the pieces of evidence against taciturn defendants. This requires other qualifications than those needed for most detective work:

Analytic capacity: Not only for hypothesis building but also for the subsequent process of information gathering in which complex social and economic relations have to be unravelled and recomposed into a 'best fit' construction. This requires another capacity than the 'hit and run' bust mentality.

Imagination and abstraction: This is implied in the previous requirement. It is not an advocacy for wild fantasies, but by this is meant a disciplined chain of 'if-then' thoughts. e.g.: 'what are the management consequences for a crime-enterprise if it has the supposed multimillion dollar turnover?' 'What is the line of development of a particular criminal trading network?'

'What are the functions of the various accomplices?' 'What happens if the police attack at a supposedly weak point?'

These requirements look more commonplace than they are. In view of the often traditional approach to crime-enterprises, it must be assumed that the qualities mentioned are not self evidently present everywhere. We wonder whether this is not frequently compensated by more staff and longer investigations?

Training

One frequently hears the lamentation that the villains are getting smarter every day. This is of course a relative development: smarter than who? If the police get sufficient on the job training and seminars which deal with the ongoing interactions between the entrepreneurial criminals and the developments in society (legislation, police methods, trading opportunities), such lamentation would be unnecessary. We believe that particularly for detectives who are engaged in organised crime investigations over a long time (sometimes for years), external courses, seminars and in-house service training are very important indeed.

These background activities of the psychologist should not be carried out in a compartmentalised way, as happens frequently when an outsider specialist fulfils certain tasks on behalf of the police. We are of the opinion that such tasks must be carried out in close interaction with the management and rank and file of the investigating crime squad. A specialist 'behind the front line' is frequently considered marginally important, consulted decreasingly (or to confirm an already held conviction) and finally forgotten, because the management feels he provides no added value to the 'real police work'.

This situation may be improved if the psychologist could also become engaged in the 'front line work' of the police, as we will elaborate in the next section.

The Investigative Psychologist at the Front-line

Much detective work of the police consists of everyday, intuitive psychology. Investigating is not merely observing, electronic surveillance and running informants, but also interpreting signs of the suspects involved, predicting what may be the next likely move of the target, finding out what his weaknesses are or how he treats his accomplices to find out whether and where there are cracks in the social structure. Also the interviewing of defendants and witnesses is more than a legal method of obtaining confessions or corroborating statements. The detective must have some insight into the psychological state and behaviour of his interviewee: when it makes no sense to continue questioning, when the defendant is 'about to break', or to what extent a witness/victim may be emotionally too confused to be of any help. The work of a detective has more psychological aspects than indeed he is aware of.

Given the contribution a psychologist may render in general and the 'human nature' tasks of the police, the experience of one of the authors being engaged in operational police work provides grounds for arguing that the participation of a psychologist can contribute to the efficiency of an organised crime investigation. Though many policemen consider only contributions leading to arrests and confessions 'real' contributions, such contributions are difficult to discern in complex teamwork operations. Just as is the case with the financial expert or the analyst, the psychologist contributes parts of the puzzle, which may lead to a better understanding of the whole picture.

We differentiate between the following aspects of the work of the psychologist.

Environmental and Situational Analysis

When one mobster remarked to his fellow mobster (being ripped of his share) that it was just 'business, nothing personal', the latter remarked 'in the crime business everything is personal', which is a correct assessment of the 'human' side of this industry. Successful crime-enterprises do not only owe their success to marketing skills, but more importantly to criminal 'human engineering', including 'human risk assessment'. Translated into simple mobster language: 'I only trade with whom I know and trust'. The social environment of central figures of an organised crime network are usually mapped by the analyst, providing only a mere skeleton of who has contacts with whom. The resulting 'organogram' or 'sociogram' may look impressive, but it frequently lacks contents (van Duyne (1995) considers such drawing 'bubblegrams'). Additional social information of the 'who with whom' is sometimes (orally) added, but unsystematically and haphazardly. However, such additional information for in-depth-analysis and concretisation of the criminal players in the field is very important indeed, because it provides the real proportions of the landscape in which they operate.

The Amsterdam criminal *Bruinsma*, a narcistic and violent personality, was considered by the police the head of organised crime in the Netherlands (van Duyne 1996). Time and again the police analysts produced huge flow diagrams in which he figures as the axis around which everything of criminal importance moved. However, a more subtle and psychological interpretation of the Bruinsma 'organisation' would have revealed a loose trading structure with a few personal spheres of influence of a 'big' boss and a few aids. Big boss Bruinsma was becoming a too flamboyant liability for his surroundings and was liquidated in the summer of 1991. Some of his aids took over his market share or simply expanded their existing share of influence and became the new captains of the crime business. Later it transpired that the big Bruinsma was only one of the wholesalers of hash and that many facts were incorrectly attributed to him. His death caused much upheaval, but did not affect the relations or the flow of goods and money on this crime-market. Instead of wondering and researching why there appeared to be so much social continuity in this market, the police simply started to chase the next target on the most-wanted-list. However, only very late the police started to look at some of the financial experts who seemed to be a constant factor in the network. The question which should have been asked is; given the modest education of the main figures, who are the brains to handle the complicated money-management? May they be considered the knots in the network? The money-managers/launderers have been targeted now, but there is still virtually no social-psychological picture of them.

Environmental analysis can also contribute to a strategy of 'outflanking movements'. It is very often difficult to approach the main target directly. By eliminating the surrounding supporting human 'satellites' the main crime-entrepreneur will encounter problems in finding replacement for his imprisoned aids and intercepted means of transport. This happened to a violent wholesaler in The Hague, who ran out of boats while he noticed that it became increasingly difficult to recruit new crew for new transports (van Duyne 1996). He finally resorted to blind violence to force the sale of a 'clean' boat, much to his final undoing, because these brutal, irrational acts provided the (wounded and terrified) witnesses the police needed.

Suspect and Group Analysis

The behavioural analysis of suspects is a second important task of the psychologist. This task has several aspects, uncertainties and difficulties. An important aspect is the expectation of the detectives, whose task it is to obtain *evidence*, not deep understanding of the inner life of the suspect. The psychologist, who is not the interrogator, cannot fulfil this expectation. However, as stated before, the psychologist can provide insight or systematise existing knowledge, which may steer the investigation towards a quicker result.

Starting with the last mentioned aspect, we believe that much everyday police insight into the character of the suspects is undervalued and insufficiently used, whether it concerns organised crime investigation, juvenile crime or sexual offences. Looking back at organised crime investigations in which we participated, we were often struck by the proliferation of knowledge about the prime suspects, however, without any systematic (written) integration of these bits and pieces of insight, or previous personal experience with the targets, into a coherent scheme. Even if the reliability of the knowledge about the character of the suspects is questionable (but this applies to all psychological knowledge), it is nevertheless a part of the mental representation of the targets, which implicitly guides the detective. Putting together these bits and pieces of 'floating knowledge' in search of more cohesion and a better psychological 'scheme' of the suspects may result in more direct action and searches. It should be mentioned that it has struck us that hardly any detective consulted the criminal files of previous investigations, which (in the Netherlands and Germany) very often contain detailed descriptions of the *modus operandi* and the 'smartness' revealed in committing other crimes, as well as expert reports of psychiatrists/psychologists on behalf of the prosecution or the defence. Disregarding all this information, except for the traditional list of previous police contacts, the police simply start anew, re-inventing the wheel.

A striking example of a crime-enterprise which the police could not penetrate using traditional means, while insufficiently elaborating old information, and ignoring social and psychological clues, has been briefly described in van Duyne (1996, p. 349).

The enterprise, called the Triumvirate is considered a global hash distributor. It is headed by *Gerald Chessplan*, but his accomplices, the musically talented charismatic *Wolfgang Soundstring* and the financially experienced *Joris Goldblood* are not his subordinates. When I analysed the first case against Chessplan in 1988 (van Duyne 1990), I was struck by his cool authority, calculating attitude and austere lifestyle. I was informed that he ordered his fellow-entrepreneurs as well as the lower ranking executives, to hand him the profits, which he would invest in Luxembourg. He demanded that they keep a low social and economic profile not indulging in the usual flashy criminal lifestyle. While this request was already remarkable, it was unprecedented (in my experience) that his staff complied in the first place. At that time my prediction was that this crime-entrepreneur would rise to the very top of the crime-trade, having the social background, education, intellect and self control to implement the necessary criminal risk management principles with due discipline. Up until now he has succeeded remarkably. He has access to the largest wholesale exporters of hash in Pakistan, to mobsters in North America and to various captains of industry in the Netherlands and Canada. The North American mobsters consider the austere Chessplan, the musical Soundstring (successful producer of CDs for his girlfriend) and Goldblood (who has bought two cigarette factories in Poland, partly as a cover) with a mixture of awe and amazement. These useful social-psychological, information fragments remained neglected and were not integrated into a hypothetical social and psychological profile for further investigation. Also neglected was the single informant, member of an exclusive gentlemen's club, who was unreliable and slimy indeed, but who could have been put under pressure by exploiting his problems with the Inland Revenue Service.

Meanwhile the surplus capital of this Triumvirate is supposed to have been invested in the energy and wood industry in Canada ($ 300 million), while a small amount may have been reinvested in the Netherlands (labour health service). The Health Firm Ltd. has recruited a former high ranking politician as President of the Board of Commissioners, who is supposed to be uninformed of the shady backgrounds of the shareholders of the Health Firm.

We do not want to claim that the Triumvirate could have been rounded up if only the police would have made use of psychological and sociological insights. However, a preparatory behavioural analysis making use of these disciplines could have led to a appropriate formulation of an investigation project.

The organised crime investigations in which the co-author psychologist participated targeted three crime-enterprises, mostly trading in the international hash market. Two enterprises also had (and still have) additional sources for illegal revenues. The psychologist's first task was to get more insight into the psychological and social status of the main suspects. Depending on the available information (and the state of investigation) the suspect analysis may encompass various traits and features. Very important are the emotional relations with the inner-circle of accomplices and aids and the intellectual level of the (prime) suspect(s). If suspects have previous convictions it is very likely that older criminal files contain the reports of intelligence tests (reasonable, reliable), personality tests (not so reliable), reports of social workers and of course, the statements of the suspect(s). Much insight can be gleaned by means of a systematic psychological analysis of this kind of 'old' information.

The leadership style of the entrepreneur of the first enterprise was characterised by delegating the operations of the various sub-groups, which worked rather autonomously. This had the advantage of creating a 'long line of evidence', making it difficult to prove his criminal responsibility for the transgressions. In normal circumstances the leader revealed a charming personality. Despite his poor educational record he showed a general interest in subjects not directly connected with his illegal trade and social surroundings. But under this veil of manliness simmered a violent ego which easily threatened to become manifest, though he had learned that outward violence could be counter productive to good criminal management.

The leader of the second crime-enterprise had not distanced himself from his streetfighter's backgrounds and revealed this character trait in his daily efforts to assert his authority. The daily management of his legitimate companies (which were of course not registered in his name) was in the hands of his 'senior' assistants who could direct the affairs without his interference. Having more feeling for the drug trade he was directly involved in the organisation of the smuggling operations.

The leader of the third crime-enterprise needed to use more violence to assert his position in the tough world of the crime-industry than he was normally inclined to. This may explain his decision to hire some bodyguards who also did the collection of money. He co-operated with two close friends and took care to maintain friendly relations to other powerful hash smugglers. In his daily management he could or would not delegate the smuggling operations or the money-management that they entailed. Despite this close supervision he was cheated by his 'staff' who carried out hidden operations for themselves.

It goes without saying that the suspect analysis has to be integrated into the environmental analysis mentioned under (a). The integrated picture should contribute to a 'weak spot' analysis of the crime-enterprise: where are the vulnerable (personal) elements; what are the limits of the human risk management of the leading figures (where does their direct control end); on whom are they dependent for the carrying out of their crime-trade? The weak spot analysis aims to concentrate the investigative resources instead of advancing on a broad front.

Investigation: Gathering Evidence and Interviewing

Most of the investigation, electronic and direct surveillance, the running of informants and the tracing of the flows of goods and moneys is plain detective work, a 'craft' in which the psychologist is an observer rather than an active participant. However, even as an 'observer' we participated in the discussions of the tactics to be used. In addition the psychologist carried out some situational studies, based on a combination and re-interpretation of information already available of the criminal sub-groups of the main targets and criminal relations they had with the media.

The situation is different when arrests have been made and the suspects are being interviewed. Here, where the personalities of the suspect and the detective are confronting each other one would expect a proper preparation on the part of the latter. However, in the circumstance of a detained suspect the police felt confident and superior enough not to make such preparations. It was observed that the detectives thought it sufficient to start interviewing by using only the available evidence which they put in front of the defendant hoping that he would surrender and start to talk. his approach may work for the majority of the usual small offenders, but frequently does not work with rationally operating calculating crime-entrepreneurs who know what is at stake. Though the more experienced detectives operated from a kind of implicit mental scheme of the suspect to direct his interview, each had his own mental representation of the criminal leading to various unharmonized approaches.

The participating psychologist in the investigation of the large hash wholesaler mentioned before, developed some measure to improve this state of affairs.

First he elaborated the idea that not every detective is capable of interviewing every suspect. The personalities of the interviewer and suspect should not be such that the latter would immediately block any psychological contact. This matching is an intuitive process, but it meant an improvement of the existing practice in which an interviewing detective could undo the work of his predecessors by adopting a poor psychological approach.

Secondly, he practised with the detective's aspects of verbal and non-verbal communication. Important aspects of this course were: how to establish contact with the suspect in the first place; developing a keener awareness of his emotional state of mind during the interview; ferreting out the verbal and non-verbal clues indicating the lies and (half) true statements of the suspect; formulating a coherent scheme of interrogation with a stepwise approach to the goals set for each session. Using a fictive, but comparable case, interview sessions were simulated and video recorded so that the detectives could monitor the improvement of their performance.

Thirdly, the author discussed with the detectives and the team leaders which detectives fitted certain defendants best to prevent the poor relations and bad results of prior interviews being maintained by a type of personality which did not suit the personality of the suspect.

Fourthly, the author made the detectives as well as the team leaders aware of the necessity of setting up a 'personality file' of the suspects right from the beginning, which can be used for preparing interviews, discussing further steps and the like.

Finally, the psychologist was involved in the crucial interrogations of the suspects for which he provided feedback to the detectives.

The adage 'know your defendant' seems most commonplace and taken for granted, but stressing time and time again that one does not know enough or that the available information was too implicit and vague helped the detectives in their practical work, structuring the preparation of their interview schemes and making them more confident about how to manoeuvre and steer between the changes in attitude (and statements) of the defendant.

Trial Preparation

One may expect that extensive and complicated organised crime investigations during which numerous suspects are often monitored and closely watched for more than a year, will yield an unambiguous 'map' of the organisation and that by the time the case goes to trial there are no more blind spots left. This may be the ideal situation, which is usually not met by reality. Most crime-enterprises do not operate like a real firm. They are characterised by a high degree of opacity and haphazard, disorderly decision making. This leaves the defence often times ample space to find weak spots in the prosecutors presentation and to cast doubts about the evidence presented to the court. In addition, the files of the investigation are usually tremendously voluminous, sometimes extending to more than ten metres. It would be a statistical miracle if such files did not contain some flaws to be used by the defence council.

In such cases, with strong evidence against the defendants, the defence strategy resembles frequently a war of attrition. First minor points in the prosecutor's presentation are attacked, questioning the legality of the means by which the evidence has been obtained. Small doubts are magnified and are linked to stronger points which then may 'share' in the atmosphere of doubt which is being extended. Secondly, a large number of legal procedural issues are raised, usually about the admissibility of the techniques of investigation. Thirdly, the large number of co-defendants, some of whom have turned into witnesses/informants, allows the defence council to play them off against each other, suggesting that the co-defendant's statements have been 'bought' by promising a lesser charge or the dropping of a prosecution.

For the investigators and their managers such trials mean spending long days in court to be called to the bench by the prosecutor or (more often) by the defence council. Even the more experienced police officer may feel moments of uncertainty when he has to testify about his role in the investigation. He is never certain whether some smart and wily barrister may pierce a little hole in his reliability and casts doubt on aspects of the evidence. Was the defendant seduced to making certain statements? Did the police officer use unfair tricks or did he pressurise the defendant unduly? Any wavering may lead to continued probing by the defence council and may weaken the case.

In order to prepare the police officers, the second author discussed what he had learned about the behaviour of the acting defence councils in other cases, either by observing their performance or by studying publications about trials in which they lead the defence. In addition court sessions were simulated in which experienced jurists acted as judge and prosecutor, which were videotaped. In this way the police officers got used to their role, learned from their mistakes or their physical appearance and got acquainted with the strategies of examination of the judges, prosecutors and defence councils. The most salient aspects of the simulated sessions were discussed with the whole detective unit, while individual detectives were counselled about uncertainties and their potential role and attitude (because of fear of failure) in court.

Inner-Group Processes of the Crime Squads

Large organised crime squads may count as many as 60-90 police officers. These crime squads are no permanent bodies. Apart from a few specialists and veterans they are composed of detectives and common policemen coming from other forces or units within the region. Some have experience with serious crime, like homicide, but in general not with organised crime-enterprises. Others come from the vice unit, the fraud squad or are simple, flatfoot policemen. This diversity of men with very different backgrounds have to be moulded into a single force aimed at most elusive targets, which may take one to two years, and sometimes more, to bring to trial. Given the fact that most police work has a short term, result-oriented nature (policemen are fond of criminal 'trophies'), the nature of organised crime investigation is very different, requiring painstaking preparations and the patient building up of evidence. From short term 'thief taker' they have to become 'organised crime strategists' of some kind.

It is predictable, that within such a context tensions within the crime squad, and between the crime squad management and the higher police officers (guarding the budget and other interests), will soon arise. Not all tensions are within the working area of the psychologist, but of a bureaucratic and political nature. The task of the psychologist concerns of course the inner-group processes.

Forming the heterogeneous members of the crime squad into some kind of operational cohesion is not easy and does not only depend on the participants. Very important is the interaction between the skills and characters of the participants and the tasks and targets. The last two determine who is fit for what, however in a very changeable way. For example during the first phases of the investigation the crime squad has to collect much basic information which can be carried out within concrete task assignments. In later investigation phases, when special criminals are targeted and are under constant observation, the mobility of the latter will make it difficult to keep certain officers allocated to one task only. Only highly specialised (and expensive) officers, like the financial specialists, are for example not sent out with a surveillance observation team, or used to transcribe the telephone tape recordings. The social composition of such an organised crime squad differs from crime squads in which 'masculine role expectation' or 'soldierly behaviour' prevail (Trompetter 1986). Action oriented officers have to work closely with patiently analysing accountants, unadventurous fiscal specialists and 'dry' jurists specialised in company law. This is a stereotype of course. During my work at the Dutch Fiscal Police (the FIOD) I rubbed shoulders with most imaginative and daring fiscal specialists, humorous accountants and witty civil jurists.

As can be deduced from the above, within the crime squad, the tasks of the psychologist can be very diverse indeed, ranging from counselling the team management to aiding individual members with personal problems. The latter individual problems were considered to be strictly private and the psychologist did not communicate them to the team management without prior consent, which required a careful balancing between the individuals and the squad's interests (Archibald 1986). However, monitoring the individual members of the squad had the advantage of making early suggestions about their performance and allocating the right man to the right place. In addition, quality improvement was attained by providing or suggesting additional individual or group training to cope with their tasks.

Inner-group processes were also improved by intermediate evaluations concerning internal and external co-operation, the technical progress made so far and in development of insight into the structure of the criminal organisation. Compared to crime squads, in which there is not only a 'division of labour', but also a 'division of knowledge' because of the rigid application of the 'need to know' rule, these presentations and evaluations contributed significantly to the cohesion between the investigators. One can say that this approach led to a feeling of belonging to a common cognitive and social space, in which agreements *not* to communicate information temporally was accepted as not unduly secretive.

The psychologist does not only have to deal with inner-group tensions. Of equal importance were the occasional threats to individual detectives, or their loved ones, by the targeted criminals themselves. This caused much emotional stress on the persons involved and on the immediate colleagues who knew they could be the next targets. Apart from the required police protection, which usually disrupts the private life of the whole family, psychological counselling and guidance was provided to cope with these traumatic experiences and to learn from them (Gentz, 1991).

Evaluation of Team Performance

It is quite natural that a team which looks back at what it has achieved will not be in the best position to evaluate the investigation of the functioning of the group. Aspects that have been evaluated by the psychologists concern the nature of internal and external co-operation, the group cohesion and 'human engineering' of the staff of detectives.

The evaluations were summarised in a number of statements and discussed during a 'crime squad day' in small groups, leading to suggestions by the participants for the improvements of observed shortcomings. For the next investigations these suggestions have been transformed into concrete new investigative approaches, for example concerning the formation of expertise and the maintenance of flexibility.

It appeared that during the first phases of the investigation, when the bits and pieces of information are unclear and widely scattered, that the formation of sub-teams around parts of the project led to expertise building, identification with tasks and better co-operation. As mentioned before, in the later phases of the investigation, with more direct and electronic surveillance, the 'little islands of expertise' lose their usefulness. The team has to adapt itself to the criminal group, which usually proves to be highly flexible (or chaotic). In this phase the detectives will have to accept being assigned to a variety of tasks.

The evaluation sessions directed to these human aspects of the investigation process served to make the group processes more transparent with more feedback and more willingness to change procedures.

Results

The active participation of a behavioural scientist in the operations of an organised crime squad is far from being a well-tested practice. Though some police forces in the Netherlands also include sociologists, psychologists and criminologists on their staff, such direct participation is still rather unique. It is therefore difficult to assess its added value in general. The remarks made in this section should therefore be regarded as highly tentative. Repetition of this experiment elsewhere may very well yield different outcomes and prove to be (locally) disappointing.

To be clear: the outcomes of this experiment were not disappointing. In various ways the involvement of the psychologist proved to be satisfactory, either concerning the more objective investigative goals or concerning the more subjective intergroups processes.

Increased Effectiveness

One of the effects of the behavioural participation is increased effectiveness in preparation and approach to the criminal targets. The social and psychological mapping of the criminal organisation and its participants reduced the time spent on analysing by the usually insufficiently trained policemen. The psychologist evaluated information from older criminal files (if present) and integrated these data into the updated 'criminal maps' of the targeted criminal figures and their social relations. This shortened the time needed to get a clearer picture of the targets and to rank order them according to their relative weights in the organisation. It also contributed to a more effective interrogation, preparing and matching the 'right detective' to the suspect. One can summarise this contribution as increasing effectiveness by 'direct targeting'.

Increasing Efficiency by Enhancing Work Satisfaction and Psychological Guidance

It is a common position that enhancing work satisfaction make people work more efficiently. The psychological guidance of work and group processes, the composition of the subteams in accordance with the available skills and phase of communication, the preparation for the trials, the feedback of information through the evaluation sessions and the trauma guidance in cases of personal threat, the execution of these tasks had positive effects on the morale of the organised crime squad. It resulted in a proper allocation of detectives to tasks and a reduction of 'communication time'. Of equal importance was the officers' training for the examinations during the trials which reduced uncertainty during the court appearance and made it easier to handle the pressure. This decreased the danger of attacks by the defending councillor, which may have resulted in suspending the trial for additional investigation into the procedures of the investigation. Such additional investigations imply much uncertainty, tension and workload, while there is always the risk that the defence succeeds in his role of 'raising doubt'.

Evaluation and Feedback

The above mentioned evaluation and feedback increased the learning capacity of the crime squad. Most organisations learn haphazardly by trial and error (if organisations learn at all). This is a time consuming undirected process with uncertain results. Frequently with the unwanted outcome of knowing better how to avoid problems instead of solving them. The evaluation sessions did stimulate problem-solving, leading to changes in the organisational approach of other organised crime cases. Because of this participation the changes were understood and accepted by 'shop' detectives.

Precipitation and Consolidation of Knowledge

As a rule the police force is quite expert in reinventing the wheel: when an investigation is finished the files are put into the archive and the detectives hurry to solve new cases: all run and none look back. The knowledge which has been generated is at best located 'in the heads' of the participating detectives and only accessible by interviewing the 'veterans' concerned. Most information and knowledge 'evaporates' when such veterans move to another force or department and new staff are requested to reinvent the wheel. The information which usually remains behind consists of the standardised criminal records of the convicted criminals. The previously described activities of evaluation and feedback of the outcomes have the important effect of making explicit, and laying down, the information generated during the criminal investigation. As a matter of fact such a consolidation of knowledge is vital for the setting up of an improved organisation for the next organised crime investigation.

Discussion

Many police forces are characterised by an inward looking culture. Police matters are police matters and those who do not come from within the forces (the born cop) are considered unqualified to deliver any contribution to solving police problems. Police work concerns *doing* things, *action* against criminals, *not* reflecting upon their psychological state of mind or the social criminal landscape. That is for probation officers and social workers who are the 'softies' and are held responsible for keeping villains out of jail, while the police are doing their job by locking them up.

During the unfolding policy against organised crime in the Netherlands this inward looking attitude proved to be fatal in its consequences when the police were facing complex cases which apparently required more talent than 'police instinct'. This may have contributed to the upheaval around some top secret investigations in which the police (and prosecution) overplayed its hand. The Dutch police recognised that contributions from other scientific disciplines are necessary in the fight against organised crime. However, most police forces restricted this broadened interest to taking in outside advice, while keeping its gates closed. Participating in *real* investigation was considered to penetrate too deeply into the heart of the police work. The innovative experience in this police force, which has an unorthodox tradition indeed, shows that a fruitful interaction between behavioural science and an organised crime squad is anything but a soft approach. Nor is it a veiled intellectual form of the regrettable 'war on crime'. It may rather be called an analytical and interdisciplinary form of law enforcement in the complex area of organised crime.

This broadened and integrated approach is worth elaborating, but it is not to be considered a general medicine that aids the police in solving all its investigative problems over night. Such naive expectations will only lead to disappointments and to the reaction that 'those scientists are no good' for the police. As stated earlier, there must develop an instructive interaction between equals with sufficient time for mutual enrichment and learning where to apply which discipline. van Duyne (1996) argued for a much broader use of scientific expertise against organised crime: economics, accountancy or anthropology in cases in which ethnic minorities are involved. Not all disciplines are required in all cases (sometimes even none of them), but they must be available and there must be a sufficient mutual intellectual understanding of the contents of each other's work to enable a correct assessment of the expected role and contribution.

References

Adler, P.A. (1985). *Wheeling and dealing. An ethnography of an upper-level drug dealing and smuggling community*. New York: Columbia University Press.

Adler, W.M. (1955). *Land of opportunity. One family's quest for the American dream in the age of crack*. New York: The Atlantic Monthly Press.

Anderson, A.G. (1979). *The business of organised crime. A Cosa Nostra Family*. Stanford: Hoover Institution Press.

Andrews, D.A. and Bonta, J. (1994). *The psychology of criminal conduct*. Cincinnati: Anderson Publishing Co.

Archibald, E.M. (1986). Confidentiality when the police psychologist is evaluator and caregiving practitioner. In: J.T. Reese and H.A. Goldstein (eds), *Psychological services for law enforcement*. Washington, D.C.: US Department of Justice.

Brenner, A.W. (1986). Psychological screening of police applicants. In: J.T. Reese and H.A. Goldstein (eds), *Psychological services for law enforcement*. Washington, D.C.: US Department of Justice.

Buchanan, D.R. and J.M. Hankins (1986). Ideology meets pragmatism: applied research in law enforcement. In: J.T. Reese and H.A. Goldstein (eds), *Psychological services for law enforcement*. Washington, D.C.: U.S. Department of Justice.

Clifford, B. (1979). Eyewitness testimony, the bridging of the credibility gap. In: D. Farrington, K. Hawkins and S.M. Lloyd-Bostock (eds), *Psychology, law and legal processes*. London: The Macmillan Press.

Duyne, P.C. (1990). *Misdaadondernemingen; ondernemende misdadigers in Nederland*. Arnhem: Gouda-Quint.

Duyne, P.C. (1995). *Het spook en de dreiging van de georganiseerde misdaad*, Den Haag: SDU-Uitgeverij.

Duyne, P.C. (1996). The phantom and threat of organized crime. *Crime, Law and Social Change,* nr. 4, p. 241-377.

Duyne, P.C. (in press). Organized crime, corruption and power. *Crime, Law and Social Change*.

Gentz, D. (1991). The psychological impact of critical incidents on police officers. In: J.T. Reese, J.M. Horn and Chr. Dunning (eds), *Critical incidents in policing*. Washington, D.C.: Department of Justice.

Hiatt, D.P. (1986). The benefits of psychological screening to applicants. In: J.T. Reese and H.A. Goldstein (eds), *Psychological services for law enforcement*. Washington, D.C.: U.S. Department of Justice.

Horn, J.M. (1988). Criminal personality profiling. In: J.T. Reese and J.M. Horn (eds), *Police psychology: operational assistance*. Washington, D.C.: U.S. Department of Justice.

Ianni, F.A. (1974). Authority, power and respect: the interplay of control systems in an organized crime "family" In: Rottenberg, S. (ed), *The economics of crime and punishment*. Washington D.C.: American Enterprise Institute for Public Policy Research.

Khster, D. (1991). Das Lagebild der organisierten Kriminalität in der Bundesrepublik Deutschland, illustriert anhad typischer Ermittlungsverfahren. In: *Organisierte Kriminalität in einem Europa durchlässiger Grenzen*. Wiesbaden: Bundeskriminalamt.

Lyng, S. (1990). Edgework, a social psychological analysis of volutary risk taking. *American Journal of Sociology, nr. 4*, p. 851-886.

Maltz, M.D. (1991). *Organized crime*, Chicago: Nelson Hall.

Rebscher, E. and Vahlenkamp, W. (1988). *Organisierte Kriminalität in der Bundesrepublik Deutschland*. Wiesbaden: BKA-Forschungsreihe.

Schoenberg, R.J. (1992). *Mr. Capone*, New York: William Morrow and Company Inc.

Trompetter, P.S. (1986). The paradox of the squad room - solitary solidarity. In: J.T. Reese and H.A. Goldstein (eds), *Psychological services for law enforcement*. Washington, D.C.: U.S. Department of Justice.

Wilson, J.Q. and J. Petersilia (eds), (1995). *Crime*. San Francisco: ICS Press.

4 Social Science Perspectives on the Analysis of Investigative Interviews

NIGEL FIELDING

Criminology is, by long-established practice, multi-disciplinary. As such it attends to areas of overlapping interest between disciplines, tending to neglect the more technical concerns of individual disciplines. This chapter aims to demonstrate the wider relevance of a methodological development in one discipline, social science, to criminology and to the practice of criminal investigation. Employing the example of suspected cases of child sexual abuse, the relevance of recent evaluations of the status of interview data is demonstrated in respect of investigators seeking legal evidence from interviews with victims, witnesses and suspect offenders. Many concerns raised by social scientists about the quality, reliability and validity of interview data apply equally to the problems faced by investigators seeking to interpret statements and non-verbal action by victims, witnesses and suspects. A profile of the micro-analysis of interview data is given, drawing on an interview with a very young suspected victim of sexual abuse. The example illustrates the interpretive work needed to carefully assess the evidence offered by an investigative interview. The approach is then related to the psychological approach to the interpretation of investigative interviews as represented by Statement Validity Analysis.

Nigel Fielding is Professor of Sociology and Director of the Institute of Social Research at the University of Surrey, England. His principal research interests are in policing, qualitative methods and new

*Offender Profiling Series: II - **Profiling in Policy and Practice***
Edited by D. Canter and L. Alison. © 1999 Ashgate Publishing, Aldershot. pp 83-101

technologies for social research. He has conducted research on police training and occupational socialisation, public order policing, community policing, the investigation of child sexual abuse, and police relations with ethnic minorities. He is an authority on computer software for the analysis of qualitative data and director of the UK national centre for qualitative software. From 1985 to 1998 he was editor of the Howard Journal of Criminal Justice and is currently editor of the Sage series "New Technologies for Social Research". He has served as consultant to the Police Training Council, Home Office, Bramshill Police Staff College, and the official Sheehy (and the independent Cassels) Inquiry on the Role and Responsibilities of the Police.

4 Social Science Perspectives on the Analysis of Investigative Interviews

NIGEL FIELDING

Tough Problems Need Multi-Disciplinary Responses

Criminology deals with some of the most intractable problems encountered in society. From its earliest days, criminology has recognised that no one discipline holds the answer to the problems of crime, victimisation and criminal justice. Law, forensic science, social and behavioural sciences have all contributed to the stock of knowledge. In this chapter, one discipline, social science, is isolated in order to consider the contribution it can make to investigators seeking to analyse interviews with victims and suspects. But the essential corollary is that its contribution is part of an effort that necessarily relies on insights from a range of disciplines.

Particular impetus to this approach has come from the author's research on the investigation of cases of child sexual abuse (Conroy, Fielding and Tunstill 1990; Fielding and Conroy 1992). The dominant emphasis in that field is on the *conduct* of the interviews and the way that investigators should be trained. Both the applied psychological literature and the legal commentaries reflect this emphasis. While social scientists also see the conduct of the interview as important, much recent attention has been devoted to the *analysis* of statements by respondents. The perspectives social scientists have applied to the debate over the status of interview data have implications for investigators seeking legal evidence from interviews.

Social Science and Police Work

Fieldwork methods, such as interviews and observation, are long-established methods of social research. Several early key studies of policing were conducted using qualitative methods (Banton 1964; Cain 1973; Reiner 1978). The social science contribution to police studies has continued to be marked by fieldwork methods and qualitative analysis. For instance, Reiner's 'Chief constables' (1991) is based on intensive interviews and several studies by police officers have drawn on qualitative methods, for example, Young's 'An inside job' (1991), an ethnography of a constabulary force.

The keynote of this fieldwork tradition has been its attention to the social context in which policing is carried out. The emphasis on social context, and the local social organisation generated by participants' orientation to that context, derives directly from the technical concerns of fieldwork methodology. Let us take the case of participant observation. The researcher seeks direct and sustained contact with the research subjects in their 'natural settings', an explicit contrast to the clinical observation of human subjects. The warrant for this lie in the idea that social action is best understood if one appreciates its meaning to those engaged in it. The argument is that such appreciation can be gained by directly experiencing the same round of daily activities, as do members. By 'introspection' the researcher assesses the differences between the persona they have adopted to get by in the setting and their persona as a researcher, to identify distinctive and characteristic constituents of the natural setting. Having been subject to the same round of constraints and contingencies, the researcher will have formed an appreciation of the ways that members' actions are oriented to features of the setting in which they operate as well as influenced by 'inner' values and attitudes.

Observational research has had an important role in policy-related research in policing. A good example is Irving's (1980) observational study of detectives for the Royal Commission on Criminal Procedure (1981), which examined the powers and duties of the police in the investigation and prosecution of crime, and the rights of suspects. The Commission believed psychological research to be particularly relevant but, as Farrington (1981) points out, Irving's research could not be characterised as 'psychological' because it did not pursue a hypothesis-testing experimental design. Such designs require random allocation to experimental and control groups, which would not be ethical where the dependent variable was a suspect's confessing to the police and the independent variable was the style of interrogation. Psychological research on human subjects often falls foul of such ethical problems.

However, the relationship between style of interrogation and likelihood of confessing could be investigated using real cases in a correlation research design. This could show that one style was *associated* with a significantly higher likelihood of confession although it could not conclusively attribute this difference to the style variable because of the other, uncontrolled variables arising from research in natural settings (as opposed to experimental ones). Experimental designs offer high *internal validity*, in demonstrating unambiguously that variation in one factor really does produce the variation in another. But such designs often have low *external validity*, because it is hard to generalise from the artificial settings of many experiments to real life. This is where social research comes in, using observation, interviews, and other basically correlation techniques to generate hypotheses. While typically low in internal validity, for the reasons given, it is usually strong on external validity, having been conducted in real life settings. These technical points again confirm the need for multi-disciplinary research combining hypothesis-generating and hypothesis-testing in a logical sequence, which would eventuate in robust analyses high on both internal and external validity.

Irving (1980) observed 76 interrogation interviews involving 60 different suspects, but acknowledged the limits of a relatively small-scale study conducted by one person in one police station, characterising the work as 'a reconnaissance exercise' (op cit:82). Irving's police were fully aware of his research and he styled himself as having adopted a policeman's role, making it unsurprising that he observed no breach of Standing Orders. His final report was subject to consultations with police before it was submitted, and his field notes were written from memory. Whilst there were good reasons for these procedures, they do suggest the constraints on internal validity in fieldwork settings. But this does not mean such research has no value, only that there are some questions it can answer and others it cannot.

Irving's hypothesis-generating research answered one question that was very important to the Commission. He reported that 'while watching any given suspect being interviewed, the observer found it impossible to judge whether the state of that suspect would have constituted sufficient grounds for excluding the statements which ensued either on the basis of involuntariness or oppression' (ibid:136). The then current Judges' Rules only permitted voluntary statements to be submitted to the court. While violence was neither threatened nor used in the interviews, Irving could not distinguish between voluntary and involuntary statements, because of the psychological state of suspects. This question, which went to the heart of officers' ability to attribute voluntariness to statements to be presented to the court, could indeed be addressed by field observation. If the distinction was obscure to Irving, a trained observer with a background in psychology and social science, it could be expected to be equally so to police. Irving recommended that the distinction between voluntary and involuntary statements should be abolished and new safeguards introduced. Irving had absorbed the social context of interrogation and reached the conclusion that officers working in it could not claim faithful adherence to the legal criterion. The Commission accepted his recommendation.

Much the same emphasis on social context can be seen in fieldwork based on intensive interviewing. The social scientist will devote considerable attention to the interaction between interviewer and respondent. It is not only what the respondent says in isolation, as it were, but the way what the respondent says may be affected by what the interviewer says (and how the interviewer behaves), which is analysed. Matters such as the rapport achieved between the two, the environment in which the interview takes place (e.g., whether there are interruptions), and the match between the interviewer's characteristics and those of the respondent, are taken into account.

A final relevant characteristic of social science approaches is the idea of 'reflexivity'. We all approach things from different perspectives, with different criteria of fact and fiction, and so on. This being so, there can be no single criterion of 'truth' equally persuasive to all in analysing human behaviour, in contrast to the axioms of natural science. The reflexivity notion suggests that it is necessary to take into account one's own biography and influence when analysing social phenomena. Another researcher may literally 'see' the phenomenon differently and be drawn to different emphases in the analysis. While some carry this to an extreme by denying the authority of *any* analysis, it does seem sensible to acknowledge the problem by making as explicit as possible the perspectives which one brings to the analysis and making as visible as possible the inferences upon which one has drawn in preferring one interpretation over another.

Interviewer Effects and Interviews as Accounts

The perspectives under discussion have developed in the literature on fieldwork methodology, particularly interviews. Many concerns social scientists have about the reliability and validity of their research data apply equally to the problems faced by investigators when they grapple with statements by victims, witnesses and suspected offenders. Further, these insights are now more readily applicable in law enforcement because victims', witnesses' and suspected offenders' statements are increasingly being recorded in a readily accessible form. Researchers have routinely audio-taped interview data since the introduction of tape recorders and were among the first professional users of video recording. With moves to record an increasing range of interviews, investigators can apply the intensive techniques developed in the analysis of research interviews. These rely on close, repeated inspection of the recorded data.

It will be obvious to any police officer that the points made earlier about the effects on response of the interviewer's manner, characteristics and modes of verbal expression, also apply to investigative interviews. The point is explicit in interrogator training, where particular interrogative tactics are identified by colourful terms, such as 'sweet and sour'. Such tactics have largely been directed to securing compliance and eliciting a statement. However, in light of concern about the quality of the evidence elicited in interrogations, there is a case to adopt analytic techniques which permit the limits of a particular interpretation to be estimated.

There is a considerable corpus of methodological literature on interviewer effects. One of the earliest concerns was the problem of 'socially desirable' responses. The early work on interviewer effects was largely done in the USA, where it emerged that the interviewer's race significantly influenced responses (Hyman 1954). White researchers interviewing black respondents were given 'socially desirable' responses that downplayed social problems experienced by respondents. Black respondents were more apt to share their criticisms, and express them more forcefully, with black researchers. The finding was borne out with other ethnic groups. Indeed, the same effect was noted with regard to gender, age and social class

This methodological research led to the conclusion that, wherever possible, there should be 'interviewer matching'; respondents should be interviewed by people as much like themselves in their broad social characteristics as possible. But these characteristics were not the only ones affecting the quality of response. The interviewer's behaviour also affected response. For instance, the respondent's 'verbosity' was affected by how aggressively the interviewer probed; aggressive interviewers elicited more information (Shapiro and Eberhart 1947).

However, it is important to note that the findings from this research are culturally-specific. They arise from research in the USA and at a particular point in time. We should not expect the findings to apply universally. What is safe to say is that the interviewer's social characteristics and behaviour need to be taken into account when interpreting what the respondent says. We can take the cultural-specificity point further. A study of the prevalence of mental disturbance in New York City initially concluded that, holding social class constant, such disturbance was more common among Hispanic people than among Jewish people, Irish-Americans and African-Americans. However, the researchers subjected the mental health inventory they were using in their interviews to a social desirability rating and found that Hispanic people were less concerned about mental disturbance and consequently felt less stigma in reporting it (Dohrenwend 1964). So the respondent's culture of origin can have effects which need to be taken into account in analysing response.

Among other important findings of the 'interviewer effects' research are that inexperienced and experienced interviewers receive distinctively different responses (the former tend to elicit terse, unelaborated responses, having difficulty achieving the rapport which leads to longer responses), and that question wording, particularly the use of prompts (which are to be avoided) and probes (which are a crucial device), and the sequence in which questions are put, affect reliability and validity (see Sudman and Bradburn 1974).

For some, these concerns undermine the value of interview data altogether. They argue that all we can usefully study is the way that interviewer and respondent work together to produce the appearance of an interview. Their attention shifts from the interview as a *resource* to the interview as a *topic*. They discount the data as affording insight into the truth of the respondent's views or reported actions, instead concerning themselves with the social organisation of interviews as occasions in which *accounts* of action are traded, none of those accounts necessarily relating to the action that really occurred (Gilbert and Mulkay 1984). Thus the last twenty years have seen a move from a positivist emphasis on interviews as information-gathering methods, with some notion of 'truth' and some effort to gauge reliability and validity, to regarding interviews as interactional accomplishments in which there is a joint construction of meaning by interviewer and respondent (Mishler 1986).

Such considerations may seem marginal in the context of investigative interviews and the collection of legal evidence. However, there is reason to attend to these considerations even here. The positivist goal of generating interview data which hold independently of both intersubjectivity and context largely proceeds by seeking to standardise the conduct of the interview, and by comparing response by individuals differently located in the research setting. This is not possible in interviews with many victims and witnesses. Standardised interview formats require a degree of compliance with set procedures which children may be unwilling or unable to grant. As to the procedure of interviewing individuals differently located in the setting (and thus 'triangulating' their opinions as a validity check), investigators are most likely to rely on interviewing the suspected victim just when other informants are lacking. Under these circumstances it is inappropriate to analyse the interview statements purely on assumptions derived from standardised interviewing methods. Closer attention to the way that questions and responses are formulated in, and shaped by, the discourse between interviewers and respondents, is called for.

The idea is not to engage investigators in a scholarly parlour game about the status of interviews, but to assist their aim of establishing what happened by means of the least intimidating possible procedures, particularly with child victims. The legal status of children's evidence remains problematic. Investigators naturally want to obtain evidence which is robust. But a report by HM Inspectorate of Constabulary and the Social Services Inspectorate (1992) on the joint investigation of child sexual abuse found that 'there had been no guidelines or training for officers involved in this activity. The equipment used was limited and the accommodation was not purpose-built. There were technical deficiencies in some of the videos' (ibid: para.9.1). Extra training was needed so staff could structure the interviews taking full account of the rules of evidence.

But while investigator training emphasises that the careful conduct of the interview is the key to reliable evidence, the complexities of interpretation which investigators encounter suggest that similar emphasis needs to be placed on the analysis of the dialogue as a product of the situated context of an interaction between investigators and victims/witnesses. Investigative attention is, understandably, first drawn to 'disclosures'. But defence lawyers also have access to child interview recordings, and locating the 'disclosure' in its context can offer them a way of discrediting the entire interview. It then becomes a matter of determining the relative quality of the inferences made by both sides when interpreting statements by the victim/witness. Statements taking the form of a 'disclosure' can be put alongside other 'factual' assertions in the interview and their relative plausibility assessed, for example by attention to their narrative structure as well as their surface content. Interviews create their own 'internal history', developing a consensual narrative whose content is constrained by previous statements. This can be an analytic resource, for example, when investigators seek to establish the degree to which the respondent has been 'led' to make a particular statement.

A Fieldwork Example

A profile can be given of the micro-sociological analysis of a victim interview, drawing on videotaped data from an interview with a suspected victim of child sexual abuse. During research into the joint investigation by police and social workers of suspected cases of child sexual abuse, a corpus of videotaped interviews with child victims and witnesses was compiled (Fielding and Conroy 1992); the extract which follows has been anonymised and various details changed to protect the identity of those involved. The extract occurs halfway through a 30 minute interview, one of several with two young brothers. It involves interviewer one (I1), a female police officer, interviewer two (I2), a female social worker, and a boy, Robin, the younger of the brothers, aged about four and suspected of having been the victim of sexual abuse in the family home. At the point where we join the interview, Robin has just been persuaded to stay to talk to the interviewers rather than go to his mother elsewhere in the building.

I1: *Come on here and sit with me (boy takes a place next to I1, who is on her knees on the floor surrounded by 6 large anatomically-detailed dolls and some stuffed animals). Oo's this, oo's this (motioning to 'adult male' doll earlier undressed by boy)?*

R: Daddy.

I1: *An' oo's this?*

R: Me.

I1: *You, right. And that's you bin playin' naughty games, have you (lightheartedly).*

R: *Yeah, my dad, my bro', my dad 'as (boy is squirming on I1's lap. I1 has left arm encircling R and right arm holding his elbow).*

I1: *Your brother and your dad. Does your daddy do those naughty things to Philip (brother)?*

R: *Yeah (quaveringly). And to me too (very quietly in a self-pitying tone, as he lies back spreadeagled and looks directly into I1's face, who is cradling him, holding his reclining head with her right forearm).*

I1: *And to you too (with emphasis). Does he? (R makes barking noise and 'chucks' chin of I1, returns to sitting position. Both talk at once, as follows).*

R: *Uuh, I mean we were right and (struggles forward off I1's lap from sitting position)...*

I1: *What does Philip say to your dad? (restrains R with left arm around his waist and right arm holding his shoulder, boy struggles)...*

R: *I'll show you what (I1 pulls boy in sitting position back on to her lap, holds his right thigh with her right arm and places her left hand past his neck to hold his shoulder).*

I1: *Tell me, tell me something, what does Philip say to your daddy when he does these things? (boy looks frustrated, attempts to push I1's right arm away irritably, pulls her arms apart with backward motion of his arms, sits back hard on her lap, I1 moves her head hard right).*

R: *Uh. (silent pause, boy looks straight ahead blankly, without looking up. Suddenly says:) Let me show you something (standing up and motioning expansively with right arm). What's along, 's down the stairs, get over (treads over dolls, exits). What's this in the middle?*

I1: *That's a cellar, that's a cellar down there.*

R: *How can you, get down there when you look out, the...cel-lar? There?*

I1: *How can you get down there? I don't think you can, you need a very very long ladder.*

R: Have you got one?

I1 and I2: No (boy wanders off to switch on light)...

After three minutes of clearing up dolls, Robin is running around the edge of the room,

I1 points to him with a grin.

I1: Did you tell your mummy that your brother had been doing naughty things?

R: Yeah (blithely as he runs past).

I1: Did you tell your mummy that your daddy had done naughty things?

R: Yeh, I'm just showing something, look.

I2: That's Snoopy, isn't it (I2 and R off camera, I1 has rueful grin).

R: And I'll show (runs past I1, who grabs him).

I1: Gotcha.

R: She's cat.

I1: I gotta ask you one or two questions, right (holds boy high on her lap, his head close to hers). Did you tell your mummy that Philip'd done naughty things to you? (I1's face is an inch from R's face. Their cheeks touch, both grinning broadly).

R: Yes (loudly, triumphant in tone, immediately struggles to get off lap, I1's arms completely enfold him).

I1: Did you tell your mummy (the boy, giggling, struggles to get off lap). Listen, wait-a-minute, one more question, then you can go, quick (spoken very quickly in rising tone as boy launches his whole frame hard left and seeks to propel himself out of the loop formed by I1's arms, then lies in cradle formed by I1's arms and looks up). Did you tell your mummy that your daddy did naughty things to you?

R: Yes (emphatically, but very quickly compared to previous 'yes').

I1: Did you?

R: Yeh.

I1: What did she say?

R : She smacked my daddy. Said (mimicking adult voice) 'don't you dare do that'.

I1: Did she?

R: Eric (father's name, completing previous phrase; boy still on I1's lap, more settled).

I1: And what did 'Eric' say?

R: Naughty things. Nothing.

I1: Nothing.

R: 'e said nothing (struggling onto his feet).

I1: Daddy said nothing.
R: No (hops away on one foot). Now I'm going back where mum is.

Earlier in the interview, the boy has variously stated that: his brother (about two years older) had 'put his bits in my bottom' while playing, that 'my brother sucked my willy' encouraged by two other boys whom he named and, the topic having been initiated by the interviewer, that his brother played these 'naughty games a lot'. He had also stated that only his brother, no other children, played these games, that the game had happened only once, that during these games they took their clothes off, that during the games they took only their shorts off, and that during these games they were in their pyjamas. He also stated that no one else did this to him, that his father played these games with him, that only his brother and mother had taken his trousers off, that his father had taken his trousers off, and that his father 'always smacked' his brother for forcing himself on the respondent. Despite these contradictions, the boy gives a perfectly competent demonstration of anal intercourse using the dolls.

Clearly, the respondent presents the investigators with a difficult task in determining the truth. These contradictions are, however, partly susceptible to 'de-coding' by reference to the context of other statements in the interview. For instance, the matter of who removed the boy's shorts can be resolved on the basis that, when first asked who removed his shorts, the boy responded in terms of who normally undressed him at bedtime (his mother) and in terms of the person who had, up to that point, been the only person 'implicated' in the sex games, his brother, whereas the later reference to his father removing his trousers is made in the context of an extended description of the father's participation in the 'naughty game'.

Another feature of the transcript is the constant movement and limited attention span of the child, qualities typical of interviews involving children of this age in our sample. While it is understandable if investigators (and defence lawyers) primarily attend to the surface content of the statements, by doing so they may be missing a substantial analytic resource. Proxemic qualities lend some insight into the context in which statements are elicited. For instance, the 'grinning' by the interviewers and respondent in the extract seems curious in the case of child abuse, but is explicable by reference to the context of the interview as it proceeded.

It may also be important in assessing whether reliable responses have been elicited because the behaviour puts the child at ease.

The extract features descriptions of the participants' movements, particularly child respondents, in some detail, on the basis that some of what is said is explicable by reference to physical actions. Some of the interviewers' physical actions are quite gross. They feature various attempts to restrain the respondent and maintain his focus on the subject under investigation. This may lead to unreliable statements because the child is concerned to use any means to escape the restraint and resume play. Gross restraint may also lead the respondent to concentrate so hard on escape that he cannot concentrate on the topic, as in the failure of the interviewer's attempt to find out from Robin what Philip said to his father when his father allegedly forced his attentions on Philip. Yet if we were to concern ourselves only with the words transcribed, we may well be content to rest with the prior statement that his father had subjected the older brother to 'naughty games'.

As noted earlier, both the professional response and psychologists' guidance in reacting to such observations has emphasised that interviews must be conducted in a particular way, with full regard to the requirements of legal evidence. However, it can plausibly be argued that, whatever investigators do to control their behaviour, young children can undermine attempts to proceed in a formal, controlled fashion. Indeed, this view is supported in research evaluating interviewer training by those who have advocated the need to conduct the interviews in a precisely controlled way; Lawrance et al (1990) found that training was ineffective in achieving such objectives. The alternative must surely be to devote attention to analysing the kind of data that is realistically available.

Returning to the extract at hand, there is also the matter of evasiveness, which may also afford a means to determine validity of response. Douglas (1976) argues that evasiveness is particularly likely in children as an alternative to outright lies, since children take injunctions about the perils of lying very literally. In the second extract, we re-joined the interview as the interviewer posed a question about whether Robin has told his mother about Philip's assaults on him. This elicits two clear, affirmative responses, but they are unelaborated, consisting of no more than 'yeah'. Robin then darts off the topic just as he utters the second 'yes', by declaring that he wants to show the interviewers something. Not to be defeated, the interviewer literally grabs him and forces him to sit down, hastily putting her agenda to him: she just has to ask a couple more questions and he can then do what he likes. Robin complies by offering the most elaborate of all his responses in the extract, an account of the alleged conversation between his mother and father following his mother's discovery of the father's alleged behaviour. Estimating the honesty of this account would involve close attention to all the occasions in which a sudden topic shift by the respondent had followed the elicitation of pertinent information. The question is whether such occasions were evasions or simply reflections of a limited span of attention.

Thus far little has yet been said about the terms in which questions are put. Some questions in the extract may be thought to have been put in leading form. But it could be argued that, with respondents of this age, it would be difficult to pursue the topic in any other way. Concern over leading questions is important, but we also need to acknowledge that the interviewer's physical actions can 'lead' or manipulate response. In this regard, it may be noted that the child's relatively detailed statement about the mother's reaction follows his settling into a limp position in the cradle formed by the interviewer's arms.

It is not being claimed that the tentative interpretations being offered here are anything more than plausible. The determination of what 'actually happened' requires that those analysing the interview state the warrant for their inferences in as much detail as they can. The evidence available for each particular interpretation can then be compared and a decision made as to the best-supported interpretation. This process of iteration (Agar and Hobbs 1985) relies on a comparison of all the data to support particular interpretations. All possible readings are made explicit so the quality of evidence supporting each can be assessed.

Attention to the character of probing and other questioning techniques is only one important check that can be performed in assessing statements made in investigative interviews. 'Content criteria' confined to the evidential statement may be distinguished from general validity checks (Raskin and Yuille 1989). The dynamic contextual considerations discussed here can be added to the content criteria summarised by Steller and Koehnken (1990) and shown in Figure 4.1.

General characteristics

1. Logical structure
2. Unstructured production
3. Quantity of details

Specific contents

4. Contextual embedding
5. Descriptions of interactions
6. Reproduction of conversation
7. Unexpected complications during the incident

Peculiarities of the content

8. Unusual details
9. Superfluous details
10. Accurately reported details not understood
11. Related external associations
12. Accounts of subjective mental state
13. Attribution of perpetrator's mental state

Motivation-related contents

14. Spontaneous corrections
15. Admitting lack of memory
16. Raising doubts about one's own testimony
17. Self-deprecation
18. Pardoning the perpetrator

Offence-specific elements

19. Details characteristic of the offence

Figure 4.1 Content Criteria for Statement Analysis

The level of detail is a criterion widely applied to plausibility. An example of 'contextual embedding' is the description of everyday occurrences as part of the story; these are facts or peripheral events that are incorporated into recall. When 'descriptions of interactions' include misperceptions by the child they are particularly consistent with validity

(Raskin and Yuille: 198). 'Reproduction of conversation' lends validity, especially when the child differentiates various roles, uses language not typical of their age, cites arguments used by the accused and so on. Validity is reinforced by mention of 'unexpected complications' like a neighbour coming to the door.

The third set of criteria reflect the 'concreteness' and vividness of the account. Invented accounts seldom include superfluous or improbable details, nor reference to the child's or perpetrators mental state. Reference to details not understood is exemplified by a child's report that the perpetrator seemed to be in pain because of groaning noises made during the sexual contact. 'Related external associations' concerns references to overlapping relationships, such as a victim's statement that the perpetrator had asked about her sexual experiences. 'Motivation-related contents' focus on the child's ability to fabricate an account. Because they tend to be seen by the speaker as undermining their account, spontaneous corrections actually heighten validity, as with admitted lack of recall, or doubts. By offering explanations of the behaviour, 'self deprecation' and 'pardoning' are also consistent with validity. The ability to assess 'offence-specific elements' is contingent on knowledge of how these offences are committed, and refers to knowledge contrary to commonly held assumptions. For instance, many incestuous relationships begin with a long period of relatively minor sexual behaviour which escalate into more serious acts (Sgroi 1982).

There is thus a great deal that may be done to assess validity through detailed scrutiny of statements. This still forms only part of the assessment. Psychological characteristics concerning the child's behaviour during interview, with attention to appropriateness of language and knowledge of the child's developmental experience are also helpful. The presence or lack of affect is also monitored; reference to a painful penetration would expectedly be accompanied by non-verbal signs of discomfort. Spontaneous and timely use of appropriate gestures, such as raising arms above the head when describing being held down, heighten validity. If the interview has been flexibly conducted it will be possible to assess susceptibility to suggestion by noting the child's reaction to incorrect interpretations posed by interviewers. Descriptions of events inconsistent with the laws of nature or previous statements, e.g., sexual acts performed in physically impossible ways, are also significant. One may also consider the circumstances under which allegations have emerged. Spontaneous provision in a typical context such as telling a teacher or friend reinforces validity, while elicitation by a parent involved in a divorce may be suspect (Raskin and Yuille op cit).

Thus, while the insights of social scientists into the contextual features of the production of talk in interviews provide investigators with a useful means of assessing the strength of evidence for the inferences supporting particular interpretations, this is by no account a replacement for the several other procedures which a stringent investigation requires.

References

Agar, M. and Hobbs, R. (1985). Growing schemata out of interviews, in R. Dougherty (ed.), *Directions in cognitive anthropology*, Homewood, Ill.: Dorsey.

Banton, M. (1964). *The policeman in the community*, London: Tavistock.

Cain, M. (1973). *Society and the policeman's role*, London: Routledge and Kegan Paul.

Conroy, S. Fielding, R and Tunstill, J. (1990). *Investigating child sexual abuse*, London: Police Foundation/Policy Studies Institut.

Dohrenwend, B. (1964). A use for leading questions in research interviewing. *Human Organization*, 23, 76-7.

Douglas, J. (1976). *Investigative social research.* London: Sage.

Farrington, D. (1981). Psychology and police interrogation. *British Journal of Law and Society*, 8(1), 97-107.

Fielding, N. and Conroy, S. (1992). Interviewing child victims: police and social work investigations of child sexual abuse. *Sociology,* 26(1), 103-24.

Gilbert, G.N. and Mulkay, M. (1984). *Opening Pandora's Box: a sociological analysis of scientists' discourse.* Cambridge: Cambridge University Press.

HM Inspectorate of Constabulary and Social Services Inspectorate (1992). *A report on joint police and social services investigation of child sexual abuse in Nottinghamshire: Executive Summary.* London: Home Office.

Hyman, H. (1954). *Interviewing in social research.* Chicago: University of Chicago Press.

Irving, B. (1980). *Police interrogation: a case study of current practice.* Research study no. 2, London: Royal Commission on Criminal Procedure.

Lawrance, K., Aldridge, J. and S. Cameron (1990). *Research into the use of video in the investigation of child abuse.* West Yorkshire Police Community Affairs Unit.

Mishler, E. (1986). *Research interviewing.* Cambridge, MA: Harvard University Press.

Raskin, D. and Yuille, J. (1989). Problems in evaluating interviews of children in child sexual abuse cases, in S. Ceci, D. Ross and M. Toglia, (eds), *Perspectives on children's testimony.* NY: Springer-Verlag.

Reiner, R. (1978). *The blue-coated worker.* Cambridge: Cambridge University Press.

Reiner, R. (1991.) *Chief Constables.* Oxford: Clarendon Press.

Royal Commission on Criminal Procedure (1981). *Report,* Cmnd. 8092, London: HMSO.

Sgroi, S. (1982). *Handbook of clinical intervention in child sexual abuse.* Lexington MA: Lexington.

Shapiro, S. and Eberhart, J. (1947). Interviewer differences in an intensive survey. *International Journal of Opinion and Attitude Research,* 2.

Steller, M. and Koehnken, G. (1990). Statement analysis: credibility assessment of children's testimonies in sexual abuse cases, in D. Raskin, (ed.), *Psychological methods for criminal investigation and evidence.* NY: Springer-Verlag.

Sudman, S. and Bradburn, N. (1974). *Response effects in surveys.* Chicago: Aldine.

Young, M. (1991). *An inside job.* Oxford: Clarendon Press.

5 False Allegations of Child Sexual Abuse

RAY ALDRIDGE-MORRIS

Controversy has always surrounded the area of child sexual abuse. Over the last decade in particular extraordinary allegations, including serial sexual satanic abuse have been made that whilst having no substantive evidence to back their claims have resulted, on some occasions in securing convictions. The following outlines some examples of these cases as well as highlighting how advocates of the claims have argued their case. Many of their beliefs rest on a poor understanding of memory and are little more than verbal legerdemain. In contrast the chapter outlines research on memory that suggests "repression" and spontaneous memory of previously forgotten serial sexual abusive events are a very unlikely phenomena. The lack of validation for any of the claims or memory-related phenomena such as repression that they are packaged with suggests a far more sceptical outlook upon such fantastical allegations should be strongly promoted.

Ray Aldridge-Morris trained as a clinical psychologist at the University of Liverpool from 1962-1967. He went on to take his doctorate at the Institute of Psychiatry under Hans Eysenck and was the first head of psychology at which is now Middlesex University from 1970 to 1983. His book "Multiple Personality: an Exercise in Deception" (1989, reprinted 1991) is a sceptical treatment of MPD which received many favourable reviews. It has led to further sceptical critiques of applied phenomena not least "false memory syndrome" and the practices of recovered memory therapists. He is a founder member of the scientific advisory board of the British False Memory Society. Ray currently

Offender Profiling Series: II - Profiling in Policy and Practice
Edited by D. Canter and L. Alison. © 1999 Ashgate Publishing, Aldershot. pp 103-122

works in clinical practice as a member of the Primary Care Psychology Team with the Hackney and City Community NHS Trust.

5   False Allegations of Child Sexual Abuse

RAY ALDRIDGE-MORRIS

This chapter is about the abuse of adult women by their counsellors and therapists. It is about allegations of child sexual abuse (CSA) for which there is no evidence other than the belated, uncorroborated, testimony of adult offspring. Typically, such revelations are presented as "insights" achieved in something called "recovered memory therapy", all too frequently in sessions with counsellors-cum-therapists with questionable professional credentials.

It is no easy task to produce accurate incidence and prevalence rates of genuine cases of CSA and estimates range from one extreme to another. Differing definitions of abuse and varying standards of criteria for acceptable, corroborative evidence make it difficult to compare studies. From the USA perspective, Levitt and Pinnell (1995) conclude that government reports probably underestimate the problem whilst independent studies overestimate it.

The reality and horror of genuine abuse is not questioned. Even in the absence of a consensus about the extent of CSA it is impossible to escape from the conclusion that it is a widespread and growing phenomenon. However, for reasons which will become progressively clear, it is argued that we should treat sceptically a particular sub-species of CSA allegations.

No one, professional or lay, can fail to have heard of the phenomenon of 'recovered memories'. The BPS working party report on recovered memories (January, 1995) defines these as memories "where adults come to report memories of childhood events having previously been in a state of total amnesia for such events".

However, Memon (1995) cautions that the "BPS report does not point out how limited the evidence is. It gives the misleading impression that total/partial memory loss is commonly associated with trauma and its occurrence cannot be explained on the basis of normal memory phenomenon (sic). There is no evidence that such memories are 'recovered' in pristine form and even if there were, there is no way of verifying accuracy... In any case it is well established that it is possible to produce clear memories of 'implanted' events".

Memon is undoubtedly referring to the research of Ceci and Bruck (1993, 1995) and Ofshe and Watters (1994). Ceci has provided convincing demonstrations that children will eventually answer "yes" to questions about incidents which did not happen, provided the question is asked repeatedly. In one procedure, for example, children were asked whether they had every caught their finger in a mouse-trap. At the outset, all children denied that such an event had ever occurred. The children were asked the same question over the ensuing ten weeks at weekly intervals. There was no coercion, not even gentle persuasion. Interviewers were at pains to avoid creating any scenario which could be described as "suggestive" and the videotaped recordings of their procedures bear this out.

Notwithstanding, all the children eventually affirmed that such an accident had indeed happened. Further, they went on to confabulate, providing rich accounts of the witnesses and admission to hospital casualty departments. In one instance, the father of a child "debriefed" him and explained that the incident really had not taken place. The only effect this had on the child's testimony was to make him more insistent, pleading, as it were, "it did so happen".

Ofshe was an expert witness in the trial of a policeman in the USA, which has become a 'cause celebre'. Paul Ingram was accused by his daughters of rape, in the role of a priest in a satanic cult. Ingram was so overwhelmed by the accusations that he decided they must be true. How could daughters whom he loved so dearly possibly tell lies about such an event? However, Ofshe suggested to Ingram that he had committed another offence, that he had forced his children to watch him have intercourse with his wife. This incident formed no part of the allegations against Ingram. It was a complete fabrication by Ofshe. Nonetheless, Ingram now admitted to this offence also. The court remained unconvinced. Ingram continues to languish in jail. False confessions are not rare as Gudjonsson (1992) points out in his "The Psychology of Interrogations, Confessions and Testimony".

A seminal book, of a very different calibre, in the history of recovered memories was "Michelle Remembers" written by one Michelle Smith and her therapist, Dr. Pazder (1980). Smith and the charismatic Pazder subsequently divorced their spouses and married one another.

Dr. Bryan Tully (1995), the British forensic psychologist summarises: "Michelle recovered memories from apparent complete amnesia of grotesque sexual abuse at the hands of a satanic cult, in which her parents participated, and was led by the devil. She described herself as a 5-year-old child naked in a cage full of snakes. She described stillborn babies butchered and burned. She described lurid sex acts and how she was subjected to surgery so that horns and a tail could be attached to her body". The book is assuredly an elaborate hoax.

The phenomena of recovered memories has had enormous media coverage beginning in, the USA, and migrating across the Atlantic and Pacific to Britain, The Netherlands and the Antipodes.

In the wake of a mass epidemic of adults in therapy accusing their parents of heinous sexual abuse (sometimes involving alleged satanic rituals) there has been a backlash in the form of national 'false memory societies'. These exist in the USA, in Australia, New Zealand and The Netherlands as well as here in the UK.

Together, these societies comprise thousands of accused parents who have formed advisory bodies consisting of leading academics in psychopathology, sociology, forensic science and the Humanities. Barristers and journalists have also joined such bodies to offer counsel and support to these beleaguered 'Victims of Memory', to borrow the title of Mark Pendergrast's (1995) recent and glowingly reviewed book. Pendergrast, himself an accused parent, has written the most accessible introduction to the recovered memory debate. It has been praised for its breadth of scholarship as well as its elegant prose and one cannot but be moved by his reaction to his daughters' accusations.

At this point, it should be pointed out that although some of the allegations refer to homicidal sabbats and cannibalism these are a minority and, of course, an extreme. At the other end of the continuum there are allegations which lack any content at all. This is the case with Pendergrast's adult daughters' accusations.

In many instances, all that parents are told (usually by letter or answerphone messages) is that their offspring have become convinced that something awful, something, which invaded sexual boundaries, took place. What actually transpired, they do not remember but it was certainly incestuous and, with their therapists' assistance, they hope, eventually, to retrieve it. I have heard such a 'victim' on a radio 'phone-in'. She reported being haunted by her vague abuse memories on a daily basis. What it was that took place, she did not know, but she was sure that she had been chronically assaulted over many years. When the programme also asked if there was ever a day when she was not plagued by such memories, she replied ingenuously, "Oh, yes, on a really bad day".

Given that families are driven asunder and parents have been sentenced to draconian lengths of imprisonment on the basis of no other evidence than the uncorroborated testimony of their adult offspring it is hardly surprising that the debates around this topic are frequently conducted with passion and acrimony. Therefore, I have little sympathy with Professor John Morton who wrote (1994) how much he admired a paper by Lindsay and Read (1994) which, he says, displays "none of the sense of outrage against individual events that has tarnished much of the public debate". I make no apology for continuing to conduct the debate with some passion and not a little indignation.

The phenomenon of these "false memories" has not arisen in a vacuum. It has a historical and an ideological context. Indeed, all social problems have such contexts and what society regards as a problem at one point in its history may stand in stark contrast to the attention given to the same issues at another time. Many commentators have drawn comparisons between the present epidemic and the Salem witch hunts and the McCarthy "reds under the beds" hysteria. Such fears about dangerous malfeasants in our midst are eternal, primitive fantasies and provide the stuff of such classic film noirs as "The Invasion of the Body Snatchers".

From this perspective then, social problems do not have absolute existences. Their identification and their ontology relate to the prevailing consciousness, to the Zeitgeist.

There are hidden agendas in this debate implying that one can address the phenomenon of false memories from a particular vantage point, namely, that of social constructivism. And I invite you to think about it in this way whilst you make up your minds where you stand.

It behoves me, therefore, to make some introductory comments about this deconstructionist intellectual position. Briefly, social constructivism has it that problems are social constructs and the way that problems are defined, the nature of the investigations which follow, the explanations that are proffered, the solutions which are devised - all these factors and more are solely dependent on the nature of the interest groups involved. Such interest groups will, by definition, have their own agendas (for that is what an interest group is) and these agendas may be explicit or implicit, public or hidden.

In a sense, the social constructivist stands aloof from the debate, from the warring factions, and tries to understand and to articulate the agendas of the parties involved. The social constructivist does not have to take sides publicly (although they will necessarily have their own private agendas).

It is also important to be aware that the social constructivist can be socially construed by others. You will be in no doubt as to what are my own agendas by the time I have finished.

Agendas, I suggest, are relatively enduring - like personality traits, a term which psychologists are much more familiar with and with which they surely have some close correlation.

Whether or not phenomenon X really exists, for example, is not the sole issue. At least as important are the motives of the protagonists in the debate. Inevitably, since we are talking partly about public opinion, social constructivists are especially interested in the role of the media when social problems are being discussed, although a considered treatment of this dimension and the social constructivist position is outside the scope of the present chapter.

However, it is important to acknowledge that, for the vast majority of people, the entirety of their "knowledge" about issues such as AIDS, child sexual abuse, Satanism, abduction by aliens, multiple personality disorder, psychoanalysis, psychotherapy, comes from what they have read in their newspapers, heard on the radio, or seen on the television.

There is a Commons select committee sitting at this moment on the problem of child labour in underdeveloped countries, notably India. Child labour, of course, is not a problem in India, any more than is cannabis smoking in Amsterdam, prostitution in Germany or multiple personality disorder in Britain.

Multiple personality disorder (MPD) is, however, a problem of epidemic proportions in the USA, and Canada follows closely behind. MPD has recently undergone a cosmetic re-christening and appears in DSMIV as Dissociative Multiple Identity Disorder. Undoubtedly this signals a partial retreat in the wake of a critical onslaught against some of the MPD faction's more extravagant claims about multiplicity.

Literally, tens of thousands of patients have been so diagnosed in the last decade and a vigorous debate about the validity of this diagnosis has followed (e.g. Fahy 1988; Aldridge-Morris, 1989 1994a, 1994b, 1995; Merskey 1992; North et al. 1993; Piper 1994; Putman 1994).

A major part of the story of False Memory Syndrome has its roots in the MPD movement and it is informative to see the topics as intertwined and to treat them together.

A major figure in the MPD movement, Colin Ross (1987) diagnosed 4.4% of psychiatric in-patients in a general hospital setting as MPD. In a recent paper Merskey (1995) extrapolates from a book by Ross (1989) the claim that MPD may afflict 1 in 20 of college students in Canada (and presumably this applies to students elsewhere).

Simple arithmetic leads us to conclude that people like Ross would have us believe that the true prevalence of this disorder, in the USA and Canada at least, lies in the millions. What credibility can we accord to Dr. Ross?

In a 1993 Canadian TV broadcast (in the "Fifth Estate Series") Ross stated that the CIA had a covert programme of implanting MPD so that some of the alter personalities "could carry more information" and that the same agency has inspired the current criticisms of MPD in order to discredit the diagnosis, so that reports of the discovery of these implanted "alters" will not be believed. Ross insists his position is scholarly and he has documentary evidence to support his claim. This has yet to be published. For the moment, however, please believe me when I tell you that I am not in the pay of the CIA.

Suffice it to say that we have come a long way from the notion of the Jekyll and Hyde, dual personality prototype. Our colleague, Colin Ross, returns to centre stage here cited in New Scientist (Cohen 1995). He reports a woman claiming "335 alter egos including rebellious teenagers and abused children". The record, however, must surely go to Dr. Richard Kluft (1988) who reported a patient with over 4000 personalities. One cannot but wonder how long the clinical interviews must have taken to provoke so many alter egos.

These data were published in the house journal of the "International Society for the Study of Dissociation" of which Ross was president and Kluft the journal editor.

What are we told of the aetiology of MPD? At the outset, in the first 73 years of this century, MPD was seen as dissociative defence occurring in individuals with a biopsychological propensity for dissociation that had endured some exogenous trauma. Dissociation is a polymorphous concept, conceived as a dimensional process ranging from moment to moment distractibility, everyday day dreaming, "highway hypnosis", somnambulism, through to the massive dissociation seen in the putative creation of multiple selves. "Dissociation" is an ill-defined notion. It is not the same as repression, about which I have something to say later.

Repression is defined as vertical splitting in contrast to the horizontal splitting involved in dissociation. I do not claim to grasp fully this distinction based as it is on some metaphysical ecology of a reified mind.

Ancestrally then, we are looking at the different heritages of Freud as contrasted with Janet and Charcot who were preoccupied with hysterical states and hypnotic phenomena.

At the outset, the nature of the precipitating trauma in MPD was non-specific. For example, Vietnam veterans were sometimes alleged to have developed MPD because of the harrowing circumstances of that war. One of the most famous cases of MPD, namely Eve White, immortalised in the book and film "The Three Faces of Eve" had a relatively happy and loving childhood.

However, in 1973, Schreiber described the case of Sybil, in her eponymous book. Sybil, allegedly had 16 personalities and catalogued a childhood of appalling physical assault and sexual abuse by her mother. CSA was now high on the agenda as a major aetiological factor. It is highly unlikely that Sybil was, in fact, suffering from MPD. Her therapist, Dr. Cornelia Wilbur was understandably fascinated by her patient's multiplicity and invited the eminent American Psychiatrist, David Spiegel, to offer her a consultation. In that consultation, Sybil asked whether Spiegel wanted her to answer his questions through the medium of one of her many alters or whether it would suffice to stay "as Sybil". Spiegel replied that staying as Sybil would do just fine and the dialogue about her past abuse and all of her anxieties continued just fine; one psychiatrist, one patient. Putnam (1986) reports that 97% of a cohort of 100 patients alleged that they were the victims of CSA. It must be said that the data was provided through the secondary source of the patients' therapists and no corroborative evidence for these claims was sought. Nonetheless, it is now the case that most clinicians who diagnose and treat

MPD believe that a major goal of therapy is to uncover CSA histories which have been repressed prior to the formation of dissociative coping strategies.

In a like vein, such clinicians, when faced with patients reporting CSA which they have always remembered, will be regarded as at risk for MPD which will figure largely in the differential diagnosis.

This relatively new emphasis on CSA has led to a treatment-orientated diagnostic bias in clinicians. It is argued that unwitting survivors can recover memories of such abuse, and if they so much as entertain the fancy that they might have been abused then they most definitely were. This extraordinary principle is enshrined in Bass and Davis's appalling book "The Courage to Heal" (1988). Such nonsense has enormously influential media role models for its promulgation. On the Oprah Winfrey Show, Roseanne Arnold said, "When someone asks you, 'Were you really sexually abused as a child' there are only two answers: one of them is 'yes,' and one of them is 'I don't know'. You can't say 'No'".

As Harvard Professor, Frederick Crews, says in his article, "The revenge of the Repressed II" in the December 1994 issue of the New York Review, these writers have no training in psychology or psychiatry. They describe themselves as radical, lesbian feminists whose knowledge base is stories heard from women who clearly remembered their own abuse histories but who had received no support from professionals or their families. The large number of such cases led them to make the extraordinary leap to the decision that repressed abuse was even more prevalent than remembered abuse. Crews tells us that "the recovered memory business"... has grown into a highly lucrative enterprise not just of therapy and publishing but also of counselling, workshop hosting, custody litigation, criminal prosecution, forced hospitalisation and insurance and 'victim compensation' claims. Manuals such as 'The Courage to Heal' keep the psychic wounds open, refusing forgiveness or reconciliation recruiting its victims into "the permanently embittered corps of 'survivors'".

Blume (1990) believes that incest "can occur through words, sounds, or even exposure of the child to sights or acts that are sexual but do not involve her". She states that you were probably molested if you speak too softly, or wear too many clothes or even "have no awareness at all of having been violated".

Unsurprisingly, Bass and Davis have never come across a woman who "suspected she might have been abused, explored it, and determined she wasn't".

John Bradshaw (an American media person also cited by Crews) says that indicators of abuse are both promiscuity and a lack of interest in sex. Crews pointedly observes that these are "sterling examples of what experimental psychologists call a 'confirmatory bias' (Merskey 1992).

We are asked to believe that counsellors lift the veil of robust repression through a variety of techniques including "feelings work", "dream work", "imagistic work", "trance work" and "group work". Also employed are sodium amytal and hypnosis - including not just age regression but "past life regression".

The master of memory therapy was, of course, Freud. In his own words, "The work keeps coming to a stop and they keep on maintaining that this time nothing has occurred to them. We must not believe what they say, we must always assume, and tell them too, that they must have kept something back... We must insist on this, we must repeat the pressure and represent ourselves as infallible, till at last we are really told something... There are cases, too, in which the patient tries to disown (the memory) even after its return" (Mason 1985). Is this psychotherapy or tyranny? Ganaway (1991) points to the already mentioned epiphenomenon whereby counsellors are recovering memories of "satanic ritual abuse ceremonies involving apparent animal and human torture and sacrifice. These crimes, allegedly, are perpetrated by a purported vast network of highly organised, extremely covert, multigenerational satanic cults led by individuals who typically would be considered pillars of the community, such as lawyers, doctors, police chiefs, mayors, school principals and government officials... the cult leaders reportedly create multiple personalities in these individuals to allow them to lead double lives".

I have heard exactly the same bizarre story from a clinical psychologist in the UK who implicates the local chief constable and clergy. I have also heard the tale from a Birmingham GP who has implicated the Royal Family. I was alarmed to read that the BPS Working Party on Recovered Memories found that 97% of their sample of clinical psychologists believe in the reality of Ritual Sexual Abuse. Strikingly, 97% also believe in the validity of their patients' recovered memories. The first author, Professor

John Morton, does not make the obvious connection, draw the obvious conclusion, that these are the same people.

As Ganaway (op. cit.) summarises, "in over eight years of Investigations reputable skilled law enforcement officials (including FBI forensic evidence specialists) have been unable to confirm either the reports of Ritual Sexual Abuse criminal activities, including supposed human sacrifices, or even the very existence of this alleged organised cult network."

Professor Jean La Fontaine (1994) drew a similar blank after a three year, Home Office funded study in the UK.

There is a network of belief systems that tend to cross the Atlantic and they are all nightmare visions. Fractionating personalities, sabbats where foetuses are aborted and eaten, even aliens from outer space (engaged in a "huge inter-species breeding programme (that) has invaded our physical reality and is affecting the lives of millions of people"). This quotation is from a book by Pulitzer prize-winning psychiatrist, Professor John Mack at Harvard (1994).

All of these socially constructed problems, all of these phenomena are rooted in the same fantastic compost. So we now have the widespread phenomenon of adults in their thirties and forties suddenly accusing their elderly parents of chronic sexual abuse for which there is not a shred of corroborative evidence and for which they claim, prior to their encounter with a recovered memory therapist, total amnesia. Such accusations have even been made in hospital wards to dying parents.

Following the accusations, therapists typically require that their clients sever all contact with the accused and begin litigation. This is the prescription of Bass and Davies. I see the rationale for this as straightforward. The vengeance is seen as therapeutic and the damages awarded pay the therapists' fees. I hope the hidden agendas are becoming progressively transparent.

The typical accuser, both here and in the USA, is female, 25 to 40, middle class and well educated. The parents are normally successful professionals and financially sound. I have read through hundreds of files housed at the headquarters of the British False Memory Society and was struck by the sterling academic success of the many complainants and the high public office occupied by so many of their accused parents. Issues of confidentiality preclude further description of the persons involved.

The complainant has entered therapy for an ill-defined, low mood, or anxiety problems in adjustment or following divorce. Some are individuals who have embarked on therapy/counselling training and have been obliged to undergo personal "therapy" as part of their courses. The accusations are not supported by other family members, e.g. the other parent or siblings, nor, until now, has the family been dysfunctional. There is not a single case in the files of the British False Memory Society which has been corroborated either by evidence or by the later admission of an accused parent. It is also striking that step-parents are almost never the alleged perpetrators. The opposite is true in corroborated cases of CSA.

The memories are said to have lain dormant for perhaps thirty years owing to massive repression, even though the number of sexual assaults may run into hundreds and be spread over ten or fifteen years. Are we to turn psychology on its head and believe that one is more likely to forget hundreds of incidents of abuse than a single traumatic assault? There are British analysts who would ask us to do just this.

Families are destroyed, of course, on the basis of nothing other than these recovered memories. Often the memories are of incidents in the first three years of life when all psychologists, conversant with the field of memory, would agree there is "infantile amnesia". The central nervous system is simply not sufficiently mature to be laying down traces at this stage.

As I have already indicated, sometimes the allegations are extraordinary ephemeral; of the kind, for example, "I felt the sexual boundaries between my father and myself were somehow transgressed".

Crews (op.cit.) directs us to a letter from Freud to Fleiss 1897 where he reports an adult patient who had a "Phonographic memory" for a seduction which occurred when the patient was 11 months old ("I could hear again the words that were exchanged between two adults at that time"). I cannot improve on the ironic observation of Crews when he says "Given that Freud here accepts a 'Phonographic memory of an adult conversation recorded at a time when the patient was probably struggling to say 'mama', this passage must rank among his most credulous ever".

It is commonplace that psychoanalysts will talk about memories being stored, not in the cortex, but in parts of the body. Once again, it is to Freud that we look for the pioneering work in uncovering body memories. Again citing Crews, "Lesions in the mouth were signs that a penis had been there first; dyspepsia or 'worm irritation' must have stemmed from the insertion of a tongue or finger in the former baby's anus; a paralysis of the lower limbs meant that the sufferer had been required to stimulate the genitals of a grown-up woman with his foot' and so forth".

The British False Memory Society was formed in 1993 and consists of some 650 accused parents, and was inspired by a similar group in the USA. Its scientific advisory body was formed 18 months ago and is chaired by Oxford Professor, Larry Weiskrantz FRS and comprises some of the UK's leading academics in cognate disciplines including distinguished professors of both psychology and psychoanalysis.

Since its inception, what can only be called a rival organisation has been formed. This calls itself AAA, Accuracy About Abuse, and is led by Marjorie Orr who describes herself as a psychotherapist. She also writes the astrology column in the British daily tabloid, the Daily Express. In an Internet communication she claims that, by analysing a client's birth chart, she can tell whether or not they have been sexually abused as a child, or indeed, whether they are likely to be perpetrator; enough said?

There are many agendas here. They relate to an obsession with people as victims and with people as survivors. They relate to a preoccupation with child abuse as the statistical norm. They relate to the demonisation of men. They relate to professional concern about the definition of a psychotherapist, the professional regulation of this title, and the abuse of psychotherapy and clients.

There is concern about defining a patient as anyone who complains and about a therapeutic ideology that says you must believe everything your patients tell you; obfuscation about "clinical truth" versus "historical truth".

There is an abysmal ignorance of the psychology literature by so many practitioners who make claims that cannot be supported. There is the disturbingly cult flavour of societies like the ISSD whose conferences parody evangelical meetings where the proselytisers meet the suggestible. There are issues about affluent societies in turmoil, projecting their endogenous ills onto phantom scapegoats.

Many commentators have made comparisons between the current hysterical epidemic and the Salem witch-hunts. Pendergrast (op. cit.) notes a disturbing similarity between "The Courage to Heal" and the "Malleus Maleficarum" the "Hammer of Witches" by Heinrich Kramer and James Sprenger, published in 1486. Fears about communist infiltration and abductions by aliens are cast in the same mould.

I want to close by saying something about the last item on my agenda, namely the validity of the concept of repression. After all, this is the bedrock of recovered memories, of MPD, of stories about satanic orgies and abduction by aliens. It could be said to be the lynch-pin of psychoanalysis, a notion bandied about by psychotherapists and counsellors of all sorts of persuasion.

In a taxi journey from Lime Street Station to the University of Liverpool, where I was due to present a paper, the driver struck up a conversation. It revolved around this case and the latest revelation in that morning's papers. With the conversational skill of all taxi drivers I was quickly identified as a psychologist. "What surprises me," volunteered my driver, "is that all these victims haven't repressed their memories." I couldn't agree more; if repression were really part of our armoury of defences.

However, I have to tell you that the emperor is quite naked. In novels and Hollywood movies, along with aliens and multiples and Satanists - only here will you find repression; and therapy based on recovered memories stands or falls with the validity of the concept of repression (Boakes 1995).

Only in the movies and novels, and perhaps our nightmares are there deeply interred memories awaiting the spades of brilliant analysts. Sadly, Ingrid Bergmans's psychoanalyst in Hitchcock's "Spellbound", like Sherlock Holmes and Cracker, is a creature of fiction.

Human beings are rather more complicated and memory does not work in this way. Memory is reconstructive and creative and selective and, above all very fallible. Memories do not lie dormant in the cortex like video cassettes waiting to be replayed when the correct button is depressed. In a very real sense, all human beings are historians and we all know how much at variance can the accounts of historians be even when there is little doubt that the events they describe actually took place.

What scientific evidence is there, then, that repression, the dynamic, motivated and unconscious forgetting of traumatic events, takes place?

Despite its uncritical absorption into our cultural consciousness and so many works of fiction in the form of novels and films it does seem to be a counter-intuitive notion. Post-traumatic stress disorder is a vibrant testimony to the fact that people are haunted by major crises. They cannot get them out of their minds. They ruminate, they are obsessed, they have flashbacks. If only such a defence strategy were available to these individuals. I refer you to a recent paper by Pope and Hudson (1995), psychiatrists based in the biological psychiatry laboratory at Harvard.

They begin by asking the straightforward question "Is it possible for victims of childhood sexual abuse to "repress" their memories?" They note how Bass and Davies state that "the human mind has tremendous powers of repression". They cite Blume (op.cit.) who says, "perhaps half of all incest survivors do not remember that the abuse occurred". Fredrickson (1992), states that "millions of people have blocked out frightening memories of abuse, years of their life, or their entire childhood". Pope and Hudson, finally cite Herman (1992) who opens her book "Trauma and Recovery" with the statement, "the ordinary response to atrocities is to banish them from consciousness". Is it any wonder that "repression" has been enshrined in both popular and professional cultures? The obvious concern of sceptics like myself is that no evidence is offered to substantiate such sweeping assertions about the reality of repression. Experimental support for the construct is sadly lacking. This is all the more surprising since child sexual abuse (as Pope and Hudson argue) probably figures in the history of some 14 million members of the USA population, surely then there ought to be a wealth of well documented cases where repression has occurred. Before presenting their trawl of the literature, Pope and Hudson delineate the criteria for an acceptable study. There must be evidence that the traumatic events actually occurred. One must exclude cases where there is clear evidence that victims derive secondary gain by alleging amnesia. One must exclude cases where victims "merely preferred not to think about the events or pretended that the events never occurred". One must, of course, exclude "amnesia developed for some biological reason - head trauma, seizures and alcohol or drug intoxication for example. These would all represent exclusionary criteria in an attempt to exhibit cases of repression. Inevitably they refer to the phenomenon of infantile amnesia, which is well documented; for example, in Fivush and Hudson's edited book (1990). Indeed, Usher and Neisser (1993) have demonstrated substantial amnesia before the age of six.

Let me be brief; Pope and Hudson could find only four relevant studies. They are most clear; "It must be emphasised that these four studies are the only applicable studies that we were able to locate. In other words, this brief review does not present merely a selection of the most important studies, but the entirety of all published studies, which to our knowledge, have systematically tested whether repression of memories of childhood sexual abuse can occur".

None of the four studies met their criteria. All were seriously methodologically flawed. Holmes (1990) examined sixty years of research into repression. I will not rehearse his readily available and comprehensive treatment here. I will only repeat some of his more salient and experimentally based observations.

Emotionally intense experiences are more likely to be recalled than those which are less emotionally intense. However, whether unpleasant or pleasant, the affect declines over time and unpleasant affect declines more rapidly than that associated with pleasant experiences. This differential slope in affective decay is a more economic explanation for the difference in recall of pleasant and unpleasant events.

Other experiments confuse differential learning with differential forgetting whilst others ignore the fact that stressful situations increase drive state which, in turn, will lead to response competition. Here, interference rather than repression accounts for difficulty in recall.

He refers to the putative dimension of the Repression-Sensitisation scale of Byrne, Barry and Nelson (1963). However, repressors were identified simply by their failure to report symptoms of psychopathology on items drawn from the Minnesota Multiphasic Personality Inventory. The procedure did not distinguish between those failing to report such symptoms and those who did not have them.

In experiments devised to demonstrate perceptual defence (where disturbing stimuli are repressed prior to conscious registration) experimenters ignored the fact that the stressful words, presented tachistoscopically, were less familiar than the neutral words. Familiarity of content influences recall and when items were equated for familiarity differences in recall disappeared.

Holmes wryly concludes by recommending that "repression" should be packaged with the warning, "The concept of repression has not been validated with experimental research and its use may be hazardous to the accurate interpretation of clinical behaviour". I would like to close with a quote from Professor Paul McHugh (1994), Director of the Department of Psychiatry and Behavioural Science at the Johns Hopkins Medical

Institutions. He describes a long-term struggle between what he calls the "empiricists" and the "romanticists" - between those who rely on the methodical study of facts and those who "rely on feelings for evidence, on metaphors for reality, on inspiration and myth for guidance."

There are those of us, the majority I am sure, who hold dearly the integrity and credibility of our professions. Let us resist as vociferously as we can these transatlantic hoaxes and these charlatan practices. Let us ensure that the crisis of credibility now affecting so many accusers and their counsellors does not spread to the very many genuine victims of abuse and responsible clinicians practising good psychotherapy who have not forgotten our guiding maxim "first do no harm".

References

Aldridge-Morris, R. (1989, 1991). *Multiple Personality: An Exercise in Deception.* UK and Hillsdale USA: Lawrence Erlbaum Associates.

Aldridge-Morris, R. (1994a). Ritualistic Abuse - A case of false memory? *Psychiatry in Practice*, 13, 2, 21-22.

Aldridge-Morris, R. (1994b). A Sceptical Reflection on the Diagnosis of Multiple personality Disorder. *Irish Journal of Psychological Medicine* 11, 3, 126-129.

Aldridge-Morris, R. (1995). Author's Reply to Putnam's Commentary On "A Sceptical Reflection on the Diagnosis of Multiple Personality Disorder". *Irish Journal of Psychological Medicine*, 12, 2, 81-82.

Baokes, J. (1995). Commentary; False Memory Syndrome. *The Lancet*, Vol. 346, 21 October.

Bass, E. and Davies, L. (1988). *The Courage to Heal: A Guide for the Women Survivors of Child Sexual Abuse.* New York: Harper & Row.

Blume, E.S. (1990). *Secret Survivors: Uncovering Incest and its After Effects in Women.* N.Y.: Ballantine.

Ceci, S.J. and Bruck, M. (1993). Suggestibility of the Child Witnesses: A Historical Review and Synthesis. *Psychological Bulletin*, 113, 403-409.

Ceci, S.J. and Bruck, M. (1995). *Jeopardy in the Courtroom.* American Psychological Association.

Cohen, D. (1995). Now We Are One, or Two, or Three... *New Scientist*, June, 14-15.

Fahy, T.H. (1988). The Diagnosis of Multiple Personality Disorder. *British Journal of Psychiatry*, 153, 597-606.

Fivush, R. and Hudson, J.A. (eds) (1990). *Knowing and Remembering in Young Children* Cambridge University Press.

Fredrickson, R. (1992). *Repressed Memories: A Journey to Recovery from Sexual Abuse.* N.Y.: Fireside/Parkside, S & S.

Ganaway, G.K. (1991). *Alternative Hypotheses Regarding Satanic Ritual Abuse Memories.* Paper presented at 99th Annual Conference of the American Psychological Association, August 1991, California.

Gudjonsson, G.H. (1992). *The Psychology of Interrogations, Confessions and Testimony.* N.Y.: John Wiley.

Herman, J.L. (1992). *Trauma and Recovery.* N.Y.: Basic Books.

Holmes, D.S. (1990). The Evidence for Repression: An Examination of Sixty Years' Research. in Singer, J. (ed.). *Repression and Dissociation,* p. 85-102 Univ. of Chicago Press.

Kluft, R.P. (1988). Phenomenology and Treatment of Extremely Complex Multiple Personality Disorder. *Dissociation* 1, 47-58.

La Fontaine, J. (1994). *The Extent and Nature of Organised Ritual Abuse.* London: H.M.S.O.

Levitt, E.E. and Pinnell, C.M. (1995). Some Additional Light on the Childhood Sexual Abuse Psychopathology Axis. *International Journal of Clinical Experimental Hypnosis,* 43, 14-16.

Lindsay, D.S. and Read, J.S. (1994). Psychotherapy and Memories of Child Sexual Abuse: A Cognitive Perspective. *Applied Cognitive Psychology* 8, 281-338.

Mack, J. (1994). *Abduction: Human Encounters with Aliens.* N.Y.:Scribner's.

Masson, J. (1985). *The Complete Letters of Sigmund Freud to Wilhelm Fleiss (1887-1904).* Harvard University Press.

McHugh, P.R. (1994). Psychotherapy Awry. *The American Scholar,* 63, 17-30.

Memon, A. (1995). Response to British Psychological Society Report on Recovered Memories *Expert Evidence,* 3, 4.

Merskey, H. (1992). The Manufacture of Personalities *British Journal of Psychiatry,* 160, 327-340.

Merskey, H. (1995). Multiple Personality Disorder and False Memory Syndrome *British Journal of Psychiatry,* 166, 281-283.

Morton, J. (1994). Cognitive Perspectives on Memory Recovery. *Applied Cognitive Psychology,* 8, 389-398.

North, C.S., Ryall, J.M., Ricci, D.A. and Wetzel, R.D. (1993). *Multiple Personalities, Multiple Disorders: Psychiatric Classification and Media Influence.* Oxford University Press.

Ofshe, R.J. and Watters, E. (1994). *Making Monsters: False Memories, Psychotherapy and Sexual Hysteria.* N.Y.: Charles Scribner & Sons.

Pendergrast, M. (1995). *Victims of Memory.* Hinesburg, Vermont: Upper Access Books.

Piper, A. Jnr (1994). Multiple Personality Disorder: A Critical Review *British Journal of Psychiatry,* 164, 600-612.

Pope, H. and Hudson, J. (1995). Can Memories of Childhood Sexual Abuse be Repressed? *Psychological Medicine,* 25, 121-126.

Powell, R.A. and Boer, D. (1994). Did Freud Mislead Patients to Confabulate Memories of Abuse? *Psychological Reports,* 74, 1283-1298.

Putnam, F.W. (1986). The Clinical Phenomenology of Multiple Personality Disorder: Review of 100 Recent Cases. *Journal of Clinical Psychiatry,* 47j, 285-293.

Putnam, F.W. (1994). Commentary on "A Sceptical Reflection on the Diagnosis of Multiple Personality Disorder". *Irish Journal of Psychological Medicine,* 11, 3, 130-131.

Ross, C.A. (1987). Inpatient Treatment of Multiple Personality Disorder. *Canadian Journal of Psychiatry,* 32, 779-781.

Ross, C.A. (1989). *Multiple Personality Disorder: Diagnosis, Clinical Features and Treatment,* p. 90-91.

Schreiber, F.R. (1973). *Sybil.* N.Y.: Warner.

Smith, M. and Pazder, L. (1980). *Michelle Remembers.* N.Y.: Congdon & Lattes.

Tully, B. (1995). *Recovered Memories of Childhood Sexual Abuse.* Briefing paper, Psychologists at Law Group.

Usher, J.A. and Neisser, V. (1993). Childhood Amnesia and the Beginnings Of Memory for Four Early Life Events. *Journal of Experimental Psychology* 122, 155-165.

6 Equivocal Death

DAVID CANTER

In cases in which a person's death was caused by means not immediately apparent a procedure known as equivocal death analysis may be employed. This consists of attempting to form a view of the mental state of the deceased from records and people who might have known the person. Whilst this relatively new procedure has some advantages over the subjective opinion that is sometimes used in such enquiries it is not a well-established and thoroughly tested technique. The present chapter discusses approaches to carrying out equivocal death analyses. It concludes that this procedure has great potential but also carries grave risks if used without considerable caution.

David Canter is Director of the Centre for Investigative Psychology at the University of Liverpool. He has published widely in Environmental and Investigative Psychology as well as many areas of Applied Social Psychology. His most recent books since his award winning *"Criminal Shadows"* have been *"Psychology in Action"* and with Laurence Alison *"Criminal Detection and the Psychology of Crime"*.

*Offender Profiling Series: II - **Profiling in Policy and Practice***
Edited by D. Canter and L. Alison. © 1999 Ashgate Publishing, Aldershot. pp 123-156

6　Equivocal Death

DAVID CANTER

Introduction

From time to time incidents of suspicious death occur in which the mental state of a deceased person needs to be assessed. If some evaluation can be made of the sort of person they were, their personality and thought processes, especially as that may throw light on any involvement they themselves had in their death, then it may assist the investigation of what is sometimes referred to as 'equivocal death'. Such an evaluation, known as a *psychological autopsy* is an attempt to reconstruct a person's psychological state prior to death. The possibilities for psychological contribution to the investigation of equivocal death are discussed and their strengths and pitfalls considered. The care that investigators need to take in assessing the accounts of the death that may be drawn from such procedures is emphasised.

Suspicious Death

When Paula Gilfoyle was found hanging in her garage, a couple of weeks before she was due to give birth, it was initially assumed that she had taken her own life. A note in her own handwriting, explaining why she felt the need to commit suicide, seemed to make the tragic occurrence understandable, if no less horrific. However, accounts of events in the previous weeks of her life began to reach the police that raised questions about whether she might have been tricked into writing the note. The possibility was even raised that she had been mislead into putting her head in the noose and murdered before she could move free. These possibilities raised questions about Paula's death that revolved around attempts to determine her mental state prior to her death. It is in such investigations, sometimes referred to as 'equivocal death scenarios', that systematic procedures for reaching a conclusion about the deceased's personality and thought processes would be of great value.

The typical case where such questions are raised, is one in which there is some doubt as to whether death was accidental, self inflicted or malicious, and if the deceased played an active role in his/her own demise. Such matters can be especially important in life insurance claims that are void if the death were suicide. They are, of course, also of potentially great significance in murder enquiries, such as that into the death of Paula Gilfoyle, in which there is a question as to whether the deceased contributed to his/her own death in some way. Fatal accident investigations, in which the technicalities of what actually lead to the accident are difficult to resolve, are other forms of equivocal death in which psychological examination aspects of the main actors/victims may be essential.

Virtually all attempts to use psychological procedures to throw light on a person's thoughts and feelings prior to their death have taken place in the USA, most of them in civil and criminal litigation rather than as part of an investigation. Dregne (1982), for example claims that "the drawing of a psychological picture of a dead person whom the expert has never met" can be a "tool for criminal defence attorneys". The expert who draws such a picture can be used in court to argue, for example, that a person accused of murder was acting in self- defence, or whether a gift is in contemplation of death and therefore of relevance in considerations of taxes due on death.

Many equivocal death examinations, however, have been part of civil proceedings in which a workers' compensation case makes it necessary to establish that certain events affected the deceased in a particular manner, or that work-related injuries contributed to the eventual suicide of an individual. Another example would be where a will is contested so that the mental state of the deceased is the major legal battleground. In the case of Howard Hughes, for instance a psychologist concluded that "psychological problems, numerous head injuries, and drug misuse had changed a vibrant millionaire into an emaciated recluse" (Fowler 1986). The possibly psychotic basis of his reclusiveness, rather than mere eccentricity, posed challenges to the probity of his estate.

A possibly less obvious circumstance in which the characteristics of a person may be usefully inferred, even though that person is not available to answer questions about him/herself is an inquiry into the report of a missing person. Another example is when it is necessary to understand the decisions made, and actions taken, by people who are no longer able to answer for themselves. For example, in the planning of care routines for demented patients (Weisman and Kastenbaum 1968), it is inevitable that some inference will be made about the mental state of the people in question. Making those inferences as systematically as possible, drawing on whatever psychological information is available, is likely to improve the decisions being taken. But when the guilt or otherwise of the deceased, or those people close to him/her, as with Paula Gilfoyle, is directly in question, then the application of any unavoidably speculative procedures has to proceed with great caution.

Psychological Autopsies

Attempts to assess the mental state and characteristics of a person who is not available for direct examination contrasts with the task that usually faces mental health professionals. As noted by Ogloff and Otto (1993) effective mental health assessments typically require the participation and co-operation of the examinee. Although in some circumstances the examinee may choose not to co-operate, it is considered essential that the examinee be available for evaluation. Furthermore, the current mental state and adjustment of the individual concerned is the focus of attention, notably in competency and capacity evaluations such as child custody, competency to plead, and competency to testify examinations. For even if the subject of the assessment is not willing to participate they can be directly observed, their demeanour considered and their transactions with others noted and other aspects of their daily lives recorded directly. If they are not present all these aspects of them, which can assist in assessing their mental state, have to be inferred at second or third hand.

Even though evaluations conducted in the absence of the examinee are fraught with challenges and problems this has not stopped a number of clinical psychologists, psychiatrists and law enforcement agents in the USA from producing such assessments. They have given them a variety of terms, including "psychological autopsies", "psychiatric autopsies", "reconstructive psychological evaluations" or "equivocal death analyses", even "offender profiles" in some cases.

Useful distinctions can be drawn between these different activities, depending on whether the target of the examination is actually known. In the case of the examination of a crime scene to infer characteristics of the offender, often referred to as "profiling", (Canter 1995) the main quest is to determine the identity of the perpetrator. But where the identity of the subject is known, as in the attempt to determine whether they died by accident, or committed suicide; the objective is to reconstruct the mental state of the deceased. If this can be based upon information obtained from people who had direct or indirect contact with the subject of the examination then it is most likely to be called a "Psychological Autopsy" (Brent 1989). In cases where the investigation is carried out by law enforcement officers, usually FBI agents, who only examine the crime scene material and other information directly available to the police enquiry, it may be called an "Equivocal Death Analysis" or EDA. Clearly an EDA is open to many more biases and distortions than a 'full' psychological autopsy. What little experience there is about EDA's casts grave doubts on their validity (Poythress et al 1993). The only people known to have used this process in a professional capacity are the Behavioral Science Unit of the FBI.

The construction of a psychological autopsy has obvious parallels with historical biographies, in which the thoughts and actions of people are reconstructed from what is known about them, or military analyses, in which the practices and motivations of enemy leaders are considered. In all these cases there is a person who is the focus of attention, but that person is not available to co-operate in the investigation. The difference between a literary autopsy, or a military character analysis, and a psychological one are likely to be differences of degree rather than kind. A psychologist would be expected to provide more systematic detail and to give clearer evidence for the conclusions reached. It might also be expected that the psychologist would more confidently express views on the motivations and personality of the target than would other authorities. However, as will become clear, the contribution of psychologists to the investigation of equivocal deaths is still very limited and probably not as different from the work of a literary biographer as some psychologists would like to think.

Perhaps the most obvious difference to hope for, between the literary recreation of a bygone celebrity and a psychological autopsy, is that the psychologist would draw upon what is known of people and processes similar to that demonstrated in the actions at the centre of the enquiry. The individual being considered would be taken as an illustration of people and processes that are known to have carried out similar actions. In this way the expert opinion would be clarified and bolstered by the empirical evidence of other known cases. For example knowledge of how adolescent suicides prepare to take their own life, or what is typically contained in a suicide note, may be drawn upon to develop the account of the individual and his/her actions, prior to death.

Unfortunately there is still very little detailed empirical evidence available on many topics that are relevant to contributing to equivocal death investigations. Perusal of the literature also indicates a lack of a comprehensive assessment and evaluation of the nature and validity of those psychological autopsies that have been carried out. It is therefore most appropriate to consider the psychological autopsy as a relatively unstructured technique in which mental health professionals attempt to describe the thought processes and personality of a deceased person prior to death, and in some cases to comment on their likely participation in their own death. Its contribution to equivocal death investigations may therefore be best regarded as the development of an organised framework for indicating the issues to be considered when forming a view about the deceased.

The most common equivocal death scenarios that are examined in the USA are those in which suicide is suspected but is not absolutely certain. The first people to contribute to such examinations are generally regarded as being Shneidman and Farberow (1961) at the Los Angeles Suicide Prevention Centre during the 1950s. They responded to requests from the Coroner that they assist in determining the cause of death in equivocal suicides. Information from persons related to the deceased was combined with the Coroner's (i.e. pathological) findings to determine the cause of death as either suicide or accident. Shneidman and Farberow gave technical definition of the psychological autopsies that they carried out for the coroner. "A retrospective reconstruction of an individual's life that focuses on lethality, that is, those features of his life that illuminate his intentions in relation to his own death, clues as to the type of death it was, the degree (if any) of his participation in his own death, and why the death occurred at that time" (p.351).

The Technique

As has been indicated, contributions to equivocal death investigations can range from an essentially informal attempt to reconstruct the thoughts of the deceased to a much more thorough exploration of everything that is known about him/her. For, although such contributions have been made over a period of approximately 40 years there are still no standardised procedures that have been agreed upon for making them. However, where more systematic methods are employed they have commonly involved obtaining information from interviews with survivors of the deceased and archival sources. Shneidman et al (1970) interviewed relatives, friends, employers, physicians and others, including teachers and in some cases even bartenders, who could provide relevant information in an attempt to reconstruct the deceased's background, personal relationships, personality traits and lifestyle. They sought significant details of the events immediately preceding the death. All of this information was subsequently reviewed by the "Death investigation team" in the Coroner's office resulting in a determination of the mode of death.

Shneidman (1976) subsequently developed an outline for conducting a psychological autopsy, which essentially consisted of a 16 point check list (see Appendix I) that is not that dissimilar to the framework that might be used by any physician in preparing a medical case history. The major differences from other forms of medical case history are the focus on what is known about the deceased's typical actions, especially reactions to stress, what might be known of their interpersonal relationships, their thought processes and their experiences surrounding the death. The procedure is based on the assumption that people close to the deceased can provide accounts of both historical and recent developments and behaviours of the deceased. Likewise, historical and recent archival information, such as physicians' records, may contribute to a determination of the individual's mental state at a particular point in time. The procedure also implies a form of corroboration in which as wide a range and variety of sources of information are collected to ensure that the bias inherent in any one source of information does not distort the whole picture.

The problem of bias is an especially important one, given the importance that may be given to the psychologist's opinion about the cause of death. Yet few writers on this process discuss it in any depth. Litman et al (1970) are possibly the most direct in drawing attention to recurring problems. They point out that there is often a lack of information about the individual, particularly information that could be used for a reliable inference regarding his/her psychological state. Secondly, the information may be distorted by the informants. They cite instances of evasion, denial, concealment and even direct suppression of evidence. Indeed it may be expected that expert advice is required precisely in those situations in which there are doubts and ambiguities surrounding the events of the death. That, after all, is what makes it 'equivocal', so the problems described by Litman et al are part of the reason why an expert is called in to help.

In an attempt to reduce these inherent difficulties Brent (1989) proposed that particular attention be paid to the choice of informants, the manner of approach to informants, the effect of the time period between death and the interview on the quality of the information obtained, and the integration of the various data sources. He suggested broadening the range of informants, particularly to include peers in the case of adolescent suicides. He also provided guidelines for approaching informants, emphasising professional distance and the avoidance of platitudinous commiseration. Brent also reports that he found no simple or consistent relationship between timing of the interview and the quality and quantity of the data obtained. He further recognised that although the integration of various data sources is a common problem in psychiatry, it is a particularly salient issue in the administration and interpretation of the psychological autopsy. Brent reviewed the relationship between direct and indirect interviews as methods of obtaining family history, suggesting that both sensitivity and specificity of data may be enhanced by increasing the number of informants and including more female informants.

Thus, one of the contributions of behavioural scientists to the formulation of opinions on a suspicious death is the greater care and systematisation that they bring to the process, drawing on sources that might not normally be considered by legal professionals or physicians. The most comprehensive set of guidelines, intended to enhance the systematisation and move towards standardisation of the psychological autopsy has been provided by Ebert (1987) (see Appendix II). This is a valuable checklist that can act as an *aide memoire* to the examiner (or even the cross-examiner wishing to challenge the conclusions of an autopsy not conducted around these guidelines!). But although it is more comprehensive than that proposed by Shneidman (1976), it only provides a framework to assist the expert whom is providing guidance to the investigation. It "provides a spectrum of factors that can be useful in formulating an opinion about the mode of death" (Ebert 1987, p.54). Examiners are encouraged to adapt the guidelines to their particular case.

Process

In keeping with a procedure that has evolved in response to practical and legal demands, there is no well-developed conceptual or theoretical basis for deriving conclusions from the various sources of information to provide guidance on equivocal deaths. It appears that the professionals involved draw upon their experience to relate the facts to symptoms or syndromes that they would draw upon in their daily practice, searching for example for evidence of psychosis, depression or organic dysfunction.

In an attempt to systematise the basis of any guidance various authorities have proposed some principles, especially for determining if a death was suicide. Perhaps the most clearly stated principle is that expressed by Faberow and Schneidman (1961) that most suicide victims communicate their intentions to others in some way. These principles have been converted into a standardised assessment protocol by Jobes et al (1991). They provide a 55 item "Death Investigation Checklist" that can be used by medical examiners. On the basis of a successful test of the validity of this checklist they developed 16 criteria that they called the Empirical Criteria for the Determination of Suicide (ECDS). This process enabled Jobes et al to clarify determination of suicide as being based on the concepts of "self-infliction" and "intention". This allowed them to derive a score from the ECDS for each of these aspects. By comparing the scores obtained in 35 known accidental deaths and 28 known suicides they were able to show that "self infliction" and "intention" scores both had to be greater than 3 for the death to be declared a suicide.

Yet although the procedure developed by Jobes et al adds a rare level of precision to what are often difficult medico-legal decisions they emphasise a caveat. Even though "medicolegal judgements may be strengthened through such tools, leading to more objective and scientific determination of suicide as a manner of death. It is critical to note that the ECDS instrument is *not* meant to be a rigid and definitive standard designed to usurp the professional's judgement and authority".

Brent (1989) provides a somewhat less mathematical approach to the consideration of the possibility of suicide, exploring the major domains to be considered when giving advice about equivocal deaths. Implicit psychological assumptions can be perceived within each of these domains. They therefore act as useful framework for revealing the theoretical perspectives on which investigative guidance may be based.

1. Stressors

An important consideration in any fatality is the circumstances surrounding it. In particular an important factor is any indication of the stressors that the deceased may have suffered. The widely held assumption here is that some form of debilitating life circumstance is usually a precursor to suicide. Paykel et al (1975) found people who had attempted suicide had more life stresses in the four weeks prior to the attempt than did psychiatric controls. Beck et al (1974) built these ideas into a Suicidal Intent Scale, which predicted actual suicides in adults. The weakness in these studies, however, is the lack of careful exploration of people with similar stressors who do not attempt suicide, or of the surrounding social and family circumstances that may consistently be associated with the stressors. Without such knowledge the pre-existence of stressors in an examination of an equivocal may be given too much weight.

2. Exposure

There has been some suggestion from police enquiries that accord with more systematic studies that teenage suicides in particular may be more likely after direct exposure, from family or friends, or indirect exposure from media coverage (Gould and Shaffer 1986). There are, inevitably, many difficulties with the simple extrapolation from a deceased having had exposure to another's suicide and their own subsequent death. If, for instance, there had been a consistent, brooding reference to the event to which they were exposed it could be assumed at the very least to have focused their thoughts. It may also have provided ideas about the actual mechanics by which the suicide could be completed. Studies have indicated that this sometimes seems to be the case when what might be considered 'unorthodox' means of suicide are used, such as setting fire to oneself or laying ones head on a railway track. There are enough examples of minor 'epidemics' of suicides following initial, widely publicised, incidents that use the same 'technology', to support the contention that some individuals decided *how* to commit suicide from these exemplars.

In contributing to the investigation into a suspicious suicide the possibility of such imitation would best be dealt with as a hypothesis. This could be refuted if there was no evidence that the deceased was aware of the example he or she was supposed to have imitated. On the other hand, morbid fascination with the example could be taken as indication that the deceased had considered the implications of the actions illustrated by the example. If the experience of the suicide was more direct, or the deceased thought in some way that the example was positively regarded, or in some senses 'heroic', then it could be hypothesised to have had the effect of 'validating' the planned action. Once again such a hypothesis is open to refutation if there were no other evidence, say in a suicide note, or comments before death, that the example was admired by the deceased or seen as appropriate in some way.

3. Availability of Lethal Agents

Writing a decade ago from the perspective of the USA, Brent (1989) commented on the then current interest in the relationship between the availability of firearms and suicide, quoting Boyd's 1983 study that claimed an increasing rate of suicide by firearms because of their increasing availability. The view seemed to be that ready and easy access to a quick cause of death increases the risk of suicide. It would certainly be expected to have an impact on the ratio of attempted to actual suicide. The number of cases may be reduced, in which a person survives a suicide attempt because of what might be regarded as 'incompetence'; being discovered before the effect of the lethal agent has been fatal, or not using enough of the lethal agent, if the pulling of a trigger is all that is needed. But it is an open question as to whether the mere availability of ready to use firearms or any other lethal agent is a strong indication that an equivocal death is suicide. Many suicides are carried out with remarkably limited means and many people live their lives in the presence of highly lethal agents without ever thinking about suicide.

As with the possibility of imitation, the important question to answer in an investigation is the interest the deceased showed in the lethal agents and their possible uses. How careful were they, typically, in the use of these agents? Had they ever commented on the consequences if they were to be used for self-harm, such as their speed of action or the pain that might be associated with their use?

4. Psychopathology

One of the major assumptions that clinical psychologists and psychiatrists seem to make in guiding an equivocal death investigation is that any evidence of prior psychopathology can be taken as an indicator of the probability that a person took their own life. Because this area of interest is such a natural part of psychiatric assessment the various structured protocols that have been developed to elicit psychiatric symptomatology (e.g. Kovaks 1985) have been adapted for use with parents and family in an attempt to complete the assessment as if the patient were present. Clearly, signs of depression or previous acts of self-harm provide *prima facie* support for suicide as opposed to accidental death. Even if there are no direct signs of depression in the deceased the many studies that point to familial correlates of mental illness can be drawn upon to explore the possibility of nascent, unrecognised aspects of disturbance indicated in the clinical history of close relatives.

It is more difficult to know what to make of a diagnosis of schizophrenia or personality disorder. Indeed, where a severe psychosis is apparent the borderline between accidental and intentional self-destruction is wide and vague. Was the person lucid enough at the time to be aware of the full consequence of their actions? Even though they had expressed a desire to commit suicide were they fully cognisant of what that meant?

Perhaps the extreme examples of the difficulties of utilising information on psychopathology in an equivocal death investigation are those cases referred to as 'suicide by cop'. These are situations in which a person creates a confrontation with the police that will inevitably lead to his being gunned down in a shoot-out. British police officers may be aware that the person they are surrounding in a siege, for example, is potentially suicidal and try to avoid giving him the opportunity to get them to execute him. The indications are that in some US jurisdictions there may appear to be fewer qualms, or there is less understanding of the possible psychopathology of the offender they are trying to disarm. The individual may see himself as heroic and look to the agents of the state to enshrine his heroism.

There are certainly many acts of suicide, across a variety of different cultures, that typically are regarded as heroic. They usually involve some confrontation with the state or a designated enemy, whether it be Biblical heroes such as Samson, World War II *kamikaze* pilots, or present day 'suicide bombers'. Without intending to be blasphemous would it be reasonable to consider what a psychological autopsy of Jesus would reveal? At the very least, the time he spent alone in the desert would lead a psychologist to suggest possible indications of psychopathology.

Evaluation of Psychological Autopsy Contributions to Equivocal Death Investigations

The brief review of the procedures and principles that may be used to guide people examining equivocal death scenarios serves to show its many areas of potential weakness. An effective model for such contributions to an investigation may therefore be a conventional scientific one. Hypotheses about the person and the cause of their death are offered. Evidence for and against those hypotheses is then carefully elicited and fully presented. Particular attention should be paid to the search for evidence that would refute those hypotheses.

I was able to explore the hypothesis testing approach when I was requested by the official enquiry into the fire in November 1987 at King's Cross underground station, in which 31 people died, to offer an opinion on whether the fire was accidental or malicious. I sought to identify the full range of options for the cause of the fire, including terrorist attack, revenge arson, pyromaniac arson, and accidental ignition. For each of these options I looked for information that would confirm it as likely and information that would refute it. So, for example, I proposed that a terrorist attack would have been of little value without some one claiming responsibility. The total absence of such claims reduced the support for this hypothesis. A pyromaniac or revenge arsonist would have been expected to ensure the fire took hold by using accelerants. No evidence of any accelerants were found. The strongest hypothesis turned out to be that the fire was started accidentally but this was dependent on the physical conditions being appropriate. Later fire tests indicated that poor maintenance had created appropriate conditions. The conclusion of the enquiry was that the fire had started accidentally.

The use of this scientific model does depend upon the effectiveness of the information collected. As has been indicated, there are many potential weaknesses in the source material that has to be drawn upon. The most obvious limitation is that the individual concerned is not available for assessment. This means that any conclusions about the individual's emotions, thoughts, attitudes and reactions have to be regarded as inferences that are no better than the information, and informants, on which they are based. Many of the subtleties, possible from having the 'patient' in front of the examiner, are lost. For example ambiguities in actions and words cannot be clarified by direct questioning. Non-verbal and paralinguistic cues cannot be utilised to add extra meaning to what is said. The context of an action or statement, that so helps to enrich its meaning, has to be gleaned indirectly. It is therefore perhaps even more important in this examination than in any other that the basic information and its sources are clearly recorded. The potential validity of these sources needs also to be carefully evaluated and the extent to which they corroborate each other thoroughly documented.

The Gilfoyle case, mentioned earlier, helps to illustrate the many pitfalls for a psychologist giving guidance on an equivocal death. I was asked to provide such guidance by the prosecution team, after they had decided that the hearsay evidence they had obtained about Paula's actions and thoughts prior to her death indicated that she had no intention of committing suicide. I attempted to seek evidence for various factors that would have been expected as precursors to suicide, as indicated above. I also did a very detailed analysis of the suicide note that Paula had written. The objective of this was to see if it indicated definite intention. It also allowed me to compare the mode of expression within it to other notes known to have been written by Paula and the person the police suspected of engineering her death, her husband Eddie Gilfoyle.

In the material the police made available to me there was no indication of any of the hypothesised antecedents to suicide. The analysis of the letter also produced results that did not accord totally with it having been written by Paula with the definite intent to kill herself. The police and the prosecution took these conclusions as strong support for their belief that Eddie was guilty. However, very sensibly in my opinion, the trial judge did not allow my evidence into court. Nonetheless, Eddie Gilfoyle was found guilty of the murder of his wife.

Mr Gilfoyle is still professing his innocence and trying to get a further appeal of his case heard, having already lost one appeal, so it is not appropriate to go into more detail at the present time. Yet it is worth drawing attention to some aspects of this case in the light of the literature reviewed here and in other chapters of this volume.

By relying on those sources made available through the police investigation, the contribution I made was rather similar to FBI 'equivocal death analyses'. The vagaries of the British legal system make it rather difficult for a 'prosecution expert' to get access to all the people or material that the defence team regard as central to their case, except through the complex and indirect process of guiding cross-examination in court. Indeed, without being a full participant in the enquiry any 'expert' may be unaware of the possible sources of information available. For example, I was never aware that Paula had kept a diary before meeting Eddie and that diary was still thought to be in existence. Perhaps the defence and/or the prosecution regarded it as having been written so long before Paula's death, and containing so little directly about her feelings and thoughts, that they regarded it as irrelevant to an opinion which they saw as being focused on the analysis of the suicide note? Yet any psychologist testing hypotheses about Paula's characteristic thoughts and feelings would have wished to see if the diary could help support or refute those hypotheses.

Similarly, as is clear from Gregory's study of suicide notes in Volume I of this series, the direct comparison of one note with the writing of two people is only the first step in testing hypotheses about the intention inherent in a suicide note. In fact Gregory's study was a direct result of my involvement in the Gilfoyle case. I encouraged him to carry out the analyses precisely because I was aware that my opinion was based on very little substantive empirical literature.

As already mentioned, psychologists are sometimes asked to give advice to precisely those investigations of fatalities in which there are many ambiguities. In an adversarial legal system they will inevitably be called upon to give guidance by one side or the other. Thus, although the expert will attempt to be as unbiased and objective as possible, without a pre-determined procedure and a clear definition of the sources of information on which their opinion should be drawn, there is always the risk that the evidence provided by the defence or the prosecution will contain hidden, and possibly unknown, biases. Yet the pressures will be on the expert to arrive at a definite conclusion, usually, in less time than the expert would wish and without all the information the expert would ideally like to have. In such circumstances careful adherence to scientific strategies and evaluations of the evidence are essential. It is also crucial to have some knowledge of the relative validity of the results produced by such means.

Validity of Psychological Contributions to Equivocal Death Investigations

Given the many difficulties associated with contributing to equivocal death investigations it might have been expected that there had been many attempts to determine how effective they actually are. Yet there has been very little research that examines the reliability or validity of psychological autopsies or related contributions to enquiries into fatalities. As mentioned, some preliminary work to develop operational criteria for determining suicide as cause of death has been conducted (Jobes et al 1991). Fifteen years earlier Shneidman (1976), rather disingenuously, referred to the increasing acceptance by Coroners of psychologists' opinions as a measure of the validity of those opinions. Barraclough et al (1974) found a high correlation between rank-ordered types of depressive symptoms in depressed suicide victims and in clinically referred depressed patients. This work in effect demonstrated the capacity of interviewers using a psychological autopsy format to elicit such information accurately, albeit across a narrow spectrum. Brent et al (1993) used the family history interview process to confirm diagnoses obtained via a psychological autopsy procedure, although he recognised that his study was subject to limitations of possible interviewer bias, interviewee bias and a limited sample.

Otto et al (1993) recognised that even before the validity of psychologists' contributions the inquiries could be sensibly explored it was important to establish if different psychologists would offer the same opinion if given the same information. This is an issue of 'reliability' rather than 'validity'. If different psychologists formed different views when presented with the same material then there is little hope that in general terms the opinions derived from the processes they used would be correct, or valid.

Otto et al (1993) examined the agreement between reports completed by 12 psychologists and two psychiatrists who reviewed materials which addressed the adjustment and psychological functioning of Clayton Hartwig, suspected of causing an explosion aboard the USS Iowa in 1989 which resulted in his own death and that of 46 other sailors. Although broad criteria were adopted, they found only moderate agreement between the findings of the 14 professionals conducting the assessment.

Otto et al's study was initiated as a reaction against an equivocal death analysis (EDA) carried out by FBI agents into the USS Iowa tragedy. The agents had formed the conclusion that Clayton Hartwig had deliberately caused the explosion in an act of suicide. Their opinion was upheld by the initial navy enquiry. However, a number of psychologists were highly critical of the EDA and the way it was carried out (Poythress et al 1993). Their examination of the facts indicated that the explosion was indeed an accident, a conclusion later supported by the technical evidence and accepted by a US Congress investigation. Poythress et al suggested that the FBI used scientific terms for a process lacking significant scientific methodology, and compounded that problem by failing to sufficiently delineate between "opinions" and "facts".

Two critical points must be made. Firstly, as emphasised earlier, the EDA technique was characterised by the examiners not conducting any interviews but relying on information provided to them based on interviews conducted by other parties. Secondly, given the nature of the initial inquiry and the subsequent review, the persons conducting the review had available to them a quantity of information significantly greater than would normally be present for most assessments. Even with this additional information, though, all panellists would have preferred more information regarding Hartwig.

Subsequent to this review, Ault et al (1993), FBI agents who provided the testimony, agreed with the view expressed by Poythress et al (1993) that "perceived utility and anecdotal evidence are mere proxies for validation, not validation itself." (p.73). Yet they rather confused the issue by asserting that EDA was an investigative technique and not a clinical-investigative method, somehow implying that the sort of detailed evidence that a 'clinician' might use in helping an investigation was irrelevant to FBI agents trying to achieve the same objectives.

The FBI agents further asserted that EDA is not a clinical but a professional opinion based on years of law enforcement experience with indirect assessment of violent death and the demands of law enforcement require that opinions be provided that do not equivocate. In other words, they are advocating opinions based merely on previous experience without any scientific support for those opinions, or even any possibility for demonstrating that hypotheses alternative to their opinions had been available for test. That they have provided a "conclusive" opinion in 42 or 45 EDA's, as they claim, is of considerable concern when viewed in the context of the technique's lack of even demonstrated reliability, and Ault's opinion that "to provide the validity is an exercise in futility" (Poythress et al 1993, p.9).

In contrast to the surprisingly cavalier view of some FBI agents, Ogloff and Otto suggest the use of blind studies to obtain an estimate of the validity of the psychological assessments of equivocal death victims. In relation to the determination of the mode of death, they propose identifying cases in which the "correct" answer to the question is known. Ideally, a group of mental health professionals should be provided with all the information except for one or two key pieces that clearly identify the correct answer (e.g. a suicide note). The subsequent opinions could then be compared to the "correct" outcome to provide an estimate of validity. Alternately, they propose evaluating "available" persons and then providing for assessment all information except that which is based on the "availability" of the examinee. Opinions could be compared to those based on comprehensive assessment (including psychometric data) of the individual. Such approaches to address the issues of reliability and validity would seem to be the minimum necessary, but do not yet seem to have been conducted. This suggests mental health professionals should be cautious when using reconstructive psychological evaluations particularly in legal and quasi-legal contexts and those major enquiries, like that in the USS Iowa tragedy, in which much of significance to many people may result from the expert's opinion. Professionals are ethically obliged not to mislead their clients about the accuracy of the conclusions they draw.

Admissibility

Despite the many weaknesses of the evidence and procedures used in psychological autopsies and the lack of definitive research to support its validity, it is clear that opinions from psychologists and other mental health professionals, about the mental state of the deceased, have been drawn upon in many courts in the United States and can strongly influence the judgements of those who read them. Jobes et al (1986) carried out an experiment that showed that the 95 medical examiners who received reports containing only physical and circumstantial evidence about a fatality, gave distinctly different judgements compared with 100 who had the same reports augmented with psychological opinion. Given such potential impact it is perhaps therefore not surprising that many jurisdictions have admitted them.

Dregne (1972) conducted a significant review of the use of the psychological autopsy in both civil and criminal cases. He cites the case of *State v. Jones,* [CR No. 98666 (Arizona Superior Court, 1978)], where the psychiatric autopsy of a murder victim was admitted on behalf of the defendant who claimed self-defence in the killing. The psychiatric autopsy was deemed to show that the defendant, a repeatedly battered wife, was not unreasonable in her assumption that the victim may have killed her. In another case, that of *State v. Carrethers*, [CR No. 100359 (Arizona Superior Court, 1978)], a psychiatric* autopsy of the defendant's deceased father was admitted. The defendant claimed defence of his mother in the killing of his father. The psychiatric autopsy indicated that the father drank heavily, routinely battered his wife and stepdaughter, and provoked numerous acts of violence at work. Again the psychiatric* autopsy revealed that the son had been reasonable in his reaction to his father's violence. Dregne, nontheless, highlights the difficulties associated with the admissibility of psychological autopsies as evidence in Court hearings, both in terms of Federal and State (USA) rules of evidence and the inconclusive debate regarding the scientific basis for the technique.

Ogloff and Otto (1997) give a very thorough review of the questions that psychological autopsy evidence needs to answer satisfactorily if it is

---

*In these criminal cases the term "psychiatric" rather than "psychological" autopsy was used. Dregne asserts the terms are interchangeable.

to be admissible in a US court. For example whether its probative value outweighs its prejudicial impact. Will it directly assist the trier of fact? Are such autopsies reasonably relied on by experts in the field? Does the proposed witness qualify as an expert? These are exactly the same questions that a British court would wish to answer, but a British court would probably look for slightly different emphasis, for example possibly being more concerned about possible prejudice and less concerned about the status of the expert.

Ogloff and Otto point out that at least one Supreme Court in the USA, that of Montana, has directly upheld the admissibility of a psychological autopsy against an appeal that the psychologist should have interviewed the deceased prior to his death in order for his expertise to be valid. The court held that the fact that the deceased "was not interviewed before his death does not render inadmissible a psychologist's opinion based on the available data". However, Ogloff and Otto emphasise that whilst many courts trying accident claims have accepted psychological evidence concerning the deceased state of mind prior to death they are more reluctant to permit experts to testify about whether the death was a suicide or an accident.

In applications challenging wills and intestate succession, Ogloff and Otto point out that the courts are reluctant even to accept psychological opinion about the intentions or state of mind of the deceased. This seems to be because such opinion is deemed to intrude too closely into the legal realm. The courts believe that given the same information available to the expert they could form a view themselves that would be just as valid. This is not far removed from the opinion with which I opened this chapter that there is indeed much that a layman can do in forming a view about a dead person that will parallel the opinion of a professional psychologist. Furthermore, as was shown in the USS Iowa case, there are definite possibilities of prejudice, whereby an opinion presented by an apparent expert is given more credence than it deserves.

All the accounts available of psychological opinion relevant to equivocal death cases, used in Court, are drawn from the USA. The examples, in the main, though, tend to be civil cases relating to insurance and worker's compensation. Even in the USA criminal cases are rarely likely to admit psychological autopsies as expert evidence. No instances of its use in courts in other English speaking countries have been identified, (Zander et al 1993). This may, partly, be a function of the data gathering or terms used. There are clearly circumstances where defence cases for example in England or Australia rely on evidence regarding the personality and mental state of a deceased victim in order to promote the issue of self defence or provocation.

Relevance to Criminal Investigations

The potential for misuse of reconstructive psychological evaluation techniques has been highlighted with reference to the paucity of the research literature and the difficulties illustrated in the Gilfoyle case and the USS Iowa inquiries. In using a technique with no well established reliability or validity the courts are appropriately cautious about allowing its use in evidence. Without doubt, the value of the procedure can be enhanced by drawing on as many and as varied direct sources of information as possible. A clearly scientific stance in which alternative hypotheses are tested would also help to reduce the influence of those agencies or other parties with a biased interest in the outcome of the investigation. Such a stance would require the following:

1. Clear statement of the alternative explanations that are feasible to account for the equivocal death.

2. Clear indication as to the evidence that would be required to support or reject each of these explanations.

3. Full account of the evidence that is available and how it relates to the evidence that would be required.

4. Evaluation of the evidence available and the processes that have been undertaken to test its accuracy and validity.

5. Clear statement of how the evidence has been drawn upon to reach conclusions about each of the explanations offered.

Such a thorough report is very demanding and time consuming to produce. It is also likely to require scholarship and research beyond obtaining the facts of the case and accounts from those closed to the deceased. In the pressures of a criminal investigation and the legal process there may not be all the resources necessary to carry out the task at as high a professional standard as all may wish. In such cases the weaknesses in the psychologist's activities need to be clearly stated, or the professional should actually refuse to undertake the task.

It must also be borne in mind that during the course of criminal investigations the burden of proof is different from that required in court. It therefore may be the case that psychological contributions can currently have a more productive role outside of the court than they have inside. Such examinations can help to draw attention to possibilities the investigating officers had not considered or provide a framework for more careful consideration of the issues salient to the case. This, after all, is the basis of the FBI claims for carrying out an EDA. The alacrity with which their opinions have been used outside of the police investigation is possibly more an indication of the thirst many authorities have for certainty in problematic situations than an indication of the validity of what FBI agents, psychologists and others try to do.

A further point that advisors to the police need to bear in mind is that police officers have no training or conceptual system for considering suicide. In the Gilfoyle case the dead woman was found hanging and a suicide note was found in her handwriting. This was taken as clear evidence of suicide, so that little further evidence was collected at the time, including no photographic record of the body *in situ* at the scene of death. If some form of psychological autopsy had been standard practice then a great deal of useful information would have been quickly collected. This would have alerted the police to the lack of the more obvious precursors for suicide, such as the fact that the woman was eight and half months pregnant and apparently making many happy plans for her baby's future. This in turn would have made the investigation more timely and thorough, avoiding the inevitable later confusions and doubts over the safety of the conviction.

Similarly, in those distressing cases, often concerning the suicide of adolescents, that emerge from time to time, in which the family and friends insist that there had been no prior indication that a suicide might occur, a systematic framework for considering the actions, emotions and mental state of the victim might enable an investigation to reach a more convincing and timely conclusion. In some cases this may reveal murders that have been disguised as suicides. In other cases it would help those touched by the death to come to terms more fully with the events surrounding it.

Conclusion

Psychologists and their cognate colleagues have responded to requests to give clear answers in equivocal circumstances. As is their custom, they have striven to convert the muddy complexity of tragic events into systematic procedures that will take some of the subjectivity and arbitrariness out of the examination of these events. Their main objectives are to remove the bias from the conclusions that may be reached about ambiguous fatalities and to facilitate the accumulation of knowledge so that others may learn from the tragedy and hopefully reduce the chances of similar future occurrences.

As so often happens with good ideas in psychology, these contributions to investigations have been used in a variety of situations before they have reached the maturity needed to be safely allowed out of the careful confines of their professional birthplace. Coroners' courts in Los Angeles, considering teenage deaths, are a far cry from enquiries of national significance into explosions on a navy warship. It is perhaps some measure of the readiness with which people in the USA embrace psychology, especially in the forensic context, that the psychological autopsy has already been tested in so many jurisdictions, long before detailed, large scale studies have been carried out to ensure its effectiveness and to determine the best way of carrying it out.

There can be little doubt that more system and less bias would be an advantage for many enquiries into suspicious deaths and ambiguous fatalities. It is also clear that psychologists, drawing upon the traditions of psychometrics, have much to offer that will reduce bias and improve the clarity of judgements. But for this emerging science to survive it is essential that it does not offer more than it can deliver.

As ever the fiction writer may have got there before the scientist, Jonathan Kellerman puts it in his 1990 book "Time Bomb " (quoted by Ogloff and Otto, in press)

"Mr Burden, what is it exactly you think I can do for you?"
"Conduct a psycho-biography. The life and times of Holly Lynn

Burden......Apply the same tools of scholarship you apply to your research and become the resident expert on my little girl – on what made her tick. Delve as deep as you like. Be unsparing with your questions. Do whatever it takes to get to the root of this mess. Learn the truth, Dr Delaware."
I took my time answering. His eyes never left me.
*"Sounds like you're talking about two separate things, Mr Burden. Reconstructing your daughter's life – what's known as a psychological autopsy. And **vindicating** her. One may not lead to the other."*

(p. 102)

References

Ault, R.L. Hazelwood, R. and Reboussin, R. (1994) Epistemological Status of Equivocal Death Analysis. *American Psychologist*, 49, 1, 72-73.

Barraclough, B.M. Bunch, J. Nelson, B. and Sainsbury, P. (1974) A Hundred Cases of Suicide: clinical aspects. *British Journal of Psychiatry*. 125, 355-373.

Beck, A. Shuyler, D. and Herman, J. (1974) "Development of suicidal intent scales" in K.Resnick and D. Leterri (eds) *The Prediction of Suicide* Bowie, Md: Charles Press.

Beskow, J., Runesow, B. and Asgard, U. (119). Ethical Aspects of Psychological Autopsy. *Acta Psychiatrica Scandinavia*. 84, 482-487.

Boyd, J.H. (1983) "The increasing rate of suicide by firearms" *New England Journal of Medicine 308,* p. 313- 317.

Brent, D.A. (1989) The Psychological Autopsy: Methodological Considerations for the Study of Adolescent Suicide. *Suicide and Life Threatening Behaviour*. 19(1) 43-57.

Brent, D.A. Perper, J.A. Maritz, G. Allman, C.J. Roth, C. Schweers, J. and Balach, L. (1993) The Validity of Diagnoses Obtained Through The Psychological Autopsy Procedure in Adolescent Suicide Victims: Use of Family History. *Acta Psyciatrica Scandinavia*, 87, 118-122.

Canter, D. (1995) "Psychology of Offender Profiling" in R.Bull and D.Carson (eds) *Handbook of Psychology in Legal Contexts*. Cichester: John Wiley and Sons p. 343- 55.

Dregne, N. (1982). Psychological Autopsy: A New Tool for Criminal Defense Attorneys? *Arizona Law Review*, 24, 421-439.

Ebert, B.W. (1987). Guide to Conducting a Psychological Autopsy. *Professional Psychology: Research and Practice*. 18, 1, 52-56.

Farberow, N. and Schneidman, E. (1961) *The Cry for Help*. New York: McGraw-Hill.

Fowler, R. (1986). Howard Hughes: a Psychological Autopsy. *Psychology Today*, May, p. 22-33.

Gould, M.S. and Shaffer, D. (1986) "The impact of suicide in television movies: Evidence of Imitation" *New England Journal of Medicine* 315, 690-694.

Jobes, D.A. Berman, A.L. and Josselson, A.R. (1986) "The Impact of Psychological Autopsies on Medical Examiners' Determination of Manner of Death" *Journal of Forensic Sciences*, 31 (1) 177 -189.

Jobes, D.A. Casey, J.O. Berman, A.L. and Wright, D.G. (1991) Empirical Criteria for the Determination of Suicide Manner of Death. *Journal of Forensic Sciences*, 36, 1, 244-256.

Kovaks, M. (1985) "The Interview Schedule for Children (ISC)" *Psychopharmacological Bulletin* 21, 991-994.

Litman, R.E. Curphey, T. Shneidman, E.S. Farberow, N.L. and Tabachnick, N. (1970). The Psychological Autopsy of Equivocal Deaths. In Snheidman, E.S., Farberow, N.L. and Litman, R.E. *The Psychology of Suicide*. New York: Science House.

Ogloff, J. and Otto, R.K. (in press). Psychological Autopsy: Clinical and Legal Perspectives. *St. Louis University Law Journal*.

Otto, R.K. Poythress, N. Starr, L. and Darkes, J. (1993). An Empirical Study of the Reports of APA's Peer Review Panel in the Congressional Review of the USS Iowa Incident. *Journal of Personality Assessment*.

Paykel, E.S. Prusoff, B.A. and Myers, J.K. (1966). "Suicide attempts and recent life events: A controlled comparison" *Archives of General Psychiatry*, 32, pp. 327-337.

Poythress, N. Otto, R.K. Darkes, J. and Starr, L. (1993). APA's Expert Panel in the Congressional Review of the USS Iowa Incident. *American Psychologist*, January, 8-15.

Rudestam, K.E. (1977). Physical and Psychological Responses to Suicide in the Family. *Journal of Consulting and Clinical Psychology*, 45, 2, 162-170.

Selkin, J. (1994). Psychological Autopsy: Scientific Psychohistory or Clinical Intuition. *American Psychologist*. 49, (1), 64-75.

Selkin, J. and Loya, F. (1979). Issues in the Psychological Autopsy of a Controversial Public Figure. *Professional Psychology*, February, 87-93.

Shafii, M. Stelz-Lenarsky, J. Derrick, A. Beckner, C. and Whittinghill, J.R. (1988). Comorbidity of Mental Disorders in the Post-Mortem Diagnosis of Completed Suicide in Children and Adolescents. *Journal of Affective Disorders*, 15, 227-233.

Shneidman, E.S. (1976). *Suicidology: Contemporary Developments*. New York: Grune and Stratton.

Shneidman, E.S. (1994). The Psychological Autopsy. *American Psychologist*, 49, 1, 75-76.

Shneidman, E.S. and Farberow, N.L. (1961). Sample Investigations of Equivocal Deaths. In Farberow, N.L. and Shneidman E.S. (eds) *The Cry For Help*. New York: McGraw-Hill.

Shneidman, E.S. and Farberow, N.L. (1970). Sample Psychological Autopsies. In Shneidman, E.S. Farberow, N.L. and Litman, R.E. *The Psychology of Suicide*. New York: Science House.

Weisman, A.D. and Kastenbaum, R. (1968). The Psychological Autopsy: A Study of the Terminal Phase of Life. *Community Mental Health Journal* (Monograph No. 4). New York: Behavioural Publications.

Zander, M. and Henderson, P. (1993). Crown Court Study. The Royal Commission on Criminal Justice. London: HMSO.

APPENDIX I

Outline for Psychological Autopsy (Shneidman, 1976)

1. Identifying information for victim (name, age, address, marital status, religious practices, occupation, and other details)

2. Details of the death (including the cause or method and other pertinent details)

3. Brief outline of victim's history (siblings, marriage, medical illnesses, medical treatment, psychotherapy, and previous suicide attempts)

4. "Death history" of victim's family (suicides, cancer, other fatal illnesses, ages at death, and other details)

5. Description of the personality and life style of the victim

6. Victim's typical patterns of reaction to stress, emotional upsets, and periods of disequilibrium.

7. Any recent – from last few days to last 12 months – upsets, pressures, tensions, or anticipations of trouble

8. Role of alcohol and drugs in (1) overall lifestyle of victim and (2) in his/her death

9. Nature of victim's interpersonal relationships (including physicians)

10. Fantasies, reams, thoughts, premonitions, or fears of victim relating to death, accident or suicide

11. Changes in the victim before death (of habits, hobbies, eating, sexual patterns and other life routines)

12. Information relating to the "life side" of victim (upswings, successes, plans)

13. Assessment of intention, i.e. role of the victim in his own demise

14. Rating of lethality

15. Reactions of informants to victim's death

16. Comments, special features, etc.

APPENDIX II

Psychological Autopsy Guidelines (Ebert, 1987)

1. Alcohol History

    a. Collect family history
    b. Research amount ingested regularly
    c. Research evidence of binge drinking
    d. Research evidence of blackouts (known from friends, family, and acquaintances)
    e. Research evidence of driving under the influence of alcohol
    f. Research evidence of alcohol-related offences
    g. Research evidence of family problems (alcohol related)
    h. Research evidence of work difficulties connected to alcohol

    i. Research evidence of blood level (BAL) g/l at time of death

2. Suicide Notes

    a. Examine content
    b. Examine style
    c. Have handwriting expert review writing style

3. Writing

    a. Review any past writing by the deceased
    b. Peruse any diary of the deceased
    c. Examine school papers for topics of essays or term papers
    d. Read letters to friends, family, co-workers, acquaintances

4. Books

    a. Examine books of the deceased
        i. Look for books on the occult, life after death, death
        ii. Look for actual books on suicide
    b. Assess books checked out of local libraries

5. Relationship Assessments

    a. Interview people who knew the deceased including:
        i. Close friends
        ii. Close intimate heterosexual or homosexual companions
        iii. Acquaintances
        iv. Mother, father, siblings
        v. Co-workers and supervisors
        vi. Other relatives
        vii. Physicians and/or mental health professionals
        viii. Teachers
    b. Construct level of intimacy on the basis of discussions with "close" friends
    c. Assess people's reactions to the victim's death
    d. Secure a history of marriages and divorces
    e. Examine relationship with children

    f. Look for anger directed to particular people

6. Marital Relationship

    a. Note any significant problems that may have made the deceased person depressed
    b. Look for history of extramarital relationships
    c. Assess the overall quality of the relationship

7. Mood

    a. Identify mood fluctuations
    b. Look for symptoms of depression:
        i. Weight loss
        ii. References to depression
        iii. Problems with memory
        iv. Fatigue
        v. Sleep disturbances
        vi. Withdrawal
        vii. Decreased libido
        viii. Appetite and/or taste changes
        ix. Constipation and diarrhoea
    c. Look for mood indicators during last few days:
        i. Interview friends and family
        ii. Interview anyone surrounding the deceased

8. Psychosocial Stressors (note and chart importance on Holmes & Rahe Scale factors)

    a. Recent loss: deaths of people or pets
    b. Relationship separations: divorce, breakups of significant relationships
    c. Loss of job
    d. Legal and financial problems
    e. Demotion, promotion and so on
    f. Reaction to stressors
    g. Move to a new location

9. Presuicidal Behaviour

a. Giving away important possessions
b. Paying up insurance policies
c. Payment of debts
d. Arrangement for children and pets
e. Sudden order in deceased's life
f. Change or initial creation of a will

10. Language

a. Identify any specific references to suicide (deceased may have stated, "Have a party in remembrance of me," or "You won't have to worry about me anymore")
b. Note any changes in language before suicide
c. Analyse language (tapes, recollections of conversations, writing) for morbid content

11. Drugs Used

a. Identify all drugs used by deceased
b. Assess interactional effects of legal and illegal drugs in use

12. Medical History

a. Review complete medical history
b. Note any unusual symptoms or diagnoses
c. Note any terminal illnesses or diagnoses

13. Reflective Mental Status Exam of Deceased's Condition Before Death

a. Orientation
b. Memory
c. Concentration
e. Mood and affect
f. Hallucinations or delusions
g. Cognition, IQ
h. Language

    i. Judgement

14. Psychological History

    a. Look for previous suicide attempts (type, method)
    b. Assess reason for treatment if involved in therapy
    c. Research evidence of depression, manic depression (bipolar disorder)
    d. Research past psychiatric hospitalizations
    e. Examine diagnoses
    f. Examine evidence of impulsive behaviour
    g. Examine any recent or past psychological tests (e.g. was the victim given the Rorschach and was the suicide constellation served via the Exner system?)

15. Laboratory Studies

    a. Examine ballistics
    b. Evaluate powder burns on hands and body

16. Coroner's Report

    a. Conduct complete drug screen
    b. Identify any poisons
    c. Read for detailed description of physical functioning/health of deceased at time of death

17. Motive Assessment

    a. Make a chart divided four ways: Murder, Suicide, Accident, and Natural, recording data to support each as it is uncovered.
    b. Report the possible reasons for suicide
    c. Report the possible reasons why subject could have been murdered (identify enemies, illicit activities)

18. Reconstruction of Events Occurring on the Day Before Deceased's Death

    a. Make a step-by-step chart of subject's movements and activities

    b. Form a chronological history of the victim that immediately preceded death

19. Assess Feelings Regarding Death as Well as Preoccupations and Fantasies

20. Military History

    a. Look for evidence of difficulty adjusting such as letters of counselling (LOC), letters of reprimand (LOR), Article 15 action (A15), or court-martial proceedings [Note: A15 is a form of nonjudicial punishment for offences not serious enough to warrant a court-martial and include repeated lateness, driving under the influence of alcohol, sleeping on duty, or negligence on duty. Punishment from an A15 can include reduction in rank, fines, or removal from duty.]

    b. Attempt to secure job ratings (airman promotion rating and officer effectiveness rating)

    c. Look for decorations or awards

    d. Notice whether deceased was in a combat zone at any time

    e. Look for evidence of posttraumatic stress disorder in Vietnam veterans

    f. Determine the number of assignments and which were at the request of the victim

21. Death History of Family

    a. Examine history for suicide by other family members

    b. List immediate deceased family members and their mode of death

22. Family History

    a. Identify family members and relationships with deceased

    b. Examine the socioeconomic status of family

    c. Identify any conflicts that occurred before death of the victim

23. Employment History

    a. Identify number and types of jobs (high- risk work may indicate the existence of subintention behavior for quite some time)
    b. Look for repetitive problems
    c. Assess whether any problems existed before death (e.g. co-worker conflict, failure to progress as planned)
    d. Note any disciplinary action

24. Educational History

    a. Assess educational level
    b. Identify any problems with teachers or subjects
    c. Note special interests or topics (e.g. in particular, look for special interests in death)

25. Familiarity With Methods of Death

    a. Examine belongings for guns, knives (e.g. the deceased may have had five or six loaded weapons around his or her house regularly)
    b. Look for lethal drugs
    c. Note deceased's interest and knowledge in weapons

26. Police Report

    a. Critical facts will be obtained by review of the police investigation
    b. Pay special attention to ballistics data

7 Approaches to the Scientific Attribution of Authorship

JOY P. AKED, DAVID CANTER, ANTHONY J. SANFORD
AND NICHOLA SMITH

Author specific linguistic patterns are present in unique combinations in the style of every writer. These underlying patterns can often be clearly described by careful linguistic observation and analysis, making author identification *(McMenamin, 1993). This chapter sets out to explore these claims and to provide an overview of the work that has been carried out by forensic linguists to determine whether two texts can be shown to be authored by the same person. It examines the assumption that there are linguistic characteristics which can be said to be unique to individuals, and reviews proposed examples of discriminating indices. The issues of genre and modality are often investigated, as well as requirements for the assessment of reliability of a discriminating index of authorship. In addition, the Cusum technique (Morton & Michaelson, 1990; Morton, 1991) is critically analysed in this context. The chapter makes several recommendations of different research objectives required by this type of research and concludes that even with stringent scientific criteria, it is unlikely that a reliable and valid measure of author identity will ever be established.

Joy P. Aked (B.Sc., PhD., University of Glasgow) is a Lecturer at the University of Paisley, where her specialist area is in Biological Psychology. She also retains her specialist interest in Forensic Linguistics. At the present time she is conducting research in the area of critical thinking, in particular, whether or not this is a skill which students can be taught at University, and whether or not there are differences in critical thinking skills across disciplines, years and Universities.

*Offender Profiling Series: II - **Profiling in Policy and Practice***
Edited by D. Canter and L. Alison. © 1999 Ashgate Publishing, Aldershot. pp. 157-187

David Canter is Director of the Institute of Investigative Psychology at the University of Liverpool. He has published widely in Environmental and Investigative Psychology as well as many areas of Applied Social Psychology. His most recent books since his award winning *"Criminal Shadows"* have been *"Psychology in Action"* and with Laurence Alison *"Criminal Detection and the Psychology of Crime"*.

Anthony J. Sanford (B.Sc. (Leeds), P.hD.,(Cantab), FPBS, Chart. Psychologist, Professor of Psychology at the University of Glasgow and Principal Investigator with the ESCR Human Communication Research Centre. Chief research interests are developing an account of human understanding and the perception of coherence. Also interested in individual styles of writing and communicating and in the communication of risk and uncertainty. He teaches in the areas of Cognition, Cognitive Science, Social Cognition and the Psychology of Language.

Nichola Smith completed her PhD entitled 'A stylistic analysis of written language behaviour with practical application to anonymous threat letters' at the University of Surrey. Dr Smith then began a three year contract for the Police Research Group's (PRG) Serious Crime Research Programme (based within the National Crime Faculty, Bramshill) as a research officer. Her principle areas of interest lie within forensic linguistics and the examination of behavioural consistency of serial serious crime. These interests are reflected, in part, within some of her allocated projects within the PRG's programme of research (evaluation of Scientific Content Analysis Technique and Comparative Case Analysis).

7 Approaches to the Scientific Attribution of Authorship

JOY P. AKED, DAVID CANTER, ANTHONY J. SANFORD
AND NICHOLA SMITH

Introduction

Whether two texts can be shown to be authored by the same person is one of the central questions of forensic linguistics. Examples include determining whether a suicide note is written by a person who died, or whether it was fabricated by another person, whether the transcript of a confession was doctored by the police or whether it is a more-or-less verbatim version of a real confession. Determining the identity of the author of a threat letter is another related example, or indeed whether two threat letters are the work of one person.

Although now appearing in a forensic guise, all these examples are clearly related to questions of the attribution of authorship in general. These questions are also important in literary research and it is therefore not surprising that many forensic studies of authorship still share much with this literary ancestry.

However, unlike the academic debates of literary historians, the application of any method in a forensic setting requires the highest standards of reliability and validity. Indeed, if a method is to be used in the case for the prosecution the need for the conclusions to be beyond any reasonable doubt requires standards beyond those that many journal articles reach. Even from the perspective of defence or appeal, where the demonstration of reasonable doubt by such methods may be sufficient, the acceptability of a method in the first place as an instrument of admissible evidence must rest on the technique itself being reputable.

Our view is that borrowing techniques from the existing field of literary analysis is not a good strategy, because most existing studies have failed to definitions or theories of language. The weakness of such a clear conceptual basis for studies meet the criteria of scientific rigour.

Furthermore, we propose that the choice of methods has tended to be largely arbitrary and lacking in a priori of authorship attribution as revealed by McMenamin (1993) in his extensive review of what he calls 'forensic linguistics'. He provides many examples of linguistic analysis used in legal cases to determine authorship, but he gives no explanation as to why the linguistic measures used should indicate authorship. Nor does he provide one single study that demonstrates against objective, external, criteria that the linguistic parameters used are reliable indicators of authorship. Despite this, he makes some remarkable claims:

> First, author-specific linguistic patterns are present in unique combination in the style of every writer. Second, these underlying patterns can often be clearly described by careful linguistic observation and analysis, making author identification possible.
>
> (p.3).

We view this statement with considerable scepticism. It is a reflection of what appears to be little more than an act of faith within linguistics that: "The totality of the possible utterances of one speaker at one time in using language to interact with one other speaker is an *idiolect*" (Bloch 1948).

As we shall describe, although idiolect has been widely accepted within linguistics as an aspect of language, the parameters that define the differences between idiolects have never been established. Perhaps more importantly for forensic application, the criteria that must be used to determine the validity of any such parameters appear not to have been closely considered.

Essentially, if authorship attribution methods are to be scientifically acceptable they have to be validated against objective criteria. This requires those involved in the study of forensic linguistics to determine and implement the highest possible standards of scientific proof. We believe that this requires genuine scientific research, and that without it authorship attribution will never be satisfactory.

The Assumption that Linguistic Characteristics are Unique to Individuals

The idea that everyone has their own unique style in discourse production is intuitively appealing, almost as appealing as the idea that we all differ from one another. It would seem that all we have to do is search for a set of descriptive parameters, which would index such discrimination. Some linguists appear to have taken it almost as an act of faith that there are identifiable differences between people in their modes of verbal expression, creating modes of expression that are unique to each person. Indeed, the analysis of the writing styles of figures in literature is the hallmark of literary criticism. There are clearly differences between some people and others, and we would scarcely be surprised if it proved possible to discriminate between an essay written by a schoolboy and an essay written by a figure from literature. But it proves more difficult to discriminate between Shakespeare and Marlowe, for example, (Mendenthall, 1891) in their 'styles' of writing even if what they choose to write about is rather different.

It is relevant to note that much of the basis of literary scholarship has derived from attempts to identify the characteristics of the particular 'styles' of leading authors. It is precisely because of that quality to their work, which is so enigmatic that the attempts to solve this enigma have produced an area of scholarship. Furthermore, much of the scholarly debate centres on trying to identify authorship where there is no objective criterion to determine who the author actually was. For example, claims to have specified which of Shakespeare's plays were not his work are treated with interest by other scholars but would not pass any scientific test of proof, and would certainly not be acceptable in a court of law as evidence of forgery. Given the difficulties of determining or recognising the work of major literary figures who have established their credentials by virtue of their linguistic capabilities, it is likely to be even more difficult to do so with the products of people who are rather less capable but who are at the heart of many forensic examples. Ultimately, the intuitive method of discerning style, so fondly cherished by literary critics, is of little use in a forensic setting because it is not amenable to direct experimental test.

Impressions of Style and Judgements 'On the Fly'

The reliance on impressions of style is unsatisfactory because it is impossible for any one else to follow the impressionistic procedure and thereby to check that they can obtain the same result, whether for the purposes of dispute or confirmation. This is the fundamental requirement of any scientific measurement; 'reliability', i.e. that any two applications of the measurement to the same material will produce similar results. The main way to achieve such reliability is the use of objective measures. Entities which are overtly describable and preferably countable, such as frequency of use of particular words or combinations of words, the distribution of sentence lengths, the sequence of themes, and so on, puts the analysis in the public domain, but only provided very clear definitions are given of what it is that is being counted or described that others can use. This essential objectivity allows any index to be tested for reliability and usefulness, and for statistical analysis to be carried out on its discriminatory effectiveness in this paper, we are only concerned with indices of the measurable kind, with procedures which are expressible as rules, or through an algorithm for the application of the test in question. However, a final word on implicit skill is in order. It is often the case that an expert is unable to fully explain a complex procedure used in judgement: he cannot describe it as an algorithm. In the Information Technology industry, attempts to produce computational procedures which mimic the decision-making behaviours of experts in a number of fields have come face to face with this problem, to the extent that it has been regarded as one of the central problems of the 'knowledge acquisition' necessary to develop expert systems. However, if the 'expertise' on which a person bases their judgements cannot be clarified, it is still essential to demonstrate that they are indeed 'experts' and that their judgements can be demonstrated to be both valid and different from those of the novice.

One should not put a drug on the market without demonstrating its safety through well-known experimental trials and statistical analysis. Simply claiming that 'experts' know it is safe is unacceptable unless evidence acceptable to other experts can be produced. By the same token, one should not put an authorship discrimination procedure into practice without demonstrating its efficacy in a methodologically appropriate way.

Consistency, Reliability, and Validity

Psychologists have been concerned with consistencies in the behaviour of individuals throughout the history of the subject: constancy of intelligence, constancy of personality, constancy of attitudes and so on. It is just as intuitively appealing to suppose that a given person has a particular level of intelligence (which is constant over time, and which may be discernibly different from her neighbour's) as it is to suppose that a given person has a fixed characteristic style of expressing themselves in discourse. The extent to which the intelligence score of an individual is the same or very similar on different occasions is the reliability of intelligence as indexed by the test in question. Even for such fundamental issues as intelligence, it is rare for a test-retest correlation, indexing reliability, to exceed 0.8, meaning that only 64% of the variance common to a measure on the two occasions is interrelated. This is the reliability for a very precise measurement made under highly controlled and constricted conditions, i.e. the intelligence test. Indeed, many of the criticisms of intelligence testing arise because of the limited generality such tests have been found to have. But those limitations are a product of the search for reliability. Other indices of a person's intellectual capabilities that derive from more open contexts, such as the level of schooling they have completed, or how highly regarded they are by their teachers are much less reliable. There are therefore *prima facie* reasons for questioning how consistent individuals will be on some style measure or set of measures in a variety of genres and registers, when they are speaking rather than writing, at different stages in their intellectual maturation, when they are consciously trying to express themselves in a particular way or not, or when they are under stress or relaxed.

Genre and Modality

Consistencies of individual style will have a maximum forensic applicability when they hold over all genres and modalities. However, there may be specific forensic applications when it appears that there is no requirement for the consistencies to be so general. For example, if a reliable index were to distinguish between a specific set of authors only for letters then it could be used to attribute authorship of some letters to the known individuals. However, this would require the development of specific indices for each context and set of authors.

The development of such specific indices is, however, fraught with problems unless a general theory was available to enable the forensic linguist to be confident of which indices were appropriate. Such a theory would have to enable the objective distinction between contexts. For example does 'letter' include business as well as personal letters, hand written as well as word processed letters? The theory would also have to be precise about which range of authors the index was applicable to. Would people brought up in the same neighbourhood and schools be excluded, or people from similar professional backgrounds? Without answers to these questions it is always possible that other material or other *individuals need* to be considered, and when considered would lead to different conclusions.

The difficulties of demonstrating stability of linguistic style under many conditions can be questioned from many studies, contradicting the claims of some that aspects of linguistic style can be identified that exist regardless of modality and genre (e.g. Morton's, 1991 claims regarding the Cusum method, considered later).

There is considerable evidence that both genre and modality influence aspects of style. Bhatia (1993) demonstrated that the choice of words made by an individual writer could differ between genres precisely because of the different nature of the genres involved. Writers bear in mind any special requirements the reader may have or any particular constraints the situation may demand, and therefore make choices to make the writing more effective. Thus, in a personal letter, the point may be to offer a graphic subjective opinion on an event. In a newspaper article the same event may be presented by the same person in the semblance of dispassionate analysis. Fowler (1982) puts it well by pointing out that genres offer "...a literary matrix by which to order experiences during compositions" (p.31, in Swales, 1990).

Modality also generates differences in writing style, as Bhatia (1993) has shown by comparing print and TV advertisements for the same products. Most comparisons of modality have examined the differences between written and spoken, showing for instance that there is a higher ratio of content words (open class) to function words (closed class) in written language than there is in spoken language (e.g. Halliday 1990). This finding, sometimes called the lexical density hypothesis, casts *a priori* doubt on any claim that written and spoken material would reflect the same habits.

Fundamental Requirements for the Assessment of Reliability

The identification of an author on the basis of his or her writing style relies on there being a characteristic which holds for that author, and which is different from the characteristic of any other possible author, or authors, with which the target author may be compared. This is true for any comparison: if deciding which of two known people have produced a piece of discourse, which one of many known people have produced a piece of discourse, whether or not more than one person contributed to a piece of discourse (where only one of the possibilities is known) and so on. Each of these comparisons does make different demands on the characteristic being examined. For instance, if two known people are being compared, then small differences between them may be of some utility, but if an attempt is made to compare one with many possibilities then the characteristic is likely to have more robust demands made upon it.

One possibility is to identify rare, 'signature' characteristics that may identify the writing of a particular person, such as the use of multiple exclamation marks and underlinings, or very unusual vocabulary or neologisms. But the problems with this approach are (i) that the very rarity may mean that not enough examples exist to make definitive statements and (ii) that without knowledge of the base rate in the population at large estimates of uniqueness may be mistaken. There are great practical difficulties in demonstrating that one particular person's rare usage is not just a small sample of the rare usage that many people would illustrate if we had a large enough set of examples of their language.

A more feasible approach is to find characteristics that are reasonably widespread in the population of interest. For such comparisons to be made, the fundamental requirement is that the variability of the characteristics in question, from one example to another is:

(1) Substantially smaller within an individual than between individuals,
(2) Not influenced by floor or ceiling effects that will make it non-discriminatory in many circumstances. It is also important that the characteristic should be widely present in the population in question,

but at a wide range of levels, so that it will be available for use under many circumstances.

What is required for testing whether an index is discriminating, is in principle very straightforward. The basic procedure for establishing (1) is to take a large number of samples from as large a group of individuals as possible and analyse them with respect to the index in question. The variation of habit within an individual can then be measured, as can the variation between individuals. A *stable index* is one that shows little variation within a person. A *discriminating index* will additionally show high variability between individuals relative to within person variation. In the case of comparing a piece of discourse with the work of two putative authors (a simple choice case), it is necessary to show that the index used is stable for each individual and discriminating between them, for the genres and modalities in question. Then it may be used on the disputed data and a probability of fit to one or the other author may be calculated.

This may seem very obvious, but no published accounts of the successful application of such a test can be found. Some claims are made that such tests have been carried out but not published. However until they are open to expert scrutiny they are not part of the body of scientific knowledge. To be able to analyse, criticise, confirm, or properly make use of a possible method, data showing its reliability, validity and robustness must be fully provided. In some cases anecdotal evidence is presented with a promise that the anecdote is typical of a larger body of data. This is not a useful way to present data, since it is no substitute for the data itself.

In the next section, we review some of the many examples of style indices that have been proposed.

Examples of Proposed Discriminating Indices

In considering the indexes that have been proposed it is useful to consider language as made up of small units, phonemes and words, that are built up into ever larger conglomerations by means of clauses, sentences and then into even larger thematic units. As the units of language considered increase in size, so issues about the relationships between components of those units become more amenable to study. Therefore characteristics of frequencies and the existence of particular types of unit, which are the dominant mode of concern at the 'lower', smaller level of words, are complemented by syntactic and other structural matters once larger units of discourse, such as sentences and sequences of sentences, are considered. Therefore it is helpful to consider the possible characteristics that may distinguish between authors along a continuum from the smallest and simplest to the largest and most complex.

Word Types

At the most elementary level, one obvious approach is to consider the distribution of word-usage by different authors. It is plausible that people have different vocabularies, and even for words which people all use, it is reasonable to assume that the frequency with which they are used will vary from person to person.

Word-Length Distribution

The simplest count to make of words is to consider how long they are, how many letters they contain. It has been supposed that word-length distribution might differ from person to person, and to a sufficient extent to be of use in discriminating between people. Indeed, this was one of the earliest kinds of analyses tried (Medenthall 1887; 1901). One of Mendenhall's attempts was to discriminate between the writings of Shakespeare and Bacon, which he claims to have done successfully. However, trying the same technique with Shakespeare and Marlowe yielded no obvious differences, there being more within sample variation than between. Obviously, to be of any use, a first necessary step is to determine stability within a set of authors, and show that the within-person variance is lower than the between-person variance. There has been no systematic investigation of such possible stability's in the distribution of word-lengths, apart from ones related to the Cusum method, described separately later.

But even at this elementary level the problems of register, genre and modality loom large. It is very likely that word length will vary between the different contexts within which words are used. Historical tragedies for example, may have more long words than romantic comedies. So in comparing Shakespeare's play with those of other dramatists it could be important to compare like with like. The nature of Shakespeare's plays may have been so different from those of Bacon that this is what produced Mendenhall's results. As a consequence, comparisons with other authors may have been confounded with the type of material they wrote.

The "Cusum" Technique

Beyond the mere counting of the average length of words it is possible to make comparisons between the frequencies of words of different length, or comparisons between words defined in some other simple, objective way such as whether they begin with a vowel or not. The cumulative-sum (or Cusum) technique, developed by Morton and his colleagues (Morton and Michaelson 1990; Morton 1991; Morton and Farringdon 1992) is based upon such comparisons.

In order to turn the numerical comparisons of the ratios of particular sub-sets of words into a form that is open to interpretation as to authorship, Morton and his colleagues have drawn upon an arithmetical technique originally designed for process monitoring in a chemical engineering context known as cumulative summation, hence 'Cusum', (Woodward and Goldsmith 1964). The types of words to which the arithmetical technique is applied includes 2 and 3 letter words, 3 and 4 letter words, nouns, vowel-initial words, or combinations of these. Morton and his colleagues refer to these sub-sets of words as 'habits'. So although that is not the usual meaning of 'habit' in English we will stay with this usage for the consideration of the Cusum approach.

Within the Cusum technique, the frequency of the 'habit' words is compared, via the cumulative summation manipulations, with the cumulative summation of the total numbers of words per sentence, producing cumulative ratios between 'habit' and total number of words, per sentence, for any piece of text. The central claim of Morton and his colleagues is that variations in these cumulative ratios can be used to distinguish between different authors who have contributed to the same piece of text.

Central to their claim is that while two people might share the same habit, i.e. cumulative ratio of one set of words to another, each person will have a characteristic set of habits of their own. That is to say, Morton and his colleagues propose that variability of habit will be less within people than between people.

In forensic applications to text, a simple procedure is carried out in which the cumulative deviation of lengths of successive sentences (in words) from the sample mean are plotted. This is then compared with the cumulative deviation of the habit rate for each successive sentence (in words) from the mean for the sample. After some scaling procedures have been applied, the two curves may be compared directly. If the fit of the curves to one another is poor, then it is proposed that that is evidence that the sample comes from two or more different authors. If the fit is good, no such claim may be made. There is a real technical problem in defining goodness of fit and the importance of deviations (Hardcastle 1993).

Aked (1994) carried out a number of simple simulations in which it was shown that the main variable influencing goodness of fit is simply how close to unity is the linear correlation between sentence length and number of instances of the target words. Deviations from linearity decreased the goodness of fit, as did any weakening of the value of the linear correlation. Essentially then, the Cusum graphs are a way of representing and testing the linear correlation of sentence length and frequency of the chosen habit. Presumably, if the work of two individuals is mixed in a text, then there is a high likelihood that the values of the regression of the habit rate onto sentence length will differ, resulting in an effective weakening of the overall correlation. This should then lead to deviations between the two Cusum curves.

Although it flies in the face of the many studies, briefly reviewed earlier, that demonstrate large variations in language as a result of register, genre and context, the proponents of the Cusum technique claim that their technique reveals consistencies, regardless of the circumstances of the individual, the point during life at which the samples are collected, or whether the samples are of spoken material or of written material (for instance, see Farrington 1996).

The most typical approach to attempting a validation of the Cusum technique is to test Morton's claims as directly as possible by using his procedures to generate Cusum curves themselves. Canter and Johnson (1993) prepared a report for the Crown Prosecution Service in which they cite seven studies which failed to show any evidence for different author material producing a bigger deviation than single author material (Beatty and Dodd 1993; Canter 1992; Hardcastle 1993; Hilton and Holmes 1993; Jamieson and Aitkin 1993; van der Heijden 1992; Sanford Aked Moxey and Mullin 1992). A variety of methods of measuring and indexing the goodness of fit of the two curves were employed over these studies, but none provided any support for Cusum. The sample sizes used in these studies were large enough to allow statistical significance to be tested, and therefore from a forensic perspective, may be deemed to have generated 'reasonable doubt'. In the subsequent, very large sample study carried out by Aked et al (1994), there was also no trace of a difference in the fit of sentence length and 'habit' Cusums. So there does not appear to be even weak evidence supporting the claims made for Cusum. Further, the comprehensiveness of the claims of Morton and his colleagues, that his Cusum technique virtually never fails to give a valid answer, must lead to any failure of the method as being fatal.

Some attempts to test the assumptions underlying Cusum moved away from attempts to apply the Cusum method *per se*, and so have been criticised as not truly reflecting the methods proposed by Morton. However, it is clearly desirable to try to test the assumptions that do appear to underlie the technique. Sanford et al. (1994) showed that there is indeed a simple increasing linear relation between sentence length and five of the 'habits' identified by Morton as useful for Cusum analysis. They went on to show that the slopes of these functions, reflecting habit-rate, appeared to vary as much within subjects as between subjects. So, at a gross level, there is no evidence that these habit-rates would have any value for differentiating cases where one versus more than one person contributed to a piece of writing.

The proponents of Cusum also examined the claim that for a given individual, it does not matter whether a sample of text is written or is spoken, the habit of the individual will be the same in both instances. Earlier we reviewed some evidence showing that there is a higher ratio of content words (open class) to function words (closed class) in written language than there is in spoken language (Lexical density difference). This finding obviously casts strong *a priori* doubt on any claim that written and spoken material would reflect the same habits. The problem would seem to be particularly severe in Morton's case, since many closed class words are 2 and 3 letter words. This would suggest that the 2/3 letter word habit rate should be lower in written than in spoken language for the same individual. In contrast, a habit like the frequency of using nouns should be higher in written than in spoken language. In short, a difference would be predicted where Morton suggests none would be found. To test this, Sanford et al (1994) compared written and verbal descriptions of a short event-filled video film, taken from the same subjects. There were indeed reliable differences in 2 and 3 letter word and noun habits as predicted by the lexical density hypothesis.

These empirical findings are the results of attempts to validate the Cusum method, and are a catalogue of lack of support. Given the evidence that there is variation as a function of genre and modality in just the kind of habits proposed for Cusum, it should be considered unsurprising that there has been a fairly widespread failure to provide any support for the claims of the technique.

A further problem with the Cusum technique as described in the currently available writings of its advocates is that the procedures to be adopted are very ill-defined and subjective in places (see, for example Hardcastle 1993, for a discussion). This is not only a major weakness for any technique, but it also always leaves open the claim on the part of its advocates that those evaluating the idea are not doing so in the correct manner (see, for example, Morton and Farringdon 1992, p. 91). Obviously the weakness needs to be rectified. It needs to be demonstrated that there is indeed a reliable technique in use by Cusum proponents that is open to systematic replication.

However, a further complication has recently arisen in understanding exactly what are the claims of Morton and his colleagues. The earlier reports by the proponents of Cusum insisted that they could determine without error whether or not a piece of text was the work of one or more authors. Levels of probability in this determination were dismissed as inappropriate for the forensic context and it was claimed that the Cusum technique had been developed to provide a decision upon which total reliance could be placed. Yet Morton (1995) has recently claimed that the application of what he calls 'weighted Cusum' allows a statistical, probability judgement to be assigned to the conclusion of whether a text is single or multiple authored. In effect, he proposes a form of analysis of variance that would demonstrate whether the variation between the indexes in question for the given text were greater than the variations within those indexes. Even in making such a proposal, Morton has not indicated the more fundamental need to demonstrate that the indexes he is using are stable for the person or persons in question across an appropriate range of texts.

Although the claims of 'weighted' Cusum do raise serious questions about the status of all the claims for Cusum prior to this innovation, they do put the Cusum technique more clearly in the scientific mould, allowing other researchers to test Cusum claims without the ambiguity of interpreting the Cusum charts. Nonetheless, tests have demonstrated that there is no more validity to weighted Cusum than to any of its forebears (for example, Canter and Chester 1995).

Given the claims by its proponents that Cusum is an objective scientifically based technique, and therefore ought to be amenable to the usual conventions of scientific study, it is quite remarkable that no successful controlled, blind trials, of any of its variants have been published by its advocates and that all those very different trials that have been published, by independent scholars in different countries, have all found totally against the technique.

In their recent attempts to challenge the findings of other researchers (Farrington 1996) the advocates of Cusum have sought to claim that other researchers have not followed their guidelines closely. They have proposed a whole series of modifications to the text prior to analysis such as removing lists or answers to questions that appear to mirror the phrasing of the questioner. However, they still only offer examples to illustrate the success of their analyses rather than fully controlled trials. The subjectivity of their approach, which initially seemed so mathematically precise, is therefore even more apparent in this recent writing. A lack of objectivity that, it must be admitted, is also revealed in their *ad hominem* attacks on their critics.

Cusum has been by far the most thoroughly studied of the 'stylistic' techniques proposed for forensic applications. The arithmetical calculations at the heart of the technique as it was originally presented do allow other researchers to check its claims. In carrying out those checks a lot has been clarified about the nature of the tests that are essential before any forensic application of a method of linguistic analysis. Morton and his colleagues could therefore justly claim to have stimulated an important debate in this area, even if their particular technique reveals within a person no discrimination between people no stability.

Distributions of Words

Beyond the number of letters in a word or the comparison of the rates of use of words with different numbers of letters, there is, of course the possibility that the frequency patterns of actual word usage varies from person to person. Ellegard (1962) carried out a study in which he attempted to determine which of a set of potential writers might have produced the Junius Letters, a set of political pamphlets written during the late 18th century. Starting with the Junius Letters, he determined which words occurred often in the Junius letters, and which did not. More recently, Mosteller and Wallace (1964) employed an analysis of the statistical distribution of word types in order to try to establish which of three possible authors had written a collection of essays known as "The Federalist Papers". Using a comparison of function word frequency from samples of work by the three putative authors and the disputed Federalist papers, Mosteller and Wallace showed that one of the writers gave a much better fit to the Federalist Papers than the others.

However, with both the Junius letters and the Federalist papers there is no objective information as to who the authors were. The analysis is being used to *propose* who the authors were, not to provide definitive proof. Furthermore, quite typically, the technique is being applied without first establishing that it is reliably sensitive to differences between authors. What is needed is a demonstration that a particular author displays constancy, (or at least low variability) with respect to the index in question and that the between author variation is indeed greater than the variation within authors. This needs to be done with known examples in which authorship is not in contention rather than making the assumption that it is valid then drawing conclusions based on that untested assumption.

Vocabulary

Even if the actual frequency of different words cannot be shown to vary reliably from one person to another, it is reasonable to suppose that people vary in the words they typically use. This may be a variation in the actual number of words they draw upon, the 'size' of their vocabulary, or in the particular mix of words they use. Even with vocabularies of the same size and mix people may have a 'dense' or less dense style - what may be regarded as the 'diversity' of their writing and speaking.

All these different aspects of vocabulary have been considered but they encounter difficulties in precise comparisons because the actual words a person uses are so clearly related to the topic about which s/he is speaking or writing. An expert on trainspotting would draw on an extended vocabulary about trains, but the same person discussing football may be very limited. One approach to the diversity of vocabulary that is potentially content free is the type-token ratio, where the first occurrence of a word specifies type, subsequent uses are additional tokens of that type. Clearly, the greater the variety of words used in a sample of discourse, the greater will be the type-token ratio, but only providing the samples used for comparison have the same number of words. The more words there are in a tract of discourse, the lower the type-token ratio will tend to be. In the extreme case, when vocabulary has been exhausted, there will be no opportunity to add a new word (type) even though there is no limit to the number of tokens produced (see, for example, Miller 1956). In general, the production of new words follows a roughly negative-exponential pattern, with the asymptote being the vocabulary size.

Despite the analytic arguments over sensitivity to sample size, it appears that this may not matter much even over quite large tracts of discourse. Apparently, most people quite quickly reach the limits of their vocabulary and thus further production of language adds relatively little in the way of new vocabulary. It also seems very likely that type-token ratios are typical of a language register rather than of a person. Therefore, the more language is produced by any two people, the closer their average type-token ratio is likely to be. However, at present there is little understanding of how genre, mode or even mood may influence these ratios in shorter lengths of text.

Thus, despite its attractions, there has still been no definitive empirical study to demonstrate that type-token ratios are both stable and discriminatory. It seems likely that for shorter samples of text the within individual variation will be too great and for larger samples the between individual variation will be too small. There may be appropriate sample sizes at which type token ratios will discriminate, but these may vary between, genre, and mode etc. and thus be very vulnerable to context.

Multivariate Indices

Type-token ratios are very simple descriptions of the structure of language that ignore the details of vocabulary. A more sophisticated possibility is to take a number of constituents of vocabulary and to examine the patterns of ways in which they vary in relation to each other for any particular person. Recently, Aked (1994) carried out a study to determine whether any or all of a set of 23 surface style and vocabulary indices were stable and discriminating within the domain of expository text - in this case, using a student essay database. These variables, outlined in table 7.1, were readily available indices obtainable by applying a standard UNIX style-checker STYLE™. They were selected from a larger set of variables in that they showed the greatest variance over the essays, thus allowing them to be potentially discriminating. The possible advantage of using such simple indices is obvious, in that they are easily obtained using relatively standard software, and therefore have been made available because the software writers at least believe these indices measure interesting or possibly important aspects of language.

Table 7.1. 23 Surface Style and Vocabulary Indices

Stylecheck	Definition
Sentence Information	
non function words	
long sentences	sentence more than 36 words
short sentences	sentence less than 21 words
Sentence Types	
simple sentences	sentence containing one verb and no dependent clause
complex sentences	sentence containing more than one verb and one or more dependent clause
compound sentences	sentence containing more than one verb and no dependent clause
compound complex sentences	sentence containing either several dependent clauses or one dependent clause plus a compound verb in either dependent or independent clause.
Word usage **Verb types as % of total verbs**	
verb "to be"	
auxillary verbs	
infinitives	
passives as % of non infinitive verbs	
Word types as % of total words	
prepositions	
conjunctions	
adverbs	
nouns	
adjectives	
pronouns	
Sentence Beginnings **Subject Openers (%)**	
prepositions	
adverbs	
verbs	
sub-conjunctions	
conjunctions	
Total	

A multivariate approach was taken in which Cluster and Factor analyses were carried out on the data. If the style variables had shown a constant (low variance) usage within a subject, then a cluster analysis should have come close to producing 25 clusters of essays, where a cluster was represented by the essays of each of the individuals. However, no evidence was found for subject constancy, as the essays were grouped not on subjects' individual scores on the variables.

Factor analysis of the same material reduced the 23 variables to 5 factors which showed no sign of identifying consistencies within individuals. Essentially, this analysis, the cluster analysis, and other analyses showed that even with 23 variables it was impossible to identify vectors of values which could be said to identify consistencies within an individual. This study shows that the obvious low-level discourse indices do not seem to be sufficiently stable and discriminating to be of any value in a forensic context, even within the restricted genre of essay-types.

Collocational and Positional Methods

Beyond mere frequencies of words, and the comparison of relative frequencies, it has been proposed that the sequence and position of words relative to one another may be of value in discriminating between authors. The majority of the research on these collocational and positional methods was carried out in the early 1970s. The authors who took this approach (e.g. Michaelson and Morton 1972; Michaelson and Morton 1973), began examining the advantages of using word positions and groups of words instead of word types as a method of authorship discrimination. They also examined the "mobility" of a word, which they defined as the whole set of positions that a word can take. Michaelson and Morton (1973) proposed that sentence length distributions were isotrophic - it does not matter whether they are counted from the first word or the last word in the sentence, since if a word is completely mobile, it will occupy each of the positions in a sentence with equal likelihood and have a mean position of the mid-point of the sentence. The mid-point is thus isotrophic. Conversely, if a word seems to occur in a preferred position for a particular author, it is termed anisotrophic. Using this assumption Morton et. al. examined Greek texts for authorship. They claimed some success in the method, which led to a further examination of collocational information within a text (Morton

Michaelson and Hamilton-Smith 1977). Morton et. al. asserted that the previously used positional methods were not as useful in English texts as in Greek texts due to the difference in phrase structure of the two languages, and thus they advocated the use of collocational analysis so that words could also be examined in their original context. The assumption was that if collocations such as the occurrence of AND with THE varied more between authors than within, then this might provide a basis for discrimination. Again, however, results were mixed. Morton returned to this method again in 1986 to examine the notion that the position of words that occur only once in a sample of text could supply information on authorship (Morton 1986). He carried out comparisons of words occurring once in the first position of the sentence with those occurring in either the first or last position of the text. Again the samples were taken from Greek texts.

Criticisms of these techniques have been many and varied (e.g. Johnson 1973; Smith 1987). Johnson (1973) takes a critical look at the method used in Michaelson and Morton (1972), where they consider words in the last position of the sentence for a sample of Greek texts. His criticisms lie mainly in the authors' application of the Chi-squared test, their lack of specification of a hypothesis, misuse of a correction factor, over-consideration of quotations and small sample sizes. Johnson found that if the figures are recalculated without these fundamental misconceptions, the conclusion of the methods should be, "that II Corinthians was homogeneous (against Michaelson and Morton) and that Romans was not homogeneous" (Johnson 1973, p.99). Johnson also suggests that there may be four things to learn from these findings:

(1) that the sentence may not be a good unit of measurement,
(2) that context may be affecting the words which appear at the end of Paul's sentences,
(3) that it is invalid to treat passages of writing as from an infinite population and
(4) that word categories have not been sufficiently well defined.

Smith, (1987), in an investigation of Morton's claims about words occurring once, additionally points out that Morton only examines works by one author. In such a case, there should be no reason to believe that for any sized sample, the numbers of once-occurring words should be able to distinguish *between* samples.

Comparison of Discourse Themes

For completeness, it is worth pointing out that a typical literary approach to considering differences between authors is to examine *what* they write about and to explore the *way* they write about it. This usually involves considerations of a more macroscopic kind than the atomistic considerations that have been reviewed so far. The problem with these approaches is to establish reliable and objective categories to begin with. For example, the use of cognitive verbs, such as 'thinking' and 'considering', or the expression of feelings, or at an even larger scale of discourse analysis, the careful laying out of an argument. Analysing statements made by rape victims to the police Canter and Heritage (1989) did show that themes in such material could be systematically demonstrated by the use of careful content analysis, and the application of multivariate statistics. It seems possible that such an approach could be fruitful in exploring authorship.

Do the Studies Reviewed Meet the Required Criteria?

Most of the approaches discussed have not been tested sufficiently on undisputed material and thus have not been shown to be a stable within authors and different between authors. Almost all of the tests reported above have treated indices as though they would be discriminating without there being any clearly presented evidence that they are even stable. In some cases there are vague statements to the effect that indices are reliable without satisfactory evidence being provided to support the claim. The studies described above are not exhaustive and neither are they meant to be. There will always be new candidates for tools of authorship diagnosis, just as there are cases that we have left out. What is universally the case is the need to demonstrate in a publicly, scientifically accessible way. Data that shows how much faith one may have in a method (in the general case) or in a method applied in a specific instance (in a particular case). We believe that at present no such demonstration exits for the general case, and that until proper standards of transparent procedure and data analysis and presentation are employed, this aspect of forensic linguistics will remain subjective and unsatisfactory from a scientific perspective.

Situation-Specific Judgements: A Test for the Notion of Expert

The approaches discussed above rely on choosing a particular index that hopefully generalises over the required range of genres and modality. The indices are transparent: anyone can make counts of the kinds of things discussed above, provided an exact specification is given. The fundamental thing about these approaches is that if a suitable index or set of indices were found, then they should have very broad applicability. To date, efforts of this sort have not been very successful.

A somewhat different approach is to take each situation independently and operate with indices that are much more restricted. The development of corpora of language produced in specific situations will greatly facilitate this approach (Coulthard 1994). Although for such a set of corpora to be of forensic use it is essential to have very clear definitions of the differences between situations. Such definitions rely in part on detailed knowledge of how language differs from one set of circumstances to another. This chicken and egg problem can only be resolved by iterative research over an extended period. The temptation to find shortcuts because of the demands of suspects and victims need to be guarded against.

Once developed, such an approach, based on the analysis of a carefully defined corpus, may exploit any feature of a discourse that deviates from expectation. An interesting example studied by Coulthard, is the use of postposed temporal 'then' in confessions. In normal spoken discourse, for example, 'temporal' then appears in the preposed position most often, as in "Then I went to the cinema." His analysis suggested that in reported speech it may be more usual to say "He said 'I went to the Cinema, then'". As a consequence, it may be possible to use the positions of 'then' to indicate whether this is genuinely recorded speech or recreated speech. However, as interesting as this approach is, it still suffers from all the unknowns discussed above. How variable is the position in which 'then' is used? Under what circumstances does it vary? Are these variations greater within a person's discourse than between the discourse of different people? Examination of corpora may provide some indication of the normal usage and therefore enable us to refine the considerations of vocabulary and frequency considered above, but without psychological examinations of how an individuals language varies or remains stable no results of forensic relevance can be proposed. Corpora, by their nature, currently emphasise few examples from many individuals and sources. This approach needs to be complemented by intensive studies of a lot of material from each of a few individuals.

Practical Problems

For the sake of clarity, it has been assumed in the above review that there are no questions about the provenance of the language in contention, even if that provenance is unknown. A questioned play, for example, is not assumed to be a letter to a friend that has been mistaken for a piece of dramatic writing. But, in fact, the considerations that are dominant in the forensic context do not allow of such simplifying assumptions.

The most obvious example of such an added complexity is the case in which a confession is challenged. The defendant may claim that he never admitted the crime, or that the details of what he is reported to have said are incorrectly recorded. Here the courts are faced with a multi-level challenge to authorship. Should they assume that the written confession presented to them is, for instance:

a) An instantaneous record, completely *verbatim,*
b) A transcript of that instantaneous record
c) A contemporaneous record that records the significant utterances exactly,
d) A written account of what was said, using the vocabulary and syntax of the written rather than the spoken mode,
e) A recreation of the intentions of the accused expressed through non-verbal means,
f) An elaboration of what was said with important additions that were not said, or
g) A complete fabrication?

Even with the advent of tape-recorded interviews these questions will not disappear, but there are enough pre tape-recording confessions that have been challenged to keep the issues alive. In relation to the matter of authorship attribution, these possibilities raise questions about what aspects of a person's style of speaking are likely to survive the various translations that are possible. Even apparently verbatim transcripts of instantaneous speech do not record the paralinguistic nuances of the speaker and usually turns the free flow of the spoken word into grammatical sentences. The question of authorship in these real life settings therefore require a consideration of what aspects of the way a person expresses himself can or do survive the retelling process. If a person's pauses are turned into commas and full stops, syntactic errors of verbs are corrected and ellipses and abbreviations are recorded in ways that relate to the recorder rather than the speaker, then any procedure that relies say on the proportion of short to long words in a sentence may be totally distorted by the recording procedure.

Most applications of linguistic measures in court currently ignore these technicalities and assume that the transcript that is being challenged can be reasonably regarded as a completely accurate verbatim transcript. Even elementary consideration of the difficulties of recording speech on the page show that such assumptions are overly optimistic in many cases and quite misleading in many others.

Written Anonymous Crimes, Threat and Extortion

There is one further important forensic application of authorship attribution that raises some interesting theoretical challenges. This is in that area in which a crime has been committed through the act of writing. The most obvious examples of this are anonymous threat letters, extortion and product-tampering demands and those cases of fraud in which written material is central, (e.g. Miron and Pascale 1978). In practical terms these cases have the advantage that the author's actual writing is available and so the problems of recording, mentioned for interviews, is not present. However, it is typically the case that the author is at pains to hide his/her true identity (Miron and Pasquale 1978).

This poses a further challenge to studies of individual styles - what aspects of a person's unique style, if such exists, may be expected to survive conscious attempts to hide the identity of the author? Of course, there are parallels to literary studies of anonymous pamphlets and the like, but in the criminal context the attempt may be to present an identity that will carry most authority in perpetrating the crime. For example, following a style that implies the author knows about a company and is thus a genuine threat, or is part of an organised team and can therefore carry out the threatened action. Simple analyses of vocabulary may not be appropriate in such cases.

Recommendations

There are then, a number of different research objectives required in a study of authorship.

As discussed earlier, the most fundamental requirement is that of reliability. Any measure identified for an author should produce very similar results when applied independently on a number of occasions, to the same material. Measures must also have been shown to discriminate between authors effectively and hence show some validity. They must have been tested on samples from more than one author and have shown that the variance between authors is greater than the variance within them.

Research objectives should also take into account the centrality of the measures. This brings to light the complex issue of style and genre. Style measures chosen must be able to discriminate between different authors, and across genres. Many of the authorship studies to date have been carried out on text samples of the same genre and thus can be regarded as context dependent.

Style measures chosen should also be overtly testable so that they are amenable to simple definition and easy replication and they must occur frequently in any given text.

In addition to these basic requirements, Wachal (1966), along with others has suggested four other objectives for authorship studies. Style measures should be:

Unconscious

It is preferable that the indices chosen are ones, which are produced by the author unconsciously and therefore are not subject to deliberate attempts at imitation of a particular writing style. This is a point raised by Morton (1991) in his analysis of the Cusum technique.

Usable on Small Samples

It is important that the indices chosen can be applied equally well to small samples of text as to large samples. Large samples of text are not always available for analysis.

Based on Already Established Indicators

Researchers who are attempting to establish indices that have the above objectives, should take into account those indicators explored by other researchers. The incorporation of previous research will not only lend credibility to the analysis, but will allow validation of indices suspected to be discriminatory of an authors style.

Robustness

To these objectives we would add that the indices are not easily open to unwitting misuse. The legal impact of any such indices is so powerful that once established they are likely to be widely used by many different individuals. If they are especially complex or technically demanding then there is more likelihood that they will be misinterpreted with consequent miscarriages of justice.

The Need for Theories

Perhaps the major weakness with all the studies described so far is that they have proceeded from a general act of faith that idiolects exist and that the various aspects of language that can be measured ought to reveal the differences between them. They have been driven by what it has been possible to measure, not by any *a priori* conceptualisations of what the basis for individual variation in language is likely to be. For example, should variations be related to an individual's cognitive processing or to their intellectual ability? Perhaps people who are more able are more capable of thinking about the world in different ways and so more likely to draw upon different vocabularies? Or perhaps the differences are more directly related to their storage capacity? People who can remember more will know more words? Or perhaps it is to do with sophistication in education, so that it would be the rarity of words that would distinguish?

Unfortunately, virtually all of the studies to date do not set out the psychological assumptions for the measures being proposed. Without such theorising it is difficult to learn anything from the many failures that have been reported. Furthermore, until clear theories of the psychological basis for individual differences in language have been articulated it is not clear in what direction the search should be continued to find such differences.

Conclusions

The importance of forensic linguistics should not be underestimated. Although it has its origins in the rarefied cloisters of academia, once it is applied to civil and criminal litigation it can have major, life and death consequences. This is probably the reason that despite at least a hundred years of failure to demonstrate scientifically individual variation in authorship there are still many linguists who believe it is possible.

However, we have shown that if the criteria of conventional science are applied to this area, not only have those criteria typically been ignored, but those few cases in which they have been used have failed to support the central hypothesis that authors can be distinguished on the basis of their language. An alternative hypothesis therefore raises its unwelcome head, unwelcome because it challenges the basis of forensic linguistics. This is the hypothesis that dialect, sociolect and language community, register, mode and genre, context and intention, are all so strong alone and in combination, in determining the speech and writing of any given individual that it is extremely unlikely that a reliable and valid measure of author identity will ever be established. As with all good scientific hypotheses it stands there to be disproved.

References

Bhatia, V.K. (1993). *Analysing Genre: Language Use in Professional Settings.* London: Longman.

Bloch, B. (1948). A set of postulates for phonemic analysis. *Language,* 24 (1), 3-46.

Canter, D. (1992). An evaluation of the "Cusum" Stylistic Analysis of Confessions. *Expert Evidence,* 1, 93-99.

Canter, D. and Heritage, R. (1989). A multivariate model of sexual offence behaviour: developments in offender profiling. *Journal of Forensic Psychiatry,* 1 (2) 185-212.

Coulthard, M. (1994).The use of corpora in the analysis of forensic texts. *Forensic Linguistics,* 1(1), 27-43.

Ellegard (1962). *Who was Junius?* Stockholm: Almquist & Wiksell.

Farrington, J. (1996). *Analysing for Authorship: A guide to the Cusum Technique.* Cardiff: University of Wales Press.

Fowler, A. (1982). *Kinds of literature.* Oxford: Oxford University Press.

Halliday, M.A.K. (1990). *Spoken and Written Language.* Oxford University Press.

Hardcastle, R. A. (1993). Forensic Linguistics: an assessment of the CUSUM method for the determination of authorship. *Journal of the Forensic Science Society*, 33, 95-106.

Hilton, M. L. and Holmes, D. I. (1993). An Assessment of the Cumulative Sum Charts for Authorship Attribution. *Literary and Linguistic Computing*, 8 (2).

Johnson, P. F. (1973). The Use of Statistics in the Analysis of the Characteristics of Pauline writing. *New Testament Studies*, 20, 92-100.

McMenamin, G. R. (1993). *Forensic Stylistics.* London, Amsterdam: Elsevier.

Mendenthall, T.C. (1887). The Characteristic Curves of Composition, *Science*, 9, 237-249. 1891, 1901).

Michaelson, S. and Morton, A.Q. (1972). Last Words. A Test of Authorship for Greek Writers. *New Testament Studies*, 18, 192-208.

Michaelson, S. and Morton, A.Q. (1973). Positional Stylometry. *The Computer and Literary Studies*, 3, 69-83.

Miller, G.A. (1956). *Language and communication.* Harvard University Press.

Miron, M.S. and Pasquale, T.A. (1978). Psycholinguistic analysis of coercive communications. *Journal Of Psycholinguistic Research*, 7(2), 95-120.

Morton, A.Q. (1986). Once. A Test of authorship Based on Words which are not repeated in the Sample. *Literary and Linguistic Computing*, 1 (1), 1-8.

Morton, A.Q. (1991). Proper Words in Proper Places. University of Glasgow, Computing Science Department, Departmental Research Report 1991/R18.

Morton, A.Q. (1995). Response to Journal of Forensic Linguistics. *Forensic Linguistics*, 2 (2), 230-233.

Morton, A.Q. and Farringdon, M.G. (1992). Identifying Utterance. *Expert Evidence*, 1, 84-92.

Morton, A. and Michaelson, S. (1990). *The Q-sum plot.* University of Edinburgh, Computing Science Department, Internal report no. CSR-3-90.

Mosteller, F. and Wallace, D. L. (1964*). Inference and Disputed Authorship: The Federalist.* Addison-Wesely Publishing Company.

Sanford, A.J., Aked, J.P., Moxey, L.M. and Mullen, J. (1994). A critical examination of the assumptions underlying the Cusum technique of forensic linguistics, Forensic Linguistics,1(2), 151-167.

Smith, M.W.A. (1987). Hapax Legomena in Prescribed Positions: An Investigation into recent Proposals to Resolve Problems of Authorship. Literary and Linguistic Computing, 2(3), 145-153.

Swales, J.M. (1990). Genre Analysis. English in academic and research settings. Cambridge: Cambridge University Press.

van der Heijden, A.W.M., Minnebo, P. and Weimar, L. (1992). Report on Morton's Cumulative Summation Analysis. National Criminal Intelligence Service Bureau, Interpol.

Wachal, R.S. (1966). Linguistic evidence, statistical inference and disputed authorship. Unpublished PhD thesis, University of Wisconsin.

Woodward, R. H. and Goldsmith, P.L. (1964). Cumulative Sum Techniques. *Mathematical and Statistical Techniques for Industry*. Monograph No. 3. Edinburgh: Oliver and Boyd.

Unpublished References

Aked, J.P. (1994). Individual differences in written language expression, unpublished PhD thesis, University of Glasgow.

Aked, J.P. Moxey, L.M. Sanford, A.J. and Mullin, J. (1994). The cumulative sum technique: a test based on a large sample of single and dual authorship materials. Unpublished report, University of Glasgow.

Beatty, F. and Dodd, N.J. (1993). A statistical evaluation of A.Q. Morton's Cusum analysis and Canter's alternative measure. Unpublished MSc report, Department of Psychology, University of Surrey.

Canter, D. and Chester, J. (1995). Investigation into the claim of weighted Cusum in authorship attribution studies. Unpublished report, University of Surrey.

Canter, D. and Johnson, P. (1993). Cusum Technique - An evaluation of the use of Cusum analysis within the legal process. Report for Crown Prosecution service, Department of Psychology, University of Surrey.

Jamison and Aitken (1993). A Survey of Approaches in Authorship Studies. Report from University of Edinburgh, Dept. of Computing Science.

Morton, A.Q. Michaelson, S. and Hamilton-Smith, N. (1977). To Couple is the Custom. Unpublished report, University of Edinburgh.

Sanford, A. J. Aked, J.P. Moxey, L.M. and Mullen, J. (1992). Discriminating one author from another through simple habits of expression: an empirical analysis. Unpublished paper, University of Glasgow.

8 Psychologists as Expert Witnesses

KATHLEEN COX

This chapter focuses on the role of psychologists in legal cases as expert witnesses. The case for using expert witnesses in court is explored, giving definitions of who the expert witness is and what they do. The development of the role of the psychologist as an expert witness is discussed highlighting the forms this can take, from submitting reports for the court, examining reports made by other psychologists or interpreting existing research in a form useful in the court. Examples of cases are given in which psychologists have been used, particularly in cases where the intelligence or ability of the accused was in question. Further examples of cases in which children are involved and need to be interviewed, and how psychologists have adapted this process for their benefit are also shown. The chapter closes by giving an insight into how courts and solicitors can operate and particularly how this can discourage psychologists acting as expert witnesses, such as being personally discredited to detract credibility from their professional judgements.

Kathleen Cox is a Chartered Psychologist with over thirty year's experience. She trained as a clinical psychologist in the NHS, worked for the British Army in Germany, worked on an employee assistance programme in the civil service and was senior educational psychologist for the secondary sector in a large metropolitan borough. She is now in private practice and a partner in Cox Associates a group of chartered psychologists who write psychological reports for legal purposes.

Offender Profiling Series: II - Profiling in Policy and Practice
Edited by D. Canter and L. Alison. © 1999 Ashgate Publishing, Aldershot. pp. 189-206

8 Psychologists as Expert Witnesses

KATHLEEN COX

Experts in the Legal System

Expert witnesses have been used in legal systems for hundreds of years; their expertise is derived from their experience as practitioners and, as in the following case, they can have considerable influence.

A young father suspected of the non-accidental injury of his daughter said he had fallen down stairs whilst carrying her. As he waited twenty-four hours before saying this he was regarded with suspicion. I saw him many months after the event in an attempt to assess what risk he posed to the child. The interview took place in his bedroom, the only place in the house free from the distraction of others, and focused on anger management and control. However as I lifted my briefcase over the child safety gate to go down the stairs at the conclusion of the interview I too slipped down the stairs. This unsophisticated assessment of the *situation* rather than the *man*, gave powerful support to his story, largely through my status as an independent expert.

In England and Wales there is no precise definition of an expert, but the principles of Rule 702 in the Federal Rules of Evidence of the United States of America (Nijboer 1995) as a person being 'qualified by knowledge, skill, experience, training or education' being allowed to testify as an expert upon 'scientific, technical or other specialised knowledge' would apply.

The first duty of the expert witness is to assist the courts in their decision making and bring expertise that is not generally in the public domain. Although in an adversarial system experts are usually instructed by one party to a dispute, they are required to be independent and objective.

An expert is established for each occasion, based on whether their expertise is relevant to the issue before the court. This can result in people who are eminent in their profession not being admitted by a court because their specific expertise was not judged likely to be of assistance with the particular problem before the court, on that occasion. A working definition of an expert is 'the person that knows the most in the room' and is just that, not the most in the world. It is pragmatic and useful in providing a context and defining the boundaries.

Traditionally, experience has been seen as the greatest asset of an expert witness, but, in a changing society that recognises professionalism and expertise, up-to-date scientific knowledge is valued increasingly. One role is to supply new facts from their discipline - "Did you know that...?"- Although the benefit of an expert can come not from providing essential factual evidence but in explaining an independent, objective opinion on facts provided by others (Gardner 1993).

Experts are the only witnesses permitted, within the limits of their expertise, to give an opinion whilst others, known as witnesses to the facts, must confine themselves to the facts. Although by demonstrating facts there is often no need to give opinions (Carson 1990 p.19). There can be a problem when the opinion borders on being a judgement, particularly when the question asked of the expert was "In your opinion was this child telling the truth in this interview?", but the distinction was neatly summarised by Lord Butler Sloss when she said that she had to remind herself it is not whether the expert believed the child but whether she believed the child (Butler Sloss 1996).

The Ikarian Reefer case heard in 1993 provided an opportunity for a restatement of the duties by Mr. Justice Cresswell, based on seven principles which the courts expect experts to fulfil. These can be summarised as independent, unbiased, including all the facts (including those which detracted from the concluded opinion), stating when the topic fell outside the claimed area of expertise, stating when the opinion reached was provisional because of being based on less than the whole truth, communicating a change of mind without delay and providing relevant plans etc. to the other side when the reports were exchanged. (For psychologists this frequently includes test proforma, which can be understood only by a psychologist on the other side).

Lord Woolf (1996) expressed concern that "...the need to engage experts was a source of excessive expense, delay and, in some cases, increased complexity through the excessive or inappropriate use of experts". However, the early appointment of an expert can save a great deal of time and money in criminal cases by exchanging reports and finding points of agreement and disagreement between experts at the pre-trial stage.

Recent years have seen the professionalisation of experts with the Academy of Expert Witnesses, the Institute of Expert Witnesses, the UK Register of Expert Witnesses and others. Experts are now treading the path of counsellors, mediators, developing codes of conduct, accreditation, etc. However, when practitioners become proficient as experts, doing little else, there is the danger of becoming 'litigation hacks', experienced in giving evidence but out of touch, being a professional witness first and an expert second, losing the expertise that they had to offer in the first place because they are no longer practising. Lawyers are increasingly aware of this and being an expert is not the lucrative retirement profession it used to be.

Psychologists as Experts

Psychologists first appeared as experts at the end of the nineteenth century in Germany where Munsterberg, an experimental psychologist, collected scientific data from which answers to problems before the courts could be obtained. He demonstrated that most 'witnesses to the fact' were in fact far from factual. His *Psychology and Crime* was published in the UK in 1908, but there is no record of psychologists as independent expert witnesses until after World War II. (Haward 1979). Until well into the 1960s psychological reports were incorporated into psychiatric reports (Castell 1966), a practice almost obsolete, due in part to arguments that such testimony was in fact hearsay and as such inadmissible (Haward 1965). Psychologists are now being used more often as independent experts and asked directly to write reports for the courts much more frequently than even ten years ago. 80% of psychological reports written for the courts are by clinical psychologists (Gudjonsson 1996).

The request to prepare a psychological report for the courts is still largely random, the result of a filtering process where the whole population of suspects is reduced to a few (Kat and Alexander 1996) starting with the custody sergeant and possibly progressing to a police surgeon and thence to a psychiatrist if mental health or handicap is suspected, before being commissioned by a solicitor. Psychologists' contribution to the justice system is frequently to identify the vulnerable members of society who commit a disproportionate number of offences, often with limited recognition of the enormity of their actions.

Psychological expertise begins at the point of enquiry. Not long ago a solicitor who thought we might help with a report for the court would say vaguely "see and assess" in the manner of a '60s' psychiatrist. Now, many are more sophisticated and make specific requests, even citing the tests they would like to have administered, although with varying degrees of accuracy and appropriateness.

More often, however, the first stage of the psychological contribution is a dialogue between psychologist and lawyer in recognition that good results come from good questions. The outcome of this dialogue can be a question that a psychologist can answer, in a form that is of value to a lawyer. The questions which lawyers want answering are often "Did the person do the deed?" (mens acta), which translates to the psychological question 'could they have done it?' and 'what did they intend?' (mens rea), to 'can they understand?'. Then questions are formulated and the psychological expertise can end at that point.

In child care cases which can involve criminal and civil proceedings if physical or sexual abuse is involved and where there can be many parties to a dispute, father, mother, child, local authority, guardian ad litem and others, the solicitors for all parties involved frequently agree the questions before jointly instructing an expert; a process which can be lengthy but helpful in itself. Also at this early stage the psychologist as scientist can give research data easily comprehensible by, but not easily accessible to, the intelligent lay person, such as a lawyer. Having established that the issue was one of parenting competencies I recently gave a reference from the psychological literature on homosexual child-rearing to a solicitor acting for a lesbian woman who wished to bring up her orphaned nephews (Campion 1995), which was the limit of the psychological contribution .

Only about 20% of psychological reports written for the courts actually lead to giving testimony in the criminal courts (Gudjonsson 1996). Sometimes the reports are not used because they are not helpful to the client or the angle the advocate wishes to take. One solicitor wished to put forward that his client was of limited intellectual ability and did not understand what was happening, as a defence. The psychological report with its standard intellectual assessment considered that he was well able to understand and so was not used.

We aim to have reports that are strong enough to be self explanatory. Reports are accepted when the other side is convinced that an expert from the same discipline, hired by them, asking the same questions, would produce a similar result.

From time to time in common with others (Gudjonsson 1996), we have been asked for reports to be changed. Clearly, if this contains inaccuracies this is done, as when there is a reference to a document a solicitor does not intend to disclose to the court. Sometimes other omissions may be sought and these too may be agreed if minor and do not affect the argument or opinion. We have never been asked to change an opinion and would regard this as an insult to our integrity. However, this is not to deny that there are experts who see themselves as advocates and solicitors know which experts will say what they wish to hear.

Another role of the psychologist expert is to look at reports written by other psychologists, particularly one acting for the other side. This can be to assess its status as a report by considering whether the tests used were appropriate for the purpose or if the conclusions follow the findings. This essentially answers the question is it a good report? They may comment on whether or not an expert has stuck to their area of expertise and not gone beyond it, e.g. the tendency of some psychiatrists to comment on psychological tests.

Additionally a psychologist may interpret an existing report, offer alternative explanations of the same information or suggest other ways of approaching the problem. This includes pointing out the strengths a report commissioned by the other side contains for the instructing lawyers. The Crown Prosecution Service in a murder case was worried that the defence would get an acquittal by virtue of having instructed a psychologist and asked for help. Interpreting and highlighting the results of the personality test given in the report of the psychologist called by the defence, where he described the accused as 'cold, emotionally unstable, impulsive and paranoid individual with high levels of anxiety', I helped the CPS to realise this was actually more helpful to them than the defence.

Psychologists study what people actually do and this can throw up surprises as they do not always do what is expected (Coleman 1988). Reference to research rather than hypothesis and precisely formulated questions in clearly defined groups can be helpful in investigative work. Whereas the best predictor of future behaviour is past behaviour and much criminal behaviour escalates from smaller crimes, one systematic study on child molesters found that their pasts were poor predictors of that crime and that an opportunistic model afforded more explanations of the offending behaviour (Canter and Kirby 1995). It is careful research like this, which assists the judicial process.

Psychological research has constructed tests, sometimes called mental measurement. They provide more accurate descriptions of people and their behaviour than words and supply a context. A tall pygmy would be one who was taller than 95% of other pygmies but may appear short on the streets of Britain. Knowing the context in which tests are developed is an important part of their choice and interpretation. Psychological tests can be used to assess competence, ability and personality but need to be interpreted within a context.

Tests vary in complexity of what they are measuring and in ease of administration. Some paper and pencil tests of personality are extremely easy to administer involving circling 'Yes' 'No' questions. However, tests that are simple to administer are not necessarily simple to interpret. Many contain scales intended to assess a continuum from lying through faking good to self-deception (Child Abuse Potential Inventory) which have to be interpreted alongside other scales before giving an opinion.

Others are more complex and involve demonstrating and teaching complex tasks (Koh's Blocks) or observing in anticipation of orally administered questions to be posed later (SIRS Rogers 1986) where what is observed is compared with what is said. Watching a subject suddenly start to fidget when routinely asked if they find it hard to sit still is useful information.

Reading tests are traditionally reported in terms of reading age. However, to say that an adult is reading at the ten year level implies a lack of competence, which does not reflect their everyday functioning and requires psychological interpretation. The "Sun" newspaper is written at the nine year reading age and read on a daily basis by many people who function efficiently as adults going to work, rearing their children and being generally competent and law abiding.

Most psychological reports are based on interview and tests within a framework of psychological knowledge. Whilst specially developed tests are not foolproof they can support or refute impressions or information gained in an interview or elsewhere. Many of the tests referred to here are actually inventories or structured interviews rather than standardised psychometric tests.

Examples of Cases

A 56-year-old woman was accused of defrauding social security, the proof of which was her signature on a document. Although many adults hide their shame at not being able to read by pretending they can, an easy defence is the inability to read. This can however be assessed with considerable reliability. From reading tests and the interview it was clear that she could not read or understand what she had signed. Our report was accepted and the case was dropped.

Another case where a reading test was used, was when a 29 year old man had taken a letter to a building society asking for £400,000 to be taken to a certain address, saying that a bomb would be exploded if this did not happen. He went home where he was rapidly picked up by the police and seen some ten days later in a prison by a psychologist. He too was unable to read as assessed by standard reading tests and said that the note had been written by his girl friend who was clearly the dominant partner. He thought he was opening an account in the building society and had been somewhat surprised to finish up in jail, as he had never been in trouble with the police before. The prosecution accepted our report that this man, although apparently committing a serious offence, did not really constitute a threat to society.

Another solicitor asked for an intellectual assessment of his client after intuitively assessing the judge. The solicitor considered the judge was inclined to attribute certain characteristics and motivations to the defendant which revealed more about the judge than his client, a German national. Herr Schmidt had first come to England about fifteen years ago, taken unskilled work, left and returned. He was typical of a new generation of Europeans who cross international boundaries in search of work and live on the margins of society committing petty crimes including not having work permits. His solicitor, a former lecturer in German, thought the judge was seeing his client as an international criminal, masterminding major crimes and liable to give him a long prison sentence. A non-verbal test of intelligence together with a semi-structured interview to obtain a life history administered in part through the German speaking solicitor showed someone functioning intellectually at about the tenth percentile, i.e. ninety percent of the population was more intelligent than he was, and who was frequently at the centre of misunderstandings of language and customs. His solicitor was able to use the psychological report to paint a verbal picture of someone who did not conform to the German stereotype, was not efficient, ambitious, early rising or well organised, for whom part of the attraction to him of living in England was just that.

The Police And Criminal Evidence Act (PACE 1984) was introduced to strengthen safeguards and ensure that people in custody understood their rights and the questions posed to them. An intelligence test can identify those who would have difficulty and when interpreted not merely by IQ, the conventional way of expressing intelligence, but by explaining what percent of the population is less intelligent than the subject, is to place it in context. The bottom 3-5% have great difficulty in understanding formal situations and need help to do so.

For those deemed to be mentally ill or mentally handicapped the concept of an 'appropriate adult' being present was introduced. We have performed intelligence tests not only on suspects but also on appropriate adults, as families on the borderline of coping have members whose knowledge and skills do not really extend to being an appropriate adult. Details from intelligence tests such as the Wechsler Adult Intelligence Scale which includes a social comprehension scale when people are asked what they would do under certain circumstances e.g. if they see smoke and fire in a public place, can further define the functional capacities of the person tested.

People who are unskilled, unintelligent or emotionally vulnerable are not able to function according to the requirements of adult society. The law recognises that they are not average and rational and psychological tests can identify them. Tests can also identify other characteristics relevant to criminal investigations.

Regardless of intellectual ability people vary in their beliefs as to how and where the factors which affect their lives are located. Some are proactive, trying to make things happen whilst others are reactive waiting to respond to events. Luck and chance are seen by others to be the main determinants in their lives. This phenomenon was described as the 'locus of control' (Craig, Franklin, and Andrews 1984) and as a style of operating can contribute to the 'mens rea'. Those who operate using an external locus of control would be reactive rather than proactive, and not be expected to plan or try to make things happen. They feel powerless. This can be a symptom of illness or trauma or a habitual response.

One woman in her mid-twenties had been an ideal school girl, achieving academically, involved in youth bands internationally and being proactive in the life of the school until she was fourteen. Then she was subjected to rape, which was dealt with unsatisfactorily. One effect of a traumatic experience is to lose feelings of control. She drifted through her youth and when referred to us for offences of breaking and entering, was totally dominated by her psychopathic husband, even from jail by his telephone calls. On tests of intelligence she scored highly but very low on locus of control. She was typical of many women who have been bullied for many years who lose their free will at 'a look' from their spouse and commit criminal acts, although not acting as free agents when they do so (Kennedy 1992). Reference to the psychological literature on classical conditioning showing that when people are rewarded and punished randomly they lose their free will, combined with her clinical history and psychological test scores, demonstrated her reduced personal agency.

A woman in her mid forties, accused of arson had set her house on fire. She had had an unfortunate history and no longer wanted to live. Generally she felt she had little control in her life. Standardised tests of depression showed she was depressed and descriptions of behaviour typical of depression made it clear that her own self absorbed misery did not enable her to consider the danger she posed to others.

Another case of arson was the ineffectual attempt of a teenage boy to help his sister get a new council house. She had been burgled frequently, deserted by the father of her children, had epilepsy and the boy felt sorry for her. He fell into the 'Compassion Trap' and tried to help. His arson of her flat was intended to get her new accommodation. There was no gain for him but was an emotional response of a powerless individual. It was a single strategy solution by a not very intelligent boy to a complex problem.

Suggestibility is a concept, which has been developed in recent years following concerns about suspects' abilities to make reliable statements to the police during interrogation (Gudjonsson 1992). Suggestibility has been defined as "the extent to which ...people come to accept messages communicated during formal questioning"; leading questions and 'negative feedback', i.e. being told that the answer is wrong. It is the tendency to accede to the demands and suggestions of another. In police investigations it can occur during questioning when people react to and agree with an idea which the interrogator has placed in their minds. It can be when people believe those in authority rather than themselves and mentally handicapped people are more vulnerable.

The tendency to suggestibility is a relatively stable trait and can be assessed using measures of suggestibility (Gudjonsson 1984). It can be interpreted in conjunction with listening to audio tapes and is possible to analyse interviews to see if the subject initiated giving the information or merely accepted or responded to implicit statements. Audio tapes have other uses in that the intonation which can be lost when the transcript is heard. When "I did that" is said emphatically, ending in a high tone it conveys incredulity and the opposite meaning to the words used.

Psychologists have assessed objectively defences of the "He would say that wouldn't he?" variety. A man accused of driving whilst under the influence of alcohol refused to give blood on the grounds that he was afraid of needles. Perusal of his medical notes along with tests of anxiety showed that this was indeed true and he was not attempting to pervert the course of justice of which he was also being accused.

One young woman claimed that she had been sexually harassed at work over several months. The police were encouraging her to bring a private prosecution as they believed her but did not feel that they had enough evidence. We were able to describe her current state of mind and relate this to both her former self and to the general population to help her case in the civil court, where what is required is the balance of probability rather than beyond all reasonable doubt.

Helpful defence is not always to the defendants liking. A man of 51 admitting to importing £100,000 worth of drugs, an offence carrying an automatic lengthy prison sentence, was shown by formal testing correlated with his life history, to lack the intellectual capacity to organise the type of crime for which he was claiming credit. The question "Could he have done this?" was answered "Extremely unlikely". In this case he was not very pleased when the charges against him were considerably reduced, as he was denied his moment of glory and being convicted of a major crime.

Similarly a clinical interview helped a sixty-six year old retired hospital sister to understand her own behaviour in the wider context.

Since her retirement she had committed repeated acts of shoplifting. She was very embarrassed by this and, although fully cognisant of the acts when she committed them, wished that no one should know of them, and in deference to her age and sixty blameless years her crimes had been kept secret. The offences, however, had started not merely when she retired but also shortly after a holiday to the other side of the world where she had been when her mother died and about which she felt extremely guilty. Our contribution related to her disposal, which had a therapeutic element when we suggested going public as there appeared to be an unconscious desire for punishment. It seemed that until her need for punishment was satisfied her offending would not stop. She did pre-empt the courts and tell her family of her offending and she did stop, although the hypothesis remains unproven.

Many psychological tests include a scale that assesses the likelihood that the respondent is telling the truth. The majority of people give reliable self-reports from their own perspectives. However this is not invariably so, particularly when criminal proceedings are involved. They can lie deliberately or they can put a gloss on themselves to 'fake good'. The reliability of the results can be assessed from this and the clinician can decide how much emphasis to place on the test. The Child Abuse Potential Inventory (Milner 1986) considers faking good in the context of admitting abuse and when abuse is admitted is more inclined to interpret this as seeking to give a good impression rather than to deceive.

It is developed to a higher degree of sophistication in personal injury claims where Structured Interview of Reported Symptoms (SIRS) (Rogers 1986) is designed to measure 'feigning, faking and malingering', major considerations when compensation is being awarded. This is an ingenious inventory which accepts that bizarre and unusual symptoms genuinely exist - a headache *may* occur at precisely 10:20 every Tuesday morning depending on what has happened every preceding Monday evening. Although this is unlikely it can be further investigated. However there is a low limit to the number of these symptoms above which the objectivity or truthfulness of the subject comes into question.

In recent years it has been recognised that children can be valuable witnesses and are no longer automatically disqualified from being such. Many people do find it hard to talk to children. They resort to 'motherese' - high pitched, repetitive, simple speech (Schachter and Strage 1989) and involved with their own concerns of detection, fail to notice when the children lose interest or stop responding. The HMSO Memorandum of Good Practice (Bull and Birch 1992) based on work by research psychologists (Spencer and Flin 1993) advises police and social workers how to interview children and provides guidelines as to how to do this.

Following the Cleveland Child Sexual Abuse enquiry when some children were repeatedly interviewed and further abused by that, children are now interviewed as little as possible, and it is intended that one interview which is recorded will satisfy the separate requirements of police and social services. Increasingly we are asked to use our knowledge and experience of child psychology to view the tapes to give an opinion on the interview and whether the child is telling the truth. Interestingly we have found when we interview children and record it that if there is more than one adult influencing the child the mechanical reproduction on the tape distinguishes the different voices used by the child.

Both knowledge of children and of situation affects the interpretation of tapes. There is an increasingly common phenomenon described as SAID (Sexual Abuse In Divorce) when parents are separating, where fathers are falsely accused by young girls living with their mothers, of sexual abuse (Wakefield and Underwager 1990). These fathers are immediately stopped from seeing their daughters and in the many months it takes the judicial system to decide the veracity or not of this accusation contact between them does not take place and the mothers are aided by the statutory system to achieve their own ends of no contact. Shortly after putting this syndrome on paper one six year old agreed that what she said was not true.

Increasingly psychologists are being asked to provide 'risk assessments', usually in connection with family courts. Their perspective differs from the criminal in being forward looking to the best interest of the child rather than backwards looking to guilt with regard to an offence. Recognising that children often love an abusing father, and do well with them if they are safe, requires an assessment of the capacity to change and the potential for minimising risk, from people convicted in the criminal courts or from those suspected but not convicted of an offence.

Problems for Psychologists

Expert witnesses are always at a disadvantage because they do not have an equal partnership with the lawyers. The court system has a life of its own and plays according to its own (strict) rules. Experts are visitors to another system which they did not devise, do not fully understand and in which they can exercise limited power. A psychiatrist with a weak report engaged by the other side, once informed his barrister that one of the most well known psychological tests I had used was 'little known' and therefore of limited value. Although it was outside his bounds of competence to comment on my tests, he had done so. I had to sit silent for over two hours when 'whether or not I had anything to offer the court' was argued by two barristers before the judge eventually decided that I did not.

It is good to see that psychologists are increasingly used in the courts and psychology in the legal domain. It is a pity that many experienced psychologists refuse to accept instructions to act as expert witnesses because they are not prepared to be discredited and at a disadvantage in an adversarial system which regards experts as 'fair game'. Discrediting personally a witness who has written a report that does not serve their client, is acceptable behaviour to lawyers. If it is a good report, that can be a ploy to take attention away from its contents.

Reports can be misused, parts deliberately misunderstood and a witness feel humiliated. An objective report demands that alternative possibilities to the conclusion being reached are considered, but there are attendant dangers that they can be picked up and used - "Could this have happened?" As there are few certainties in psychology the answer is almost always "Yes if unlikely", and the experience professionally unsatisfying.

Psychologists as experts have special problems. First psychologists and lawyers have different ways of regarding people (models of man). Lawyers speak of free will, psychologists recognise predetermination; lawyers act as if people's behaviour was driven by reason, psychologists (even cognitive psychologists) recognise the part played by feelings and emotion. Unconscious motivation is not recognised by lawyers only conscious will. Questions such as "Could he have formed the intent?" requiring a "yes" "no" answer which are central to lawyers' thinking would be answered "It depends" by psychologists.

Secondly the confusion with psychiatrists. How does a clinical psychologist differ from a psychiatrist? Psychologists are scientists and psychiatrists are doctors. Psychologists base their opinions on research and use standardised tests to assist their opinion. Psychiatrists base their opinions on a clinical examination only and will name a clinical condition or its absence.

The problem for psychologists is that lawyers tend to prefer psychiatrists even when psychological expertise is more appropriate; psychology is a 'new' science and the ancient alliance between the old disciplines of medicine and law feels more comfortable to practitioners steeped in tradition and precedent. In addition psychiatrists fees are paid more easily as there is an established system for doing so. One group of magistrates was recently advised to order a psychological report with caution as "the courts have no authority to pay psychologists fees *since psychologists are not medically qualified people*" sic! (italics mine).

Finally there is the "Psychology is common sense" approach, enshrined in case law in the iniquitous 'Turner ruling' (1975 Q.B.834). Then Lord Justice Lawton ruled that psychologists have no special expertise to offer the judge and jury to help them make their decisions because they study normal behaviour and the judge and jury as ordinary people do not need expert help to understand ordinary behaviour. One excellent introduction to psychology debunking this, is based entirely on twenty psychological findings which are contrary to the common sense expectations of ordinary people (Coleman, 1988). He includes the finding that contrary to expectation in groups, from committees comprised of the great and the good, to random mobs, people do not moderate each others behaviour but are more inclined to extremes than when on their own (the risky shift phenomenon, or group polarisation).

Even if psychology were common sense, there would still be problems of definition; "common to whom?" The life styles of the accused and the agents of law and order often contain little in common. Einstein said that 'common sense' consists of those layers of knowledge and beliefs laid down before the age of eighteen and experience itself teaches that 'common sense' is not very common.

References

Bull, R. and Birch, D. (1992). *Memorandum of Good Practice.* Home Office, Dept of Health.

Butler Sloss (1996). Family Law Reports Vol 2 p.158.

Campion, M.J. (1995). *Who's Fit to Parent?* London: Routledge.

Canter, D. and Kirby, S. (1995). Prior Convictions of child molesters, *Science and Justice;* 35 (1) p.73-78.

Carson, D. (1990). *Professional and the Courts; A Handbook for Expert Witnesses.* Birmingham: Ventura Press.

Castell, J.H.F. (1966). *The Court Work of Educational and Clinical Psychologists.*London: British Psychological Society (EDPP).

Coleman, A. (1988). *What is Psychology?* London: Routledge.

Craig A.R., Franklin A.J. and Andrews, G. (1984). A scale to measure locus of control behaviour*British Journal of Medical Psychology* 57, p.173-180.

Gardner, C. (1993). Agreeing to Disagree. *The Lawyer* 12 October 1993.

Gudjonsson, G.H. (1996). Psychological Evidence in Court. *The Psychologist,* p.213-217, May 1996.

Gudjonsson, G. H. (1992). *The Psychology of Interrogations, Confession and Testimony.*Chichester: Wiley.

Gudjonsson, G. H. (1984). A new Scale of Interrogative Suggestibility; *Personality and Individual Differences,* 5 p.303-314.

Haward, L.R.C. (1965). Hearsay and Psychological Reports. *Bulletin of the BPS,* Vol 18, 58 p.21.

Haward, L.R.C. (1979). The Psychologist as Expert Witness, in Farrington, D.P., Hawkins, K. and Lloyd-Bostock, S. (eds). *Psychology, Law and Legal Processes.* London: Macmillan.

Ikarian Reefer Case, Responsibilities of expert witnesses. *Law Report* March 5 1993. Queen's Bench Division.

Kat, B. and Alexander, J. (1996). Mentally disordered offenders: outcome of an audit, *ClinicalPsychology Forum* No.97 p.40.

Kennedy, H. (1992). *Eve was Framed.* London: Chatto and Windus.

Milner, J.S. (1986). *Child Abuse Potential Inventory.* De Kalb Ill. USA.

Munsterberg, H. (1908). *Psychology and Crime.* London: T. Fisher Unwin.

Nijboer, H. (1995). Expert Evidence, in Bull, R. and Carson, (eds). *Handbook of Psychology in Legal Contexts.* D. Wiley.

Rogers, R. (1986). *Structured Interview of Reported Symptoms.* Florida: Psychological Assessment Resources Inc.

Schachter, F.F.and Strage, A.A.(1989). *The Developing Child* (5th edn) in Helen Bee, Harper Collins p.299.

Spencer, J.and Flin R. (1993). *The Evidence of Children; the Law and the Psychology.* London: Blackstock.

Wakefield, H.and Underwager, R. (1990). Personality Characteristics of Parents Making False Accusations of Sexual Abuse in Custody Disputes. *Issues in Child Abuse Accusations,* Vol 2. No.3 p.121-136.

Woolf (1996). *Access to Justice* (Report by Rt. Hon. The Lord Woolf).

9 Criminal Profiling: Trial by Judge and Jury, not Criminal Psychologist
DAVID ORMEROD

This chapter examines the numerous difficulties facing any party seeking to adduce an offender profile in a criminal trial in England. An offender profile is likely to conflict with some of the most fundamental rules of the law of evidence such as the rules of legal relevance, opinion, hearsay, and the rules guarding against prejudicial evidence. This chapter explains these rules and how they would affect the admissibility of the profile, whether adduced by the prosecution or the defence. It identifies the dangers in criminal psychologists being treated as expert witnesses and the legal hurdle profiles would face if they sought to rely on earlier research to support a particular profile. By providing an explanation of the relevant rules of the law of evidence and how they impinge on the admissibility of the profile, the aim is for psychologists to be better equipped to address requests from the investigating authorities for profiles.

David Ormerod read law at Essex University and lectured there before being appointed to a lectureship at the University of Nottingham in 1990. He was promoted to senior lecturer in 1998. His main research interests are Criminal law and the law of Evidence. He has written a number of articles on topics within these fields including items on expert evidence, the use of documentary evidence, computer evidence, psychological profiling, and psychiatric harm in the criminal law. In addition to his work in the Law School at Nottingham, David Ormerod has presented

*Offender Profiling Series: II - **Profiling in Policy and Practice***
Edited by D. Canter and L. Alison. © 1999 Ashgate Publishing, Aldershot. pp. 207-261

lectures to the legal profession, (especially the Crown Prosecution Service) and has acted as a consultant to the Law Commission and the Criminal Bar Association. He writes monthly case commentaries for the *Criminal Law Review* and is a member of the Editorial Board of the *International Journal of Evidence and Proof.*

9 Criminal Profiling: Trial by Judge and Jury, not Criminal Psychologist

DAVID ORMEROD[1]

Introduction

R v Colin Stagg remains the only English criminal case in which psychological profiling has been considered directly.[2] In that notorious case the trial judge, Ognall J, not only rejected the prosecution evidence but also made notably pessimistic statements about the use of profiles as evidence. His lordship was not wholly dismissive of the work of the criminal psychologist, acknowledging that "in certain cases the assistance of a psychologist of that kind can prove a very useful investigative tool".[3] But, the idea that this material could be put in evidence in a criminal trial met with a much colder reception. His lordship stressed that the court "[w]ould not wish to give encouragement either to investigating or prosecuting authorities to construct or seek to supplement their cases on this kind of basis".[4]

Is the picture necessarily so bleak? Is the criminal psychologist restricted to helping police with their inquiries or may he also have his say in court? Despite the decision in *R v Stagg*, and the negative comments made, the admissibility of criminal profile evidence is, for a number of reasons, still open for the courts to decide. First, the decision in *R v Stagg* is that of a Crown Court, not one of the appellate courts. The binding precedent of Crown Court decisions on any future court is very limited.[5] Furthermore, the evidence against Stagg was rejected by Ognall J on grounds unrelated to the admissibility of the profile: that the investigation was conducted in such a manner as to render the evidence unreliable. Mr Justice Ognall's statements concerning the admissibility of the profile evidence were merely asides, or *obiter dicta*, that do not bind any future court. Moreover, Ognall J's *dicta* are less persuasive because they are expressed in such broad terms. That is not to criticise the decision of that judge, who was faced with an appalling case in which the abuse of the profile technique was blatant. The case was described as "so bad even a moron in a hurry could see it could never stand up".[6] Mr Justice Ognall was, quite understandably in that context, erring on the side of caution.

If the issue is still open for decision, as it appears it must be, is a court ever likely to accept the evidence of the criminal psychologist in the future? This chapter tries to identify the many reasons which prevent a court relying on the evidence of the criminal psychologist. The aim is to paint a positive, yet realistic picture, including an attempt to identify the very rare circumstances in which the evidence could be admitted.

It has been argued elsewhere that the admissibility in a criminal trial of a profile would be unlikely, largely because of a number of rules of evidence.[7] The specific goals of this chapter are, first, to assist the psychologist in understanding these rules of criminal evidence. Unravelling some of the complexities of the rule will at least provide the psychologists with an idea of the law's major concerns and expectation. In this way, psychologists will be better equipped to address requests to testify from investigating authorities. In addition, by drawing on the experience of the use of DNA profiling in the criminal courts, it will be possible to highlight analogous dangers and how some of them may be avoided in the unlikely event that the profiler testifies in court. Given the (understandably) negative judicial attitude following *R v Stagg*, the criminal psychologist must be as well prepared as possible for any further attempts to rely on his work in court. The further goal is then that when a future criminal trial presents an opportunity to admit such evidence, there will be a greater likelihood that the psychologist will have generated the sorts of evidence to which the courts will be receptive.

Reasons for Rejecting the Profile as Evidence in Court

One reason that the concept of a criminal profile is so attractive in both fact and fiction,[8] is the idea that from the seemingly few clues it is possible to create a *complete* picture of the offender. This not only makes profiles potentially powerful in the fight against crime, but also gives them an air of mystique.[9] The long and varied list of characteristics which it is claimed will be catalogued reinforce this belief. Thus, a "typical profile will include most, or all, of the following descriptive criteria: age, race, occupational level, marital status, intelligence, education level, arrest history, military history, family background, social interests, socio-economic level, residence in relation to crime and with whom residing, personality characteristics (rigid, passive, manipulative, aggressive), colour, age, and description of vehicle, suggested interview technique for offender".[10] This almost exhaustive detail about the offender can be seen in Professor Canter's extremely successful profile of the Railway Murderer - Duffy. Out of the seventeen pointers Canter put forward, thirteen were accurate.[11]

"The Profile (M denotes the Murderer)	*The Match*
M lived in the Kilburn or Cricklewood area of London.	Duffy lived in Kilburn.
M was married but had no children.	Duffy was married, and a low sperm count meant he was infertile.
The marriage was in serious trouble.	Duffy was separated from his wife.
M was a loner with few friends.	Duffy had only two male friends.
M was a physically small man who felt himself to be unattractive.	Duffy was five feet four inches tall, and had acne.
M was interested in martial arts or body building.	Duffy spent much of his time at a martial arts club.
M felt the need to dominate women.	Duffy was a violent man who had already attacked his wife.
M fantasized about rape and enjoyed bondage.	Duffy liked tying his wife up before intercourse.

M had a fascination for weapons, particularly knives and swords.	Duffy had many 'Kung Fu' style weapons in his home.
M indulged his fantasies of sex and violence with videos and magazines.	Duffy collected hard-core porn and martial arts videos.
M was a man who kept some sort of souvenir of his crimes.	Duffy had 33 door keys, each taken from a victim as a souvenir.
M had a semi-skilled job as a plumber, carpenter, or similar.	Duffy trained as a carpenter with British Rail.
M was in the age range 20 to 30.	Duffy was 28 when arrested and had been a rapist for four years".[12]

It will be useful to return to this profile, which proved successful, to illustrate various points throughout the ensuing discussion of the numerous reasons why the court should reject evidence of this kind in a criminal trial.

1. Intuition

Although many aspects of a profile will be based on scientific data, the gaps are filled, to varying degrees,[13] with intuition to give a fuller picture. As once commentator put it this "lend[s] to the colour, hue and tint" of the portrait of the offender.[14] The completeness of this picture which at first makes the profile so attractive is also what leads to its rejection as a piece of evidence as a whole. The court is not prepared to hear testimony from any person, no matter how well qualified or experienced, that he has an intuition that the offender will have a certain characteristic. It is for this reason that the courts would refuse to hear the evidence of say an astrologer (unless of course he were testifying about the customs and activities of astrologers should that be relevant to the trial).

2. Legal Relevance

(a) Relevance Explained

Every criminal trail involves an attempt to reconstruct and analyse a past event. One function of the rules of evidence is to regulate how much information should be admitted in attempting this reconstruction. This is not merely to ensure that the trial does not go on for an unduly protracted period, but also that the trier of fact (the jury or magistrate) are not distracted from their central enquiry by a limitless clutter of material. The first concern with any potential item of evidence is to ensure that it is "legally relevant". This term has taken on a particular meaning in the law of evidence, but it is essentially one of common sense. Stephen's classic definition of relevance from the last century is widely adopted: "any two facts to which it is applied are so related to each other that according to the common course of events one either taken by itself or in connection with other facts proves or renders probable the past, present, or future existence or non-existence of the other".[15] This definition is not restricted to English law, and can be found in the American Federal Rules of Evidence r.401: Relevant evidence is "evidence having any tendency to make the existence of any fact that is of consequence to the determination of the action more probable or less probable than it would be without the evidence".

The definition is clear enough, but it begs the obvious question: relevant to what? In any criminal trial, the issues which must be proved by the prosecution (or in some rare instances, as in a case of insanity, by the defence) to succeed can be labelled the "facts in issue". This is the agenda for the trial, but it is never a fixed agenda. If the elements of murder which the prosecution must prove include an intentional unlawful killing of a person, those issues are all on the agenda; facts in issue. If the defendant, at trial, pleads that he killed intentionally, but that he was provoked into doing so, all the issues on the original agenda are redundant, and the new agenda is whether he satisfies the legal requirements of the defence of provocation. It will be noticed that the "facts in issue" in any case are derived not from the procedural rules of evidence but from the substantive criminal law; that is the law defining offences and defences, not procedure. From all of this, it becomes obvious that the answer to the question posed above, "relevant to what?" is simply "relevant to the facts in issue".

One further aspect of the rules about relevance can be best explained by way of an example. If D is charged with the murder of V, it is clear from the discussion above, that the facts in issue will be whether he intentionally killed. Using Stephen's definition, any fact which makes it more likely (or less likely) that these facts in issue occurred (i.e. that D intentionally killed V) is a relevant fact. This would include, for example, D's fingerprints on a weapon with V's blood on it. Common sense dictates that a court inquiring into this charge would also want to hear about the fact that an eyewitness, W, has very poor eyesight. That fact is neither a fact in issue, nor a relevant fact: W's poor eyesight does not make it more likely or less likely that D stabbed V. Another example would be the reliability of a computer that processed information relevant to an investigation. Such facts are acknowledged to be relevant, and are labelled "collateral facts" and will often be relevant only to credit (i.e. the credibility of a witness) rather than relevant to the issue (i.e. relevant directly to guilt).

In addition to taking a strict stance on what constitutes legal relevance, the courts will reject as insufficiently relevant evidence likely to lead to the trier of fact being distracted.[16] In the context of the criminal profile, this could give rise to significant problems. If the criminal psychologist wishes to testify that, for example, a certain percentage of rapes are intraracial,[17] or that the age of a rapist is likely to be between 20 and 30 (as in Duffy), this could lead into may side-issues, such as the size of sample in the study, the reliability of methodology etc. These would all distract the jury from the primary purpose of assessing the guilt of the accused on trial for this particular rape.

The courts' strict approach to the question of relevance can be seen in the course taken by the House of Lords in the leading case of *R v Blastland*.[18] Blastland was convicted of murdering a 12 year old boy. Having admitted that he had been engaged in sexual activity with the boy, Blastland claimed that they had been disturbed by a third party and that he had run away leaving the boy alive and well. The description of the third party fitted that of Mark, someone who had actually confessed to the murder but then retracted his confession. Blastland sought to rely in his defence on the fact that Mark had detailed knowledge about the murder at a time when the body had not been discovered. The House of Lords held that since there was no evidence as to how Mark might have acquired his knowledge, the evidence was "irrelevant" to Blastland's defence. This seems unduly harsh, but on strict application of Stephen's test above, it is the right decision. The fact that Mark knew about the existence of a dead body does not make it more or less likely that Blastland killed that person. Mark could have killed the boy, seen Blastland do it, or even seen a fourth party do it. What is necessary is to know how Mark came by his knowledge. As Lord Bridge said: "Mark's knowledge that [the boy] had been murdered was neither itself in issue, not was it, per se, of any relevance to the issue".[19]

The decision has been heavily criticised for, at the very least, failing to ensure that justice is seen to be done.[20] The decision, coupled with other recent appellate court decisions in similar vein have led one commentator to suggest the term relevance is not a simple question of logic or common sense as in Stephen's definition. Professor Choo has argued that the courts have, in applying the rules of relevance, paid insufficient attention to the fundamental rights of an accused to be protected from wrongful conviction.[21] This is a powerful claim, particularly in the light of cases such as *Blastland*, but it can be countered by the equally persuasive argument from Adrian Zuckerman that "[i]n piling up evidence, albeit relevant, a point will come where any further piece of evidence may detract from, rather than increase, the correctness of the final assessment".[22] It would seem that the idea of legal relevance, as applied by the courts is, first and foremost a question of logic, but also involves an assessment of other factors such as the likelihood of distraction for the trier of fact, the risk of increasing the length of trial etc. Relevance is then not simply a question of probability.[23]

Implicit within the decision about relevance are a number of questions about the sufficiency of the evidence and how appropriate it is for the jury to hear it. These are really issues of exclusion that should be tackled explicitly once the question of relevance has been resolved. The rules of evidence do go on to regulate explicitly the *admissibility* of *legally relevant* evidence. Relevant evidence will be excluded if it is unreliable, unfair, too prejudicial or privileged. Before addressing these rules of exclusion and how they affect the use of a criminal profile, it is necessary to consider whether a profile (or part thereof) is legally relevant as defined.

(b) Relevance and the Profile

If all that a profile can do is to suggest that, in the opinion of a criminal psychologist, the perpetrator will have certain characteristics (age, residence in a certain area, etc.) that will be insufficiently relevant to be received by the court. The psychological profile, as a whole, is tendered to help prove the facts in issue. It is tendered as a relevant fact. However, before we are able to rely upon this relevant fact (the profile) to render more probable the facts in issue (killing by D) we must be satisfied that the relevant fact (the profile) is indeed a "fact" or "true". This can never be done: it is an opinion. Although the profile may well be based upon statistical data, that foundation alone will not make *the entire profile* "a fact" that is "true".

Would a part of a profile be accepted as legally relevant? If a criminal psychologist has, as a result of reliable research, concluded that, say 90% of rapes are intraracial, would that statistic be legally relevant in the trial of a white defendant for the rape of a black woman? The statistic suggests that it is less likely that the man is guilty. According to the leading American commentator, "[i]t is enough if the item [of evidence] could reasonably show that the fact is slightly more probable than it would appear without that evidence".[24] However, in view of the strict approach of the English courts, it is far from clear whether even this part-profile would be accepted as legally relevant. The dangers of collateral issues arising (how accurate was the statistic? Was the methodology reliable? etc.) would *probably* lead a court to conclude that even this evidence was insufficiently relevant to be admitted.[25] In *R v Mohan*,[26] the Supreme Court of Canada upheld the trial judge's decision to exclude profile evidence where the defendant sought to call a psychiatrist to testify that the typical offender in the cases in question would have certain abnormal characteristics (paedophilia) and that the accused did not have these characteristics. Sopinka J stated that "there was no material in the record to support a finding that the profile of a paedophile or psychopath has been standardized to the extent that it could be said that it matched the suggested profile of the offender depicted in the charges".[27]

It has been argued that the reliance on such normative data should *never* be accepted as sufficiently relevant.

The findings derived from empirical research are used by psychologists to formulate 'norms' of human behaviour. From observations and experiments, psychologists may conclude that in circumstance X there is a likelihood that an individual or group member will behave in manner Y. But "normative data" of this sort are of little use to the courts. The courts are concerned to determine the past behaviour of accused individuals, and in carrying out that function, information about the past behaviour of *other* individuals is wholly irrelevant. What the courts require is information, direct or circumstantial, about the alleged criminal acts or omissions of the *accused*. Such information might be termed "positive data". Such data are (or may be) legally relevant because they "attach" to the person of the individual accused. Normative data, in contrast do not "attach" to the accused because they are not relevant about that particular individual's conduct. To become legally relevant (and practically helpful), the findings from psychological research must in some way be connected to the particular case.[28]

But surely this is how all criminal trials are decided - on the basis of people making judgements founded on their experiences of life.

The profile as a whole will then be deemed legally irrelevant and thus rejected by the judge in a criminal trial,[29] but there is a slightly better chance of admitting a number of individual items of evidence, possibly generated by a number of different experts. This idea of a "profiling team", where individual members of the team would be responsible for analysing specific aspects of the crime, may be viewed more favourably by the court. It would certainly represent a move away from a single individual acting on intuition. Furthermore, it has been recognised that a more accurate report may be produced in this way: "certain profilers were more accurate and more keenly perceptive with certain tasks than they were with others. ... Since individual profilers appear to enjoy certain areas of expertise within the general field of profiling, it seems plausible that more accurate and richer profiles would result from "group profiling" than from individual profiling".[30]

However, all that has been considered thus far is the most basic rule which filters out the irrelevant, it remains to consider the exclusionary rules which exclude the concededly relevant evidence. Specific rules create problems for the admissibility of a profile, and even a part profile. The most important rule, and that to be considered first, relates to the undue prejudice which may be created.

3. Rules of Exclusion: Similar Fact Evidence[31]

An accused is charged with murdering a young girl by strangulation, and there is no sexual interference with the girl, nor any attempt to conceal the body. In such a case, it is surely relevant that the accused has twice previously killed in identical circumstances. Applying the test of relevance above, it is obvious that this information makes it more likely that *this* accused rather than a member of the general public selected at random committed the act.[32] The evidence creates a greater likelihood of his being convicted and as such can be described as prejudicial to the accused, as could any piece of incriminating evidence such as a fingerprint or DNA evidence. However, the evidence of the previous convictions, or other discreditable conduct not amounting to a crime, also creates in the minds of the jury more sinister prejudices: "he did it before so he deserves to be punished anyway" etc. The most important of these prejudices have recently been described as "moral prejudice" and "reasoning prejudice".[33] The first label is being used to describe the danger that the fact-finders might treat the evidence as being more probative of guilt than it really is, and the second, that it might lead them to convict the defendant without being properly satisfied that he is guilty as charged.[34] There is the potential for these prejudices to be exacerbated in two ways in the context of the criminal profile. First, the risk of moral prejudice is increased in cases involving deviant crimes[35] - and there is an argument that profiles are used more in relation to deviant crimes than others.[36] The Law Commission's research with a mock jury led to the conclusion that the prejudice created by certain types of crime was significantly greater than others. Second, the risk of reasoning prejudice is increased in cases of serial crimes, and there are many who argue that profiles are most often called upon in relation to serial activity.[37] Other well-rehearsed dangers justifying the exclusion of this type of evidence are also apparent, including the danger that the evidence of discreditable attributes leads the police to "round up the usual suspects".[38] Finally, there is a risk that evidence of previous misconduct will not only create prejudice, but might "mislead, confuse or distract the fact-finders, or cause undue waste of time."[39]

The rules of evidence provide a general safeguard against such prejudices in the rule against similar fact evidence. In the leading authority on the similar fact evidence rules (*D.P.P v P*)[40] Lord Mackay, the Lord Chancellor, said that the key was the "probative force" of the evidence. This had to be so great as to make it just to admit the evidence, *notwithstanding* the prejudice to the accused. In the case of the strangler, the proof of his previous convictions will, undoubtedly create the prejudices, but the evidence is *so* probative of guilt (without reference to such prejudice) that to exclude it would be, as one distinguished Law Lord once said, "an affront to common sense".[41]

As the discussion focuses more specifically on the similar fact rule and profile evidence, it is worth bearing in mind the two elements that must be balanced. First the judge will have to be satisfied that the evidence has probative force, i.e. relevance, and then secondly, that the probative force is sufficient to outweigh the prejudicial effect on the jury.

Using Similar Facts to Identify the Offender

There is no limit to the use of similar fact evidence once it is admissible under the test. There are cases where it is used to rebut a defence or an innocent explanation raised by the defendant.[42]   More importantly for profiling, similar fact evidence may be used to prove the identity of the perpetrator. This use is the most controversial, and can operate by one of two distinct methods: cumulative or sequential.[43]   The sequential approach works by the prosecution first proving that the defendant performed an act A (usually a crime) before turning to the second act B. Having established that acts A and B share such peculiarity that there is no doubt they were the work of the same person, it is legitimate for the jury to conclude that this defendant performed both.[44]   Unless the prejudicial effect (i.e. the jury engaging in moral or reasoning prejudice) of admitting the evidence is outweighed by its probative force (e.g. the peculiarity of the *modus operandi*) the similar fact rule will lead to the exclusion of the evidence. With the cumulative approach the prosecution must first prove that the two (or more) activities or offences are the work of the same person. This will usually depend on there being a sufficient peculiarity in the activity or manner of performance. Thereafter, the jury will be allowed to combine items of inconclusive evidence (e.g. identification) from each individual offence to prove that this defendant was the offender on both occasions.[45]

The use of a criminal profile relies on a very different sort of reasoning from either of these accepted techniques, and yet it falls foul of the general prohibition on similar fact evidence. Reliance is on the reasoning that X% of those who commit this type of crime have a certain characteristic or trait (e.g. possession of a collection of hard-core pornography as in Duffy). The accused has that certain characteristic, therefore, he is more likely to be the perpetrator of the offence. It is simply an attempt to assist in focusing investigative attention on individuals whose personality traits match those of others who have been convicted of such crimes. This tells us nothing about *the accused* i.e. the man in the dock. It tells us that there is an X% likelihood that *the perpetrator* is of a certain type.[46] There is insufficient probative force in such evidence (irrespective of the prejudicial effect that will be considered shortly). Even if in a rape case, the statistics say that the likelihood of a rapist being between 20 and 30 years old is 80%, that does not, as noted above, have tremendous probative value in the question whether it is more likely that his accused committed this particular rape.

The danger is even more obvious where, rather than as one individual statistic, the profile is relied upon *as a whole*. The tendency then is towards ambiguity:

> Nine out of ten profiles are vapid. They play at blind man's bluff, groping in all directions in the hope of touching a sleeve. Occasionally they do, but not firmly enough to seize it, for the behaviourists producing them must necessarily deal in generalities and types. But policemen can't arrest a type. They require hard data: names, dates, none of which the psychiatrists [or others involved in creating profile evidence] can offer.[47]

For the purposes of the criminal trial, and the rules of evidence, the evidence of the criminal psychologist will usually be insufficiently relevant. They will identify a type of person likely to have committed the offence(s) in question. This is inadequate for the purposes of the criminal trial. This highlights a major distinction between the values of profiles in investigation as opposed to evidence:

> The requirements for investigation and proof are very different. The use of offender profiling can be compared with the use of screening techniques in medicine. Here the tests required for diagnosis must be far more rigorous than the tests for screening: a doctor does not rely on an abnormal mass X-ray to make an individual diagnosis of tuberculosis. The same distinction should apply between information that directs an investigation and information that

proves guilt. The success of offender profiling as an investigative tool depends first on its sensitivity in identifying the characteristics of anyone capable of committing the crime in question. If people without these characteristics could also commit this crime, then use of the profile will focus the search for suspects too narrowly so that possible culprits will be missed. Also the initial scan will inevitably, as in preventive medicine, include many false positives. However, if profiling is to be used to determine guilt, specificity becomes more important than sensitivity. The profile must identify factors that are specific to those who commit he type of crime in question and are not shared by the rest of the population.[48]

This difference was recognised recently in the US Supreme Court in the context of novel techniques and expert evidence:

...there are important differences between the quest for truth in the courtroom and the quest for truth in the laboratory. Scientific conclusions are subject to perpetual revision. Law, on the other hand, must resolve disputes finally and quickly. The scientific project is advance by broad and wide-ranging consideration of a multitude of hypotheses, for those that are incorrect will eventually be shown to be so, and that in itself is an advance. Conjectures that are probably wrong are of little use, however, in the project of reaching a quick, final, and binding legal judgment - often of great consequence - about a particular set of events in the past.... Rules of evidence [are] designed not for the exhaustive search for cosmic understanding but for the particularised resolution of legal disputes".[49]

The probative value of the evidence of the criminal psychologist does not weigh too heavily, and when it comes to considering the other side of the similar fact balance - the prejudicial effect - the profile fairs no better. All the hazards of the prejudices noted above can be demonstrated by reference to the successful profile of Duffy. The reception of evidence about the *accused's* collection of hard-core pornography, his violence towards his wife and collection of Kung-fu weapons would certainly create (moral and reasoning) prejudice against him in the minds of the jury: "[t]here is all the difference in the world between evidence proving that the accused is a bad man and evidence proving that he is *the* man".[50]

The other potential prejudices are all too obvious. If the police are led to believe that the offender in such cases will, on the basis of proven statistics, have an interest in martial arts, they may well simply round up the local enthusiasts. To take a different example, if the profiler relies on a statistic that, for example, rapes are usually committed by men of the same racial group as the victim and most likely of an age between 20-30, there is a risk that the police will *only* direct their enquiries towards such people, therefore leading to proportionately higher conviction rates of such people, thus feeding back into the statistical data from which we began. This is exacerbated by the accumulation of self-reports from convicted criminals to provide material from which profiles can be drawn:[51] "Offender profiling as an activity carries with it the danger of creating new, apparently scientifically-reinforced, stereotypes, hence criminalising sections of the population".[52] In addition to all of this there is the acknowledged possibility that the perpetrator may have staged the crime scene[53] (i.e. altered it to confuse investigators) or has altered his *modus operandi* if he is a repeat offender.[54] Finally, returning to the Duffy case, the evidence of facts such as the accused's violence towards his wife could give rise to collateral issues - how often, how badly, were the events proven? etc. - which could create confusion for the jury by distracting them from the central inquiry.

All in all, the similar fact rule seems to present a significant obstacle to the admissibility of both the criminal profile as a whole, and even the limited use of a single item of statistical evidence adduced by a criminal psychologist. The best that could be hoped for is that a court would accept statistical evidence such as the hypothetical intraracial rape statistic discussed above. It is submitted that even this evidence lacks sufficient probative force. But in case that opinion is wrong, and a criminal court is prepared to accept such a statistic, it remains to explain how these items will be presented to the court and to identify the host of hidden perils which might prevent the acceptance of even this limited evidence. These should make every criminal psychologist extremely wary of testifying.

Receiving the Opinion of the Criminal Psychologist

The Criminal Psychologist as an Expert

(a) Expertise[55] It has long been established that for a court to hear expert testimony, it must be satisfied that the expert witness is suitably qualified.[56] This question is one to be decided by the judge alone.

"Qualification" in this context is not limited to formal academic qualification, but includes practical experience. This was illustrated in the recent case of *Clare*,[57] in which the Court of Appeal accepted expert evidence from a police officer who had watched a video-recording approximately 40 times. He was an expert as to the identify of those on the film although, clearly, the officer had no "formal qualification". Similarly in another recent Court of Appeal decision, an expert was allowed to testify although he had no scientific training, no formal qualification and was not affiliated to any professional body.[58] Although the Royal Commission on Criminal Justice recommended that professional bodies should maintain a register of those members who were suitably qualified to act as expert witnesses, no action has been taken to implement the suggestion.[59]

There is considerable scepticism exhibited by many towards expert evidence of criminal profiles. One commentator has stated recently that "psychiatrists or psychologists have [no] business pretending to be experts in profiling criminal suspects".[60] The flexibility of the approach seen above in *Clare* and *Stockwell* could work, in the long term, to the disadvantage of the criminal psychologist by allowing any person who claimed to have practised the "art" of profiling to testify. Such amateurs could leave a poor impression resulting in a negative attitude to all involved including the true experts. Worse still, the evidence of such amateurs could easily result in a miscarriage of justice.[61] This, coupled with the courts' acknowledged suspicion of all experts[62] and particularly psychologists becoming involved in the criminal trial[63] suggests that only those who are in fact specialists in criminal psychology and profile work will be likely to be permitted to give expert evidence.

(b) The expert opinion must deal with matters beyond the jury's knowledge Expert evidence will be admissible in any criminal trial only "to furnish the Court with ... information which is likely to be *outside the experience and knowledge of a judge or jury*".[64] This requirement has been the subject of considerable academic comment. It has recently been claimed that

> The true test of admissibility is whether the evidence that is proposed to give will be sufficiently helpful to the jury to offset any disadvantages that its admission is likely to entail, in terms of lengthening the proceedings,

increasing their complexity, or diverting the jury's attention away from the main issues in the case and the proper way to evaluate them.[65]

This compares with the approach of the US Federal Rules of Evidence, r.702[66] in which the true test rests on how helpful the expert's evidence will be. Such vague tests give the courts considerable discretion, which has often been exercised against psychological evidence. However, it must be noted here that the expert in the context of this discussion would be testifying about the offender not the defendant. In most cases where expert psychological evidence has been considered by the courts, the question has been about the defendant's mental normality or otherwise.[67] Psychiatric or psychological evidence about the defendant's state of mind will be inadmissible unless he is abnormal and therefore beyond the jury's experience and understanding.

The construction of an entire profile in the sense discussed above is certainly a technique beyond the scope of the ordinary person or juror. Even if reduced to its essential elements, this must be the case:[68]

> The process used by an investigative profiler in developing a criminal profile is quite similar to that used by clinicians to make a diagnosis and treatment plan: data are collected and assessed, the situation reconstructed, hypotheses formulated, a profile developed and tested, and the results reported back. Investigators traditionally have learned profiling through brainstorming, intuition and educated guesswork. Their expertise is the result of years of accumulated wisdom, extensive experience in the field, and familiarity with a large number of cases.[69]

A part-profile such as a statistic related to the likelihood of an offender bearing a specific characteristic will also, in general, lie outside the scope of the juror's knowledge. This will be a question of degree. While the average juror applying his common-sense will realise that there is a (slightly) greater likelihood of a murderer who kills in the middle of the afternoon being a shift-worker than someone who works regular office hours, the same is not true of other characteristics (e.g. a collection of pornography or interest in martial arts). Where the research and experience of the psychologist enables him to provide an opinion as to the likelihood of the offender being interested in martial arts or separated from his wife, the information is clearly beyond the scope of the jury's knowledge. There is a possible challenge even to statistics of this type being beyond the knowledge of the jury. Research in the USA by Pinizzotto and Finkel showed that, in controlled conditions, professional profilers were found not to "process material in a way *qualitatively different*"[70] from untrained psychologists, detectives and first-year psychology students.[71] All that the research shows is that at least some of the jury may be able to construct a profile. That is not to say that they have knowledge and experience of the way the particular profile before the court was constructed. That the profile is beyond the knowledge of the jury is even more clearly apparent where the crime involved is one of particular deviance, as most profiled crimes are.

(c) Additional safeguards for novel techniques? Ognall J. in *R v Stagg* stated that any prosecutor wishing to rely upon profile evidence would face "formidable difficulties" in proving that such a profile was in fact expert evidence. His lordship was also doubtful that the psychological profile evidence is sufficiently well established or "generally accepted" as a scientific method to be received as expert evidence.[72] He went on to suggest that such a novel technique must satisfy tests such as those developed in the USA in cases such as *Frye v US* (1923)[73] and *Daubert v Merrell Dow* (1993)[74]. Similarly, the Supreme Court of Canada ruled that "expert evidence which advances a novel scientific theory or technique is subjected to special scrutiny to determine whether it meets a basic threshold of reliability and whether it is essential in the sense that the trier of fact will be unable to come to a satisfactory conclusion without the assistance of the expert".[75]

There is no authority in English law that applies such a test.[76] The preferred English approach is well illustrated by the case of *R v Robb*[77] in which the Court of Appeal accepted evidence of techniques of voice identification, which had minority support amongst the relevant scientific community. Bingham L.J., as he then was, stated that

> Expert evidence is not... limited to the core areas. Expert evidence of finger-printing, handwriting, and accident reconstruction is regularly given. Opinion may be given of the market value of land, ships, pictures, or rights. Expert opinions may be given of the quality of commodities, or on the literary, artistic, scientific or other merit of works alleged to be obscene... Some of these fields are far removed from anything which could be called a formal scientific discipline. Yet while receiving this evidence the courts would not accept the evidence of an astrologer, a soothsayer, a witch-doctor[78] or an

amateur psychologist and might hesitate to receive evidence of attributed authorship based on stylometric analysis.[79]

In a similar vein, in *R v Stockwell*[80], a case concerning facial-mapping, Lord Taylor C.J. approved the trial judge's statement that "[o]ne should not set one's face against fresh developments, *provided they have a proper foundation*".[81]

Daubert requires a court to consider whether the method is reliable and relevant, tried and tested, has been subjected to peer review, has a known potential error rate, and has some support in the scientific community. These factors will not be considered explicitly by English courts. Nevertheless, the English courts will be influence by a number of these factors in determining whether the method has a "proper foundation".

(i) Reliability "Perhaps the most controversial aspect of psychological expertise... is the problem of knowing when the specialised knowledge is sufficiently reliable and valid to quality either scientifically or legally, as expertise".[82]

The reliability and source of the profile must be established. There are two points here. First, if the profile is not reliable it will not pass as "expert" evidence even under the test in *R v Robb* or *R v Stockwell*. Secondly, even if it is admitted as expert evidence, it will not be strong enough to withstand critical examination in court. As observed earlier, opinion evidence does not necessarily attract a great deal of weight; it is not conclusive proof of anything. The more reliable the procedure is perceived to be, the more weight is likely to be attached to it by the trier of fact.[83] It is arguable that the reliability issue would go to weight and not admissibility, but there must be a cut-off point below which, evidence is of such unreliability as to be of no assistance to the court, and indeed may be a positive impediment.

Both of these points indicate a need for profiling to be established as reliable. But can this ever be proved? Profiling has been under constant scrutiny for reliability for a number of years. The FBI's success rate has been put as high as 46%,[84] others have claimed success rates of up to 80%.[85] In England, Canter's Offender Profiling Research Unit was judged to be successful by detectives in "most of the 30-plus profiles thus far produced".[86] These claims are open to attack given the impossibility of an objective assessment of reliability.[87] Given the nature of the exercise, a controlled experiment is out of the question.[88] Similarly, practical difficulties would be encountered in any retrospective evaluation of trial outcomes. It would simply not be possible to disentangle from the ultimate profile what information came from guess work, what was forensic input, crime scene analysis etc. An equally cogent criticism of the claims for reliability is that many relate only to success as an investigative tool rather than as admissible evidence: profiles are usually intended to assist investigation rather than prove guilt. There is an important point behind this attack, as noted by Mair[89] and discussed above. Whereas investigation calls for sensitivity to all possible material, the criminal trial is concerned only with very specific evidence.

This inability to establish, categorically, that the procedure is reliable is problematic even for the use of part-profiles such as statistical data. If the statistic is not capable of proof as an uncontroverted fact, it could be rejected as being of insufficient relevance. A court could rule that such matters were likely to divert the attention of the tribunal into too many side issues as discussed above.[90] In one decided US case this was the basis upon which the profile evidence was rejected. In *State v Cavallo*[91] the defendant was charged with rape and sought to introduce expert evidence that he lacked the psychological traits common to rapists. The court rejected the evidence, noting that "the testimony was based on two unproven and unreliable premises: (a) rapists have particular mental characteristics, and (b) psychiatrists can, by examination, determine the presence or absence of these characteristics".[92]

Finally, there is the danger of the lack of reliability owing to the poor knowledge and/or technique of the profiler himself.[93] As Grubin has noted:

> An increasing number of individuals are now claiming expertise in offender profiling, and most are not shy in offering their services to the police. Their techniques are often poorly articulated, if articulated at all, with intuition and 'brainstorming' often playing a prominent role.[94]

(ii) A uniform method of profiling? In *Robb*, it was not fatal to the reception of the evidence that the method used to identify voices by this particular method was different to the majority of others in that scientific community. There would seem to be no need to establish a uniform

method of profiling. Nevertheless, the more scientific the approach can be made to appear, the more acceptable it is likely to be to the court; it will have greater objectivity. As noted, there are so many different approaches to creating a profile that it is difficult to discern any uniform methodology. There have been efforts to establish a uniformity of definition of types of crime: for example the publication of the Crime Classification Manual.[95] Such attempts to produce a definitive catalogue of aspects of human behaviour are never likely to result in universal acceptance. There is, for example, widespread scepticism as the reliability of the approach used in the famous Diagnostic and Statistical Manual of Mental Disorders: DSM IV.[96] In *R v Mohan* the Supreme Court of Canada excluded profile evidence precisely because of this failure to prove that the psychological characteristics listed in a profile had been "standardized" to a satisfactory extent.[97]

(iii) Profiling as a science?[98] Once again, the English authorities are clear that expert evidence may be received on issues of art, taxation, accounting practice, stylometry[99] and even foreign law, none of which could really be described as a science. Nevertheless, the more scientific, the more objective it appears the less sceptical courts will be. It has been noted above that the profile produced as a whole may appear less scientific than a part-profile and thus be less well received. In general, profiles "... are the result of statistics. In other words, given many incidents of a similar nature, the investigators have discovered that the individuals who often committed "this particular type of offence" displayed specific characteristics or traits".[100] Material such as that in the studies conducted as the residence of rapists,[101] could not be sensibly distinguished, *in this scientific sense*, from statistical evidence about the likelihood of a voice-match for identification of the accused as in *Stockwell*. The statistical evidence will, if properly constructed, be consistent, cumulative, methodical and predictive, and as such will qualify, in the view of one leading commentator, as a science.[102] The difference will lie, if at all, in the question of the legal relevance of such evidence.

(iv) Avoiding the trial by expert One other factor which will influence the court's decision whether to receive expert testimony of profile evidence is the likelihood that the issues raised by that testimony will

become the substance of a debate between competing experts. This could distract the jury, waste time and, rather than assisting the court as it is designed to do, could simply create confusion. In *Stagg*, Mr Paul Britton was the main instigator of the prosecution case, while the defence were to rely on a formidable team of experts including Gisli Gudjonsson, Glenn Wilson and David Canter to discredit the profile.[103]

Although it is not possible to address the issue of the neutral expert[104] and the dangers of trial by expert[105] in full, it is possible to highlight the particular hazard with the criminal psychologist testifying for the prosecution. Because the profiler will have helped *throughout the investigation*, bias is even more likely than in the usual case of an expert witness hired by one party to testify to their cause.[106] The psychologist may well, at the very least, be perceived to be more anxious to get a conviction because of his close involvement in the investigation and because the conviction would reflect positively on his work in general.

(v) The "ultimate issue" rule There is a technical rule which prohibits the expert giving his opinion on the very matter on which the tribunal of fact will ultimately have to arbitrate - the "ultimate issue" - as this would be to usurp their function.[107] The rule is now regarded as a "matter of form rather than substance": *Stockwell*.[108] Nevertheless, the jury must be reminded that they are the decision-makers and are not bound by the opinion of the expert.

> Refusing to allow experts to express opinions on material questions reflects our fears that [the jury] will pay undue attention to those opinions. In effect we are saying that they may be overborne by the articulateness, the impressiveness of the jargon of the expert.[109]

It is a fear of the usurption of the jury's function which results in the rule preventing an expert from testifying as to whether an accused had the requisite mental state (e.g. intention or recklessness) at the time of the commission of the offence charged. This concern, and the general rule of relevance, also lies behind the prohibition on any witness (including an expert) testifying as to the credibility of any other witness (including the accused).[110]

Finally in relation to expert evidence, it is worth noting that the *Royal Commission on Criminal Justice* Cm. 2263 (1993) and the Law

Commission (*Report No 245 Evidence in Criminal Proceedings: Hearsay and Related Topics* (1997)) have both made recommendations which attempt to facilitate more reliable expert evidence which is not time-consumingly and confusingly contested at trial unless it is disputed.

From this detailed review of the current position, it would seem that a profile is the opinion[111] of an expert based on material gleaned from reports of other investigations, prosecutions and from reports of those convicted (self-reports). The mechanics of admissibility are being continually simplified by legislation.[112] Section 9 of the Criminal Justice Act 1967 permits any witness evidence, including the evidence of an expert, to be admitted subject to certain procedural formalities. Section 30 of the Criminal Justice Act 1988 renders expert reports admissible in criminal proceedings (with leave of the court required where the expert does not testify). Section 31 provides that "for the purpose of helping members of juries to understand complicated issues of fact or technical terms Crown Court rules make provision: (a) as to the furnishing of evidence in any form".[113]

Before such an opinion can be admitted as evidence, there are a number of other factors of which the criminal psychologist ought to be aware. These apply equally to expert opinion adduced by the defence or the prosecution.

Other Perils for the Expert Criminal Psychologist[114]

1. Transposing the Conditional

One of the gravest sins for the expert witness whose testimony contains statistical material is to transpose the conditional. This is lesson to be learnt from the use of expert evidence on DNA.[115] The courts have been so troubled by this that they have recently provided a model direction for trial judges to follow in cases involving DNA: *R v Doheny* (1996)

> Members of the jury, if you accept the scientific evidence called by the Crown, that indicates that there are probably only four or five white males in the United Kingdom from whom that semen stain could have come. The defendant is one of them. The decision you have to reach on all the evidence is whether you are sure that it was the defendant who left that stain or whether

it is possible that it was one of that other small group of men who share the same DNA characteristics.[116]

The dangerous process of reasoning is to take the statements relating to the *offender* and transpose them to the *accused*. If the compiler of a profile were permitted to testify, he could only venture an opinion as to the likelihood of the offender having a specific characteristic. Under no circumstances must the opinion relate to the likelihood of the accused being guilty because he has that characteristic.

The problem usually arises when it comes to questions being put to the witness in court.[117] There are two questions with a crucial distinction:

1. What is the probability that D's profile matches the sample profile, assuming he is innocent?
2. What is the probability that D is innocent assuming that his profile matches the sample profile?

The most famous example used to demonstrate the difference is by reference to a card game with the Archbishop. What is the probability of the Archbishop dealing himself a straight-flush if he is playing honestly? (Answer: 3/216,580) What is the probability of the Archbishop playing honestly is he has dealt himself a straight-flush? (Answer: depends on the assessment of this Archbishop's morality.)[118]

The expert can answer question 1, but the court is interested in the answers to question 2. The expert is not able to answer the second question: that is a matter for the jury. Whereas question 1 assumes the innocence of the accused (as is appropriate with the presumption of innocence in a criminal trial) and asks about the likelihood of an accurate match, question 2 assumes a match and asks about the likelihood of innocence. The fact that an answer to question 1 gives a very small statistical probability does not necessarily lead to a similarly small probability in answer to question 2. The prosecutor's fallacy, as it became known in DNA cases, is for the expert to give an answer to question 1 that purports to be an answer to question 2.

A related problem in which the courts have demonstrated an equally cautionary approach to statistics, recently came into the open for the first time in England.[119] This is the argument; that all issues in a criminal trial could be processed by the jury using a mathematical formula: Bayes theorem. The Court of Appeal's rejection of this theory demonstrates a clear reluctance to have the courtroom turned into a mathematics seminar.

This links in with the courts' long acknowledged worries about the use of scientific jargon by expert witnesses in general. Theories such as Bayes Theorem are ill suited to the criminal trial. The theorem requires that values for each item, "prior probabilities", be multiplied together to produce a final probability. In the recent case *R v Adams*,[120] figures were being suggested for items of evidence including "the likelihood that the perpetrator was a local man" and the "likelihood that the alibi evidence was true". It is obvious that no precise figure can be place on the accuracy of any such evidence. A further danger lies in attaching a numerical value to each item of evidence with a view to multiplying the values together to produce an overall probability. This hazardous assumption that each item of evidence is statistically independent is often labelled the "Kouskas fallacy". To take a well known example, in an armed robbery the offender drove a red sports car to escape and had a blond passenger. It is wrong to assume that the two facts were statistically independent and assign values to each to produce an overall probability: blondes may prefer red cars.

These types of objection could arise in the case of the criminal psychologist's work. Although there is no reported instance of a psychologist calculating the likelihood of an offender possessing a particular profile, there is always a danger that such a technique could be attempted in an effort to render the evidence more credible. Certainly where the evidence relates to the less-scientific evidence, the courts will object to the possibility that (as with Bayes Theorem) it could lead jurors to assume (falsely) that it was possible to represent the accuracy of an item of non-scientific evidence by a precise numerical value.

2. Hearsay

Any expert's testimony must be based upon facts which can themselves be proved by admissible evidence.[121]

> Before a court can assess the value of an opinion it must know the facts upon which it is based. If the expert has been misinformed about the facts or has taken irrelevant facts into consideration or has omitted to consider relevant ones, the opinion is likely to be valueless. In our judgment, counsel calling an expert should in examination-in-chief ask his witness to state the facts upon which his opinion is based.[122]

One of the major problems is to ensure that the facts upon which the opinion is based do not offend the rule against hearsay. The now accepted definition of hearsay is:

an assertion other than one made by a person while giving evidence in the proceedings, is inadmissible as evidence of any fact asserted.[123]

This unduly technical rule has taken on a logic of its own, and it would be inappropriate to do more than attempt the briefest of outlines here. The key problem to bear in mind is that even though the information (statements made by a person otherwise than while testifying) may be the most reliable and trustworthy source of information, it will still constitute hearsay if someone seeks to rely on it in court.[124] It is not possible to prove such material as "true", although the expert is permitted to rely upon the material to form his opinion.[125]

How does all this bear on the expert evidence of the criminal psychologist? Canter and Kirby recently wrote that "By working with records of convicted offenders it was thus possible to ensure that the evidence for the offence had been evaluated through the legal process before being incorporated into the research."[126] This may be true, but the information (assertions made by others) in the police records or documents is still hearsay! The hearsay rule is especially problematic in relation to all data collected by self-report. It matters not that the material for the report was compiled from police sources or even from the transcripts of an earlier trial.

Further problems are created by the technical possibility of counsel insisting on all who had a hand in the preparation of a report or profile attending as a witness. If A, B and C had been working on the collation of material and statistics, and only C gave evidence, it would be hearsay for C to report anything he had not witnessed with his own eyes. The work of A and B, if conducted independently could not be relied upon unless they testified. This could, at face value, render the profile inadmissible, but the Court of Appeal has recently acknowledged that a strict application of the rule would be unworkable. In *Jackson*,[127] it was accepted that there is a widespread practice of adducing Crown expert evidence without calling each of the technicians or others involved in the creation of the report: plainly this is with a view to saving costs on uncontroversial matters. The Law Commission's recommendations in

Report No. 245, *Evidence in Criminal Proceedings: Hearsay and Related Topics*[128] will, if enacted, reduce the opportunity for such pointless and time-consuming cross-examination of assistants.

The hearsay rule may be a hindrance to the expert, but it has not been allowed to create absurdity. It is well established that once the primary facts on which the expert's opinion is based have been proved by admissible evidence, the expert is entitled to draw on the work of others (i.e. published and unpublished works, articles and textbooks) as part of the process of drawing conclusions from those facts. For example, in the case of *Abadom*,[129] a forensic expert was able to refer to statistics collated by the Home Office Central Research Establishment in order to demonstrate that the refractive index of glass found in two samples was uncommon. The difficulty for the criminal psychologist is that while he will be allowed to refer to the works of others to form his opinion, that, say, the rapist resided in an area close to the attack, it will not be possible to probe the specific statistic as a fact unless he has conducted that research himself.

A much wider hearsay exception might well prove useful in many cases: section 24 of the 1988 Criminal Justice Act. This admits documents "created or received by a person in the course of a trade, business, profession or other occupation or as the holder of a paid or unpaid office; and [provided] all information contained in the document was supplied by a person (whether or not the maker of the document) who had, or who may reasonably be supposed to have had personal knowledge of the matters dealt with". There are many drafting deficiencies with the statute which could cause problems, but they lie beyond the scope of this chapter, and would be removed by the Law Commission's proposed reform.[130]

There is no requirement that the document form part of a record, nor that it be created by someone acting under a duty. Any work compiled by a criminal psychologist in the course of his business would be covered. The statement in the document will be admissible subject to the judge's discretion (under section 25 or 26) not to receive such evidence unless it is in the interests of justice to do so. The application of the section should apply to material such as the police records, which formed the basis of the Canter and Kirby study above.[131]

3. Computers

Computers are playing an increasingly important role[132] in the work of the criminal psychologist. In the USA, the famous VICAP programme of the FBI is the most prominent,[133] but there are many others including: the AIMS - Arson Information Management System; HALT - New York State's Homicide Assessment and Lead Tracking System; HITS - Michigan's Homicide Investigative Tracking System. Although it has been said that in the UK, "[a]ttempts to produce computerised 'M.O. indexes' at great expense [have] ... been found to be qualified failures",[134] there seems little doubt that computers will take on a greater role for the criminal psychologist here as in the USA.[135] The use of computers can be seen in a significant amount of the academic work published by criminal psychologists. Recent examples include the work of Canter on rape locations and on previous records of offenders.

Unfortunately, the rules of evidence include a provision which hinders reliance on computer generated material as evidence in a criminal trial. Section 69 of the Police and Criminal Evidence Act 1984 (PACE) requires that *all* computer evidence is admissible only where it has been shown that the computer(s) is/are, being operated properly and operating properly. Reliability may be proved by a written certificate (para 8 of Schedule 3), or, where required by the trial judge, by oral evidence (para 9 of Schedule 3). The s.69 requirements will be unnecessary where the other party consents to the admission of the evidence, but if, as in most reported cases, the issue is contested there will be a trial within a trial, where legal argument is conducted in the absence of the jury, to decide on admissibility. Furthermore, it was held in the case of *Cochrane*[136] that it is necessary to explain the function and working of the computer in all cases. The burden of proof always lies on the party wishing to adduce the computer evidence, and the normal criminal standard applies: beyond reasonable doubt for the prosecution, and on the balance of probabilities for the defence.

As if these undiscriminating requirements were not enough, there are many problems with the drafting of the section. Section 69(1)(b) is concerned with the accuracy of the contents of the computer evidence. Where there is an error in relation to an aspect of the information supplied to the computer, the whole will be admissible if the erroneous part has no bearing on the way the computer functions. Thus in *McKeown v D.P.P.;*

Jones v D.P.P.[137] the clock of an intoximeter (treated here as a computer) was operating incorrectly, yet the documentary evidence produced by that device was admissible because the accuracy of the clock had no bearing upon the accuracy of the alcohol reading. If a computer printout containing the information forming part of the criminal psychologist's expert evidence was incorrect, for example, as to the date, s.69 would not render the whole document inadmissible.

Numerous other difficulties have arisen because of the nature of computers. These include the difficulties of proving reliability where there is networking of machines. This problem has proved particularly acute where large mainframes are concerned (e.g. a bank mainframe or the police computer network). It may be difficult or even impossible to find anyone who can certify the reliability of such a complex system. As with any very complex piece of technology, it is not too difficult to raise such a doubt in the minds of the trier of fact. The effect of even the most scientifically reliable data can be severely damaged by counsel's suggestions about computer error.

One advantageous aspect of section 69 is that it applies *only* to documents *actually tendered*. In *Sophocleus v Ringer*[138] the Divisional Court held that s.69 was "wholly reserved to cases in which the prosecution choose to put before the justices, without any other evidence attached to it, a computer record or document which contains some statement". Thus where, in *Golizadeh*[139] an expert relied on evidence which has been prepared with the assistance of computers which were not subjected to s.69 scrutiny, but has not actually adduced the computer printout as evidence, the expert's opinion will be admitted.[140]

Finally it must be noted that this position may not be around to trouble the criminal profilers for too much longer. In Report No.245, *Evidence in Criminal Proceedings: Hearsay and Related Topics* (1997) the Law Commission's recommendation is to repeal s.69.

Exclusionary Discretion

Even if the profile(r) has jumped all these hurdles, there is still the chance that the court will exclude the evidence under its general discretion. Exclusion would be most likely to occur under this head by virtue of section 78 of PACE:

In any proceedings the court may refuse to allow evidence on which the prosecution proposes to rely to be given if it appears to the court that, having regard to all the circumstances, including the circumstances in which the evidence was obtained, the admission of the evidence would have such an adverse effect on the fairness of the proceedings that the court ought not to admit it.

Section 78 focuses on unfairness in the proceedings as the criterion for exclusion.

This can include the way in which the evidence was obtained. Unfairness in the gathering of evidence could have a "knock-on" effect on the fairness of the trial. The central ruling in Stagg was that the evidence obtained by the undercover police operation would have such an adverse effect upon the fairness of the proceedings as to require its exclusion.

Ognall J reviewed the law in this area, and in particular a number of recent decisions relating evidence obtained as a result of police "entrapment".[141] The principles to be derived from the earlier cases are concerned mainly with the question of whether the police have tricked the defendant. These principles are unlikely to arise in properly conducted profiles.[142] One other principle which can be derived from the recent case law is more worthy of note, this is the fact that "public policy is in favour of the proposition that the more serious the offence, the more unusual form of investigation may be justified."[143] Since it is widely claimed that criminal profiles can generally be compiled only in relation to serious crimes, this principle is unlikely to represent a hindrance to the use of profile evidence. In the most recent pronouncement, *Latif*,[144] the House of Lords once again drew attention to this with an instruction to judges to:

weigh in the balance the public interest in ensuring that those that are charged with grave crimes should be tried and the competing public interest in not conveying the impression that the court will adopt the approach that the end justifies the means.[145]

Would Evidence of the Criminal Psychologist Ever Be Received

There are three possible situations in which the potential for a court to receive a criminal psychologist's opinion evidence deserves special consideration.

1. Similar Fact Cases

In cases in which the prosecution seek to prove the identity of the offender by similar fact evidence, it might be appropriate for a criminal psychologist to testify. As discussed above, there are two distinct approaches to the proof of identity by similar facts: cumulative and sequential. In both approaches it is vital that the court is satisfied that the two acts (usually crimes) are the work of the same offender. It is submitted that there would be nothing to stop a criminal psychologist testifying as to how similar two offences are in his opinion. Normally, there would be no need to hear evidence as to the degree of similarity since it would be something which the jury could itself perceive. However, in some cases, it would be useful for the court to hear precisely how peculiar is a particular *modus operandi*. The jury could then assess how likely it would be that the offences were committed in such a peculiar way by different people. If satisfied that the offences were the work of the same person they would be able to apply either the cumulative or sequential line of reasoning as appropriate. There is some judicial support for such evidence. In *R v Mullen*[146] evidence was received of the statistical fact that notionally, only 13 burglars used a blow torch to crack the glass windows to effect entry.[147] The criminal psychologist would simply be using his expertise to draw more clearly to the attention of the court, the particular aspects of the crime(s) in question. Care must be taken here since it will not be possible for an expert to testify that, for example, the offence in question is a "classic sadistic rape". The courts would not be prepared to accept such expert evidence unless satisfied that the classification system used was sufficiently precise and reliable. What will be permitted is evidence highlighting similarities or, for that matter discrepancies between the offences. In the Canadian case of *R v Mohan*, the Supreme Court accepted that a "psychiatrist's testimony was admissible to show that the offences alleged were *unlikely* to have been committed by the same person".[148]

2. As Evidence in Support of the Defence

It is not difficult to conceive of a case in which an accused wishes to rely upon a profile in an attempt to raise reasonable doubt as to his guilt. The right of the accused to meet the charge against him by all legitimate means is "fundamental to the administration of criminal justice."[149] Colin Stagg, had the case gone to full trial, would certainly have sought to introduce evidence from a criminal psychologist to rebut the prosecution profile. Specifically, the accused would wish first to identify aspects of the profile of the offender, and second to draw attention to this own personality and its incompatibility with the profile. In both instances there would be problems of admissibility.

First, the psychologist's evidence as to what constitutes a profile of the *offender* will be unlikely to be admissible for the many reasons already considered. Secondly, the psychologist's comments as to the *accused's* character would also be likely to be excluded. In so far as such evidence related to the accused's mental state, it would be inadmissible unless the accused were abnormal (thus beyond the jury's understanding and experience). Thus, in the Canadian case of *R v Mohan*,[150] the Supreme Court upheld the trial judge's decision to exclude profile evidence on which the accused proposed to rely. The charge was one of sexual assault on young women, and the evidence of the profiler was that a typical offender in such cases would be a paedophile and that the accused was not. Sopinka J stated that "such [e]vidence of an expert witness that the accused by reason of his or her mental make-up or condition of the mind, would be incapable of committing or disposed to commit the crime would be inadmisssible".[151]

A more fundamental objection to the testimony on the accused's character is that the decision in *R v Rowton*[152] forbids the accused calling evidence of particular acts or witnesses' opinions at to *his disposition*. The accused may bring only evidence of his general reputation in the neighbourhood. Thus, if an accused is charged with a homosexual offence, this rule prevents him calling specific evidence of his heterosexuality by reference to particular incidents or by calling his female partner(s).[153] To take a further example, the rule would, if applied strictly, prevent an accused on trial for gross indecency calling a psychologist to testify that he had examined the accused and found him to be a heterosexual with a marked intolerance to homosexuality.[154] The rule seems unduly harsh and impractical, but as one commentator observes "[th]ere would appear to be five reasons for limiting evidence as to character, namely, that such evidence (a) is easy to fabricate; (b) is often irrelevant; (c) may lead to the investigation of side issues of little relevance to the case; (d) amounts frequently to evidence of opinion which is generally excluded; and (e) may create a risk that the function of the jury will be usurped".[155] The rule in *Rowton*, despite being cogently criticised,[156] still represents the law. It would prohibit an accused from relying upon a psychological profile, or any part thereof, which related to his particular disposition. It is only avoided in practice, in cases in which the courts show particular "indulgence" to an accused.[157]

Finally, it should be noted here that there is a common law rule which would prohibit a witness testifying as to the credibility of any other witnesses, including the accused.[158]

Where One of Two Accused Must Have Done It

When one defendant wishes to draw upon a profile to show that he is less likely to have committed the offence than a co-accused things become more difficult. In any case involving multiple accused, the rules of evidence have to applied with much more care.

One case which presents particular difficulty here is the decision of the Privy Council in *Lowery v R*.[159] In that case one accused, K, was permitted to adduce psychological opinion evidence to establish that he was less likely than L, his co-accused, to have committed the horrific murder with which the two were charged. This case might be taken to lend support for the use of defence profile evidence. However, there are a number of reasons why it is submitted that *Lowery* should not be held to support such a proposition. First, the case has been distinguished as being "decided on special facts".[160] The Privy Council stressed that the evidence was not being received as evidence of criminal tendency. Lord Morris of Borthy-Gest stated that the evidence "was not related to crime or criminal tendencies: it was scientific evidence as to the respective personalities of the two accused".[161] Second, as Thornton has pointed out "it may also be a decision which was fashioned by the peculiar jurisdiction of the Privy Council in which a conviction will not be quashed unless the court concludes that there is a serious likelihood of a miscarriage of justice".[162] Third, the evidence was only admitted to rebut the specific allegations of the co-accused.[163] Finally, the victim in *Lowery* was definitely killed by one of the accused (or both), and both had been subjected to the same psychological examination. The facts are very different from a situation in which a profile seeks to identify the killer from the population at large, or even to distinguish the accused from a general type of person capable of committing the crime.

In a situation such as this the court *might* be prepared to accept the profile evidence of the criminal psychologist, thought the words of Lawton L.J. in *R v Turner* (rejecting *Lowery*) should not be ignored:

> We do not consider that [Lowery] is an authority for the proposition that in all cases psychologists and psychiatrists can be called to prove the probability of the accused's veracity. If any such rule was applied in our courts, trial by psychiatrists would be likely to take the place of trial by jury... We do not find that prospect attractive and the law does not at present provide for it.[164]

There are a number of these cases where one accused has sought to introduce evidence of the propensity of a co-accused to commit the offence with which they are both charged. The central question will be one of relevance and, as Devlin J noted in *Miller*,[165] "the character of the accused is no more relevant at the hands of a co-accused than it is at the hands of the prosecution". The question of relevance takes on a more prominent role in the cases involving the co-accused because, the court has no discretion to exclude evidence of a defendant as it does when the prosecution seek to rely on such evidence. The courts are therefore more likely to rule the evidence inadmissible on grounds of relevance.[166] *R v Neale*[167] provides a good example. N was charged with arson and sought to support his defence that he was not a participant to the attack by adducing evidence that his co-accused, B, was a known fire-raiser. This was held to be insufficiently relevant, since it did not prove that B had started this fire alone. The court interpreted *Miller*, as requiring as strict a test of relevance to defence evidence as prosecution evidence in these cases. This strict attitude is also apparent in a number of other cases,[168] but it has been doubted by academic commentators whether there ought to be such a rigid application of relevance.[169]

A more complicated scenario is one in which D is on trial for an offence, and a third person, has also been investigated by the police but not charged. The decision in *R v Blastland*[170] discussed above provides an example. If the third party, Mark, fitted a profile prepared for he police, could Blastland have relied upon it to support his claim that Mark was the murderer? The case is very easily distinguishable from *Lowery* on the basis that Mark is not a co-accused; he is not on trial. On the other hand it would bear similarity to *Lowery* provided the criminal psychologist had compared the profile to both the two people investigated. Returning to first principles of evidence, there can be no question of prejudice rendering the evidence inadmissible. Furthermore, the rule in *R v Rowton* and other exclusionary rules would appear not to apply. Thus the sole question would be one of relevance. The question can be posed as follows: Does the fact that an expert witness is of the opinion that a specific person other than the accused is more likely to be the perpetrator make it more (or less) likely that the accused committed the crime? It is submitted that, subject to the arguments about reliability above, the evidence is logically relevant. However, given the courts' recent strict approach to legal relevance,[171] the acceptance of such an opinion is by no means beyond doubt. In particular, the court would be wary of the numerous side issues which would arise. Even here it is doubtful that the criminal psychologist will have his day in court.

Conclusion

In *Stagg*, Ognall J made broad and perhaps unnecessary statements doubting the admissibility of psychological profile evidence in the English criminal trial. A detailed review of the rules of evidence suggests that his lordship was right to sound this more of discouragement to those traditionally involved in the investigation and prosecution of crime and to criminal psychologists who might be persuaded to become involved in any such prosecution.

The prosecutor seeking to rely on a profile (if such a thing exists) or even part of a profile will have to navigate his way through practically all of the most difficult rules of the law of evidence. The most fundamental and primary question of what relevance a profile has to the facts in issue may well be as far the legal argument gets before being rejected. This rule of relevance, although not expressly tackled by Ognall J in *Stagg*, also underpins the further difficulties facing the prosecutor: rules against the admissibility of highly prejudicial similar fact evidence, and against admitting the opinion evidence of an expert on so controversial a subject. The rules of evidence are clearly stacked against the admissibility of this material except in very rare cases. The legal argument would be equally foreboding in the case of a defence application to admit such evidence.

The rules of evidence also present difficulties for the criminal psychologist. If involved in the presentation of the case the criminal psychologist will have to face extensive questioning as to his expertise, the reliability of his methodology and working practices, the availability of alternative methodologies and their success rates. There would also be the inevitably detailed and testing questions in the light of evidence provided by the opposing party's own criminal psychologist who will have cast doubt on the methodology, the interpretations etc. In addition, the psychologist will have been constrained by the evidential rules even before setting foot in court. The hearsay rule will inhibit reliance on data even though it may be the most reliable available, the provisions of the Police and Criminal Evidence Act 1984 will also necessitate the proof of computer reliability.

In the case of a prosecution profile, the story does not end there. In the event that all of these problems are overcome by both the psychologist and the prosecutor, the court may still exclude the evidence, in its discretion, on the ground that it would be unfair to the accused.

It will be most unlikely that counsel can persuade the court of the relevance of this potentially highly prejudicial opinion. If it should happen, the opinion evidence of the psychologist will be admitted as mere circumstantial evidence. Admittedly, there is no rule preventing a conviction based on circumstantial evidence alone,[172] but in view of all the hazards addressed above, one question then has to be asked: was it worth it? Perhaps Ognall J saved the criminal psychologists considerable strife with his suggestion that they limit their activities to helping the police with the investigation.

On a more positive note, one of the aims stated above was to explain the rules of evidence to the psychologist, but there is also a clear need for judicial training so as to be aware of progress in science and other fields of expertise.[173]

Psychologists and other behavioural scientists might be more usefully employed outside the witness box, assisting, not only in the earlier stages of criminal investigation and prosecution, but also in the training of lawyers and judges. This might at least ensure that not too much would be expected of them in court.[174]

Index of Abbreviations Used

The style of citation adopted in this chapter is an orthodox one which will be familiar to lawyers. For a complete guide, non-legal readers are referred to Raistrick, D., *Index to Legal Citations and Abbreviations*. 2nd ed, 1993, Bowker-Saur: London. The following is a list of the more common abbreviations used:

A.C.	*Appeal Cases (Law Reports)*
All E.R.	*All England Law Reports*
C.L.J.	*Cambridge Law Journal*
Cr. App. R.	*Criminal Appeal Reports*
Crim. L.Q.	*Criminal Law Quarterly*
Crim. L.R.	*Criminal Law Review*
D.L.R.	*Dominion Law Reports*
Harv. L.R.	*Harvard Law Review*
J. For. Sci. Soc.	*Journal of the Forensic Science Society*
L.Ed	*Lawyer's Edition, United States Supreme Court Reports*
L.Q.R.	*Law Quarterly Review*
L.S.	*Legal Studies*
L.T.	*Law Times*
M.L.R.	*Modern Law Review*
Med. Sci. Law	*Medicine Science and the Law*
N.L.J.	*New Law Journal*
O.J.L.S.	*Oxford Journal of Legal Studies*
Q.B.	*Queen's Bench (Law Reports)*
R.T.R.	*Road Traffic Reports*
S.C.R.	*Supreme Court Reports (Canada)*
V.R.	*Law Reports of Victoria (Australia)*
W.L.R.	*Weekly Law Reports*

Bibliography

Allan, T.R.S. (1988). Some favourite fallacies about similar facts. 8 *L.S.* 35.

Alldridge, P. (1992). Recognizing Novel Scientific Techniques: DNA as a test case. *Crim L.R.* 687.

Allen, R.J. (1994). Expertise and the *Daubert* Decision. 84(4) *J. Crim Law and Criminology* 1157.

Andrews, J.A. and Hirst, M. (1992). *Criminal Evidence* (2nd ed) London: Sweet and Maxwell.

Ashworth, A. (1980). The Binding Effect of Crown Court Decisions. *Crim. L.R.* 402.

Badcock, R. (1997). Developmental and Clinical Issues in Relation to Offending in the Individual. In J.L. Jackson and D.A. Bekerian (eds) *Offender Profiling: Theory, Research and Practice*. Chichester, UK: Wiley.

Balding, D.J. and Donnelly, P. (1994). The Prosecutor's Fallacy and DNA Evidence. *Crim. L.R.* 711.

Bernstein, D.E. (1996). Junk Science in the United States and the Commonwealth. 21 *Yale Journal of International Law* 123.

Bessner, R. (1987-88). The Admissibility of Novel Scientific Techniques in Criminal Trials: Voice Spectroscopy 30 *Crim. L.Q.* 294.

Birch, D.J. (1987). Hearsay-logic and hearsay-fiddles: *Blastland* revisited. in P.F. Smith (ed) *Criminal law: Essays in Honour of J.C. Smith*. London: Butterworths.

Boon, J.C.W. (1997). The Contribution of Personality Theories to Psychological Profiling. In J.L. Jackson and D.A. Bekerian (eds) *Offender Profiling: Theory, Research and Practice*. Chichester, UK: Wiley.

Boon, J. and Davies, G. (1993). Criminal Profiling. *Policing* 218.

Britton, P. (1997). *The Jigsaw Man*. London: Bantam Press.

Canter, D. (1994). *Criminal Shadows*. London: Harper Collins.

Canter, D. and Kirby, S. (1995). Prior Convictions of Child Molesters. *Science and Justice* 73.

Canter, D. and Gregory, A. (1994) Identifying the residential location of rapists. 34(3) *J. For. Sci. Soc.* 169.

Carson, D. (1990). *Professionals and the Courts: A Handbook for Expert Witnesses*. Birmingham: Venture Press.

Carson, D. (1992). Expert Evidence in the Courts. 1 *Expert Evidence* 13.

Carter, P.B. (1987). Hearsay, relevance and admissibility: declarations as to state of mind and declarations against penal interest. 103 *L.Q.R.* 106.

Cellmark Diagnostics (1993). 143 *N.L.J.* 1596.

Choo, A.L.-T. (1993). The Notion of Relevance and Defence Evidence. *Crim. L.R.* 114.

Clapham, B. (1981). Introducing Psychological Evidence in the Courts: Impediments and Opportunities. in S.M.A. Lloyd-Bostock (ed) *Psychology in Legal Contexts*. London: Macmillan.

Cleary, E.W. (1984). *McCormick on Evidence* (3rd ed) West: St Paul.

Confronting the New Challenges of Scientific Evidence (1995). 108 *Harv. L.R.* 1481-1605.

Cowen. Z. and Carter, P.B. (1956). *Essays in the Law of Evidence.* Oxford: Clarendon.

Cross, R. (1975). Fourth time lucky - similar fact evidence in the House of Lords. *Crim L.R.* 62.

Davies, A. (1994). Editorial: Offender Profiling. 34(3) *Med. Sci. and Law* 185.

Davies, A. (1997). Specific Profile Analysis: A Data-based Approach to Offender Profiling. in J.L. Jackson and D.A. Bekerian (eds) *Offender Profiling: Theory, Research and Practice.* Chichester, UK: Wiley.

Davies, A. and Dale, A. (1996). Locating the Stranger Rapist. *Med. Sci. Law* 146

Diagnostic and Statistical Manual of Mental Disorder, 4th ed, (1994) American Psychiatric Association: Washington DC.

Douglas, J.E., Burgess, A.W., Burgess, A.G. and Ressler, R.K. (1992). *Crime Classification Manual.* New York: Lexington.

Douglas, J.E., Ressler, R.K., Burgess, A.W. and Hartman, C.R. (1986). Criminal Profiling from Crime Scene Analysis. 4(4) *Behavioural Sciences and the Law* 401.

Editorial Introduction. (1992). Some Legal Issues Affecting Novel Firms of Expert Evidence. 1 *Expert Evidence* 79.

Edmond, G. and Mercer, D. (1997). Recognising Daubert. What judges need to know about falsificationism. *Expert Evidence* 29.

Eggleston, R. (1983) *Evidence, Proof and Probability* (2nd ed). London: Weidenfield.

Farrington, D.P. and Lambert, S. (1997). Predicting Offender Profiles from Victims and Witness Descriptions. in J.L. Jackson and D.A. Bekerian (eds) *Offender Profiling: Theory, Research and Practice.* Chichester, UK: Wiley.

Farrington, L. (1993). Unacceptable Evidence. 143 *N.L.J.* 806.

Freckleton, I.R. (1987). *The Trial of the Expert: A Study of Expert Evidence and Forensic Experts.* Melbourne: OUP.

Giannelli, P.C. (1980). The Admissibility of Novel Scientific Evidence: *Frye v United States,* a Half Century Later. 80 *Columbia Law Rev.* 1197.

Gill, P. and Fedor, T. (1993). DNA Profiling: Is It Reliable? *Sol. J* 3 Dec 26.

Goldring, S.L. (1992). Increasing the reliability, validity and relevance of psychological expert evidence; An introduction to the special issue on expert evidence. 16 *Law and Human Behaviour* 253.

Grubin, D. (1995). Offender Profiling. 6(2) *Journal of Forensic Psychiatry* 259.

Gudjonsson, G.H. (1993). The Implications of Poor Psychological Evidence in Court. 2(3) *Expert Evidence* 120.

Gudjonsson, G.H. and Copson, G. (1997). The Role of the Expert in the Criminal Investigation. in J.L. Jackson and D.A. Bekerian (eds) *Offender Profiling: Theory, Research and Practice.* Chichester, UK: Wiley.

Harmon, R.P. (1993). Legal Criticisms of DNA Typing: Where's the Beef? 84 *J. Crim. Law and Criminology.*

Haward, L.R.C. (1964). A Psychologist's Contribution to Legal Procedure. 27 *M.L.R.* 656.

Haward, L.R.C. (1979). The Psychologist as Expert Witness. in D.P. Farrington, K. Hawkins and S.M.A. Lloyd-Bostock (eds) *Psychology, Law and Legal Process.* London: MacMillan.

Hazelwood, R.R. and Douglas, J.E. (1983). The lust murderer. 49(4) *FBI Law Enforcement Bulletin* 18.

Higgins, M. (1997). Looking the Part. *American Bar Association Journal.* p.48.

Hodgkinson, T. (1990). *Expert Evidence: Law and Practice.* London: Sweet and Maxwell.

Hoffman, L. (1975). Similar facts after *Boardman.* 91 *L.Q.R.* 193.

Holmes, R.M. and Holmes, S.M. (1996). *Profiling Violent Crimes: an investigative tool.* New York: Sage Publications.

House, J.C. (1997). Towards a Practical Application of Offender Profiling: the RNC's Criminal Suspect Prioritization System. in J.L. Jackson and D.A. Bekerian (eds) *Offender Profiling: Theory, Research and Practice.* Chichester, UK: Wiley.

Howard, M.N. (1991). The Neutral Expert: A Plausible Threat to Justice. *Crim. L.R.* 98.

Jackson, J.D. (1984). The Ultimate Issue Rule: One rule too many. *Crim. L.R.* 74.

Jackson, J.L. and Bekerian, D.A. (1997). Does Offender Profiling Have a Role to Play? in J.L. Jackson and D.A. Bekerian (eds) *Offender Profiling: Theory, Research and Practice.* Chichester, UK: Wiley.

Jackson, J.L., van den Eshof, P. and de Kleuver, E.E. (1997). A Research Approach to Offender Profiling. in J.L. Jackson and D.A. Bekerian (eds) *Offender Profiling: Theory, Research and Practice.* Chichester, UK: Wiley.

Jones, C.A.G. (1994). *Expert Witnesses: Science, Medicine and the Practice of Law.* Oxford: Clarendon Press.

Kenny, A. (1983). The Expert in Court. 99 *L.Q.R.* 197.

Law Commission, report No.245. (1997). *Evidence in Criminal Proceedings: Hearsay and Related Topics.* London: H.M.S.O.

Law Commission Consultation Paper No.141. (1996). *Evidence in Criminal Proceedings: Previous Misconduct of a Defendant.* London: H.M.S.O.

Lawton, F. (1980). The Limitations of Expert Scientific Evidence. 20 *J. For. Sci. Soc.* 237.

Mackay, R.D. and Colman, A.M. (1996). Equivocal Rulings on Expert Psychological and Psychiatric Evidence: Turning a Muddle into a Nonsense. *Crim. L.R.* 88.

Mair, K. (1995). Can profile prove a sex offender guilty? *Expert Evidence* 139.

May, R. (1995). *Criminal Evidence* (3rd ed). London: Sweet and Maxwell.

McCann, J. (1992). Criminal Personality Profiling in the Investigation of Violent Crime. 10 *Behavioural Sciences and the Law* 475.

McEwan, J. (1994). 'Similar Fact' Evidence and Psychology: Personality and Guilt. *Expert Evidence* 113.

McEwan, J. (1992). *Evidence and the Adversarial Process: The Modern Law.* London: Blackwell.

McLeod, N. (1991). English DNA Evidence Held Inadmissible. *Crim. L.R.* 58.

Mewett, A.W. (1984). Character as a Fact in Issue in Criminal Cases. 27 *Crim. Law Q.* 29.

Mirfield, P. (1987). Similar facts - *Makin' Out. C.L.J.* 83.

Monahan, J, and Walker, L. (1990). *Social Science in Law; Cases and Materials* (2nd ed) Foundation Press: New York.

Nair, R. (1993). Similar Fact Evidence - prejudice and irrelevance. *Crim. L.R.* 432.

Neufeld, P.J. (1993). Have You No Sense of Decency. 84 *J. Crim. Law and Criminology* 863.

Oldfield, D. (1997). What Help Do the Police Need with their Enquiries? in J.L. Jackson and D.A. Bekerian (eds) *Offender Profiling: Theory, Research and Practice.* Chichester, UK: Wiley.

Ormerod, D.C. (1996). The Evidential Implications of Psychological Profiling. *Crim. L.R.* 863.

Pattenden, R. (1986). Conflicting Approaches to Psychiatric Evidence in Criminal Trials: England, Canada and Australia. *Crim L.R.* 92.

Pinizzotto, A.J. (1984). Forensic Psychology: Criminal Personality Profiling. 12(1) *Journal of Police Science and Administration* 32.

Pinizzotto, A.J. and Finkel, N.J. (1990). Criminal Personality Profiling: An Outcome and Process Study. *Law and Human Behaviour* 215.

Porter, B. (1993). Mind Hunters. *Psychology Today* (April) 44.

Redmayne, M (1995). Doubts and Burdens: DNA Evidence, Probability and the Courts. *Crim. L.R.* 464.

Redmayne, M. (1996). Science, Evidence and Logic. *M.L.R.* 747.

Report of the Royal Commission on Criminal Justice (1993). Cmnd.2263 London: H.M.S.O.

Ressler, R.K., Burgess, A.W. and Douglas, J.E. (1988). *Sexual Homicide: Patterns and Motives.* New York: Lexington.

Roberts, P. (1996). Will You Stand Up In Court? On the Admissibility of Psychiatric and Psychological Evidence. *J. For. Psy.* 63.

Robertson, B. and Vignaux, G.A. (1993). Probability - The Law of Logic. 13 *O.J.L.S.* 457.

Robertson, B., Vignaux, G.A. and Egerton, I. (1994). Stylometric Evidence. *Crim. L.R.* 645.

Robertson, B., Vignaux, G.A. and Egerton, I. (1995). *Interpreting Evidence: Evaluating Forensic Science in the Courtroom.* Chichester, UK: Wiley.

Rossmo, D.K. (1997). Geographic Profiling. in J.L. Jackson and D.A. Bekerian (eds) *Offender Profiling: Theory, Research and Practice.* Chichester, UK: Wiley.

Sheldon, D.H. and MacLeod, M.D. (1991). From Normative to Positive Data: Expert Psychological Evidence Re-Examined. *Crim. L.R.* 811.

Slovenko, R. (1993). Expert Testimony: Use and Abuse. 12 *Med. and Law* 627.

Smith, C. (1993). Psychological Offender Profiling. *The Criminologist* 244.

Smith, J.C. (1995). *Criminal Evidence.* London: Sweet and Maxwell.

Spencer, J.R. (1991). The Neutral Expert: An Implausible Bogey. *Crim. L.R.* 106.

Stephen, J.F.J. (1948). *Digest of Law of Evidence.* (12th ed). London: MacMillan.

Stevens, J.A. (1997). Standard Investigatory Tools and Offender Profiling. in J.L. Jackson and D.A. Bekerian (eds) *Offender Profiling: Theory, Research and Practice.* Chichester, UK: Wiley.

Tapper, C. (1995). *Cross and Tapper on Evidence* (8th ed). London: Butterworths.

Thompson, W.C. (1993). Evaluating the Admissibility of New Genetic Identification Tests: Lessons from the 'DNA Wars'. 84 *J. Crim. Law and Criminology* 22.

Thornton, P. (1995). The Admissibility of Expert Psychiatric and Psychological Evidence: Judicial Training. 35 *Med. Sci. Law* 143.

Turco, R.N. (1990). Psychological Profiling. *International Journal of Offender Therapy and Comparative Criminology* 147.

Vorpagel, R.E. (1982). Painting Psychological Profiles: Charlatanism, Coincidence, Charisma, Chance or a New Science. *The Police Chief* 157.

Wigmore, J.H. (1983 rev.). *Evidence in Trials at Common Law (Vol 1A).* Tillers, P.

Wolbert, A. (ed) (1985). *Rape and Sexual Assault A Research Handbook.* Garland: New York.

Young, S.J. (1991). DNA Evidence - Beyond Reasonable Doubt? *Crim. L.R.* 264.

Zuckerman, A.A.S. (1987). Similar fact evidence - the unobservable rule. 104 *L.Q.R.* 187.

Zuckerman, A.A.S. (1989). *Principles of Criminal Evidence.* Oxford: Clarendon.

Zuckerman, A.A.S. (1992). Miscarriage of Justice: A Root Treatment. *Crim. L.R.* 323.

Notes

[1] I am grateful to Ms T.K. Baxter for her excellent research assistance.

²   (1994) Central Criminal Court 14th September. See Grubin, D., "Offender Profiling" (1995) 6(2) *Journal of Forensic Psychiatry* 259. See also Britton, P., *The Jigsaw Man* (1997) Bantam Press: London.

³   Transcript p.29.

⁴   *Ibid.*

⁵   See further Ashworth, A., "The Binding Effect of Crown Court Decisions" [1980] Crim. L.R. 402.

⁶   Mark Stephens, leading criminal solicitor, quoted in *The Independent on Sunday* 18 September 1994 p.15.

⁷   See Ormerod, D.C., "The Evidential Implications of Psychological Profiling" [1996] Crim. L.R. 863. This chapter draws upon and develops many of the issues raised therein.

⁸   See Holmes, R.M., and Holmes, S.M., *Profiling Violent Crimes: an investigative tool.* (1996) Sage Publications: New York, Ch.2.

⁹   See the discussions of the famous Brussel profile of the Mad Bomber of New York: Porter, B., "Mind Hunters" (1993) (April) Psychology Today 44, p.46; Boon, J., and Davies, G., "Criminal Profiling" (1993) Policing 218.

¹⁰ Vorpagel, R.E., "Painting Psychological Profiles: Charlatanism, Coincidence, Charisma, Chance or a New Science" (1982) The Police Chief 157, p.159.

¹¹ Canter, D., *Criminal Shadows* (1994) Harper Collins: London, Ch.2. See pp. 84-87 in Stevens, J.A. (1997) Standard Investigatory Tools and Offender Profiling. in Jackson, J.L. and Bekerian, D.A. (eds) *Offender Profiling: Theory, Research and Practice.* Wiley: Chichester, UK.

¹² As tabulated in Smith, C., "Psychological Offender Profiling" (1993) The Criminologist 244. See also Canter, D., *op cit.* n11.

¹³ Canter, *op cit.* n11, p.65; Pinizzotto, A.J., "Forensic Psychology: Criminal Personality Profiling" (1984) 12(1) Journal of Police Science and Administration 32, p.39.; Boon J., and Davies, G., *op cit.* n9, p.224. Many different methods of profiling have been described. See McCann, J., "Criminal Personality Profiling in the Investigation of Violent Crime" (1992) 10 Behavioural Sciences and the Law 475, p.478; Turco, R.N., "Psychological Profiling" (1990) International Journal of Offender Therapy and Comparative Criminology 147 and Holmes and Holmes, *op cit.* n8, Ch.3.

¹⁴ Vorpagel, *op cit.* n10, p.156.

¹⁵ See Tapper C., *Cross and Tapper on Evidence* (8th ed 1995) Butterworths: London, p.56; Stephen, J.F.J., *Digest of Law of Evidence* (12 ed 1948) MacMillan: London, Art 1. See also *R v Kilbourne* [1973] A.C. 729 "...relevant (i.e. logical probative or disprobative) evidence is evidence which makes the matter which requires proof more of less probable" *per* Lord Simon of Glaisdale, p.756.

¹⁶ *Agassiz v London Tramway Co.* (1872) 27 L.T. 492.

17 Such a claim is doubted by Canter, *op cit.* n11, p.188.
18 [1986] A.C. 41. See also *R v Kearley* [1992] 2 A.C. 228; Choo, A. L.-T., "The Notion of Relevance and Defence Evidence" [1993] Crim. L.R. 114.
19 [1986] A.C. 41, 54.
20 See further, Birch, D.J., "Hearsay-logic and hearsay-fiddles: *Blastland* revisited" in P.F. Smith (ed) *Criminal law: Essays in Honour of J.C. Smith* (1987) Butterworths: London; Carter, P.B., "Hearsay, relevance and admissibility: declarations as to state of mind and declarations against penal interest" (1987) 103 L.Q.R 106.
21 Choo, A.L.-T., *op cit.* n18. A very detailed examination of the concept of evidence) Wigmore, J.H., *Evidence in Trials at Common Law (Vol 1A)*, Tillers, P., (1983 rev).
22 *Principles of Criminal Evidence* (1989 Clarendon: Oxford, p.49.
23 For a fascinating discussion of the relationship between these concepts see Eggleston, R., *Evidence, Proof and Probability* (2nd ed 1983) London: Weidenfield.
24 Cleary, E.W., *McCormick on Evidence* (3rd ed 1984) West: St Paul, p.542.
25 This provides an example of the exclusionary approach implicit in the question of relevance. If the defence sought to adduce the evidence and were denied, this would raise the issues Choo considers *op cit.* n18.
26 [1994] 2 S.C.R. 9.
27 At p.38.
28 Sheldon, D.H., and MacLeod, M.D., "From Normative to Positive Data: Expert Psychological Evidence Re-Examined" [1991] Crim. L.R. 811, p.815.
29 In the absence of the jury at a *"voir dire"*.
30 Pinizzotto, A.J., and Finkel, N.J., "Criminal Personality Profiling: An Outcome and Process Study" (1990) 14 (3) Law and Human Behaviour 215, p.230.
31 This is an extremely controversial area with a wealth of literature including: Hoffman, L., "Similar facts after *Boardman*" (1975) 91 L.Q.R. 193; Cross, R., "Fourth time lucky - similar fact evidence in the House of Lords" [1975] Crim. L.R 62; Zuckerman, A.A.S., "Similar fact evidence - the unobservable rule" (1987) 104 L.Q.R. 187; Mirfield, P., "Similar facts - *Makin'* Out?" [1987] C.L.J. 83; Allan, T.R.S., "Some favourite fallacies about similar facts" (1988) 8 L.S. 35; Nair, R., "Similar Fact Evidence - prejudice and irrelevance" [1993] Crim. L.R. 432; McEwan, J., *Evidence and the Adversarial Process: The Modern Law* (1992) Blackwell: London.
32 See *R v Straffen* [1952] 1 Q.B. 911. For an interesting account of the rule and it's relationship with probability see Eggleston *op cit.* n23, Ch.7.
33 See Law Commission Consultation Paper No.141 *Evidence in Criminal Proceedings: Previous Misconduct of a Defendant* (1996) H.M.S.O: London

and the *Report of the Royal Commission on Criminal Justice* (1993) Cmnd. 2263 H.M.S.O.: London which described this rule as "difficult to comprehend embodied as it is in a series of judgements that are not always readily reconcilable". Chapter 8 para 30.

[34] Law Commission Consultation Paper No. 141, para 9.92.

[35] "The more revolting the suggestion, the more the jury may be likely to lose sight of the fact that it may not be true." Cowen, Z., and Carter, P.B., *Essays in the Law of Evidence* (1956) Clarendon: Oxford p.146.

[36] Porter, B., *op cit.* n9, p.45; Holmes and Holmes, *op cit.* n8, p.2; McEwan., "'Similar Fact' Evidence and Psychology: Personality and Guilt" (1994) Expert Evidence 113. See also Pinizzotto, *op cit.* n13, p.33; Smith, *op cit.* n12, p.249; Davies, A., "Editorial: Offender Profiling" 91994) 34(3) Med. Sci. Law 185.

[37] See McEwan, *op cit.* n36. See also Pinizzotto, *op cit.* n13; p.33; Smith, *op cit.* n12, p.249; Davies, A., "Editorial: Offender Profiling" (1994) 34(3) Med. Sci. Law 185.

[38] See Zuckerman, *op cit.* n31, p.224; Law Commission, *Consultation Paper No. 141*, paras 7.36-7.41; Canter, *op cit.* n11, Ch.7.

[39] Law Commission Consultation Paper No.141, para 10.85. See McEwan, J. (1997) *Law Commission Dodges the Nettles in Consultation Paper No 141.* Crim. L.R. 93.

[40] [1991] 2 A.C. 447.

[41] Lord Cross of Chelsea in *R v Boardman* [1975] A.C. 421, p.457. There need not be similarity e.g. where D steals from house A and then drops his swag in house B where he commits a murder, the prosecution will be allowed to reveal his conviction for the burglary at the trial for the murder, even though this reveals a criminal conviction which has no similarity whatsoever. See *R v O'Meally* [1953] V.L.R. 30.

[42] As in a famous case such as *R v Smith* (1913) 11 Cr App R 229, and *Makin v Attorney General for New South Wales* [1894] A.C. 57.

[43] See Pattenden, R., "Similar Fact Evidence and the Proof of Identity" (1996) 112 L.Q.R. 446.

[44] *Barnes* [1996] Crim L.R. 39; [1995] 2 Cr App R 491. *R v Wharton* (1998) Crim. L.R. (Sept)

[45] *Downey* [1995] Crim L.R. 414; [1995] 1 Cr App R 547.

[46] This distinction is crucial: see the discussion of transposing the conditional below.

[47] Holmes and Holmes *op cit.* n8, p.44.

[48] Mair, K., "Can a profile prove a sex offender guilty?" (1995) Expert Evidence 139. On investigation and profiles see also Stevens, J.A. Standard Investigatory Tools and Offender Profiling. in Jackson, J.L. and Bekerian,

D.A. *op cit.* n11 and Oldfield, D. What Help Do the Police Need with their Enquiries? in Jackson, J.L. and Bekerian, D.A. *op cit.* n11

49 *Daubert v Merrel Dow Pharmaceutical Ltd* (1993) 1265 Led 2d 469, 485.

50 *per* Lord Sumner in *Thompson* [1918] A.C. 221, p.234.

51 See especially Mair *op cit.* n48, p.140; Canter, *op cit.* n11, Ch.3. See p.119 in Jackson, J.L. and Berian, D.A. Does Offender Profiling Have a Role to Play? Jackson, J.L. and Berkerian, D.A. *op cit.* n11.

52 McEwan, *op cit.* n36, p.118. On the potential for bias in the profile(r) see also the discussion of racial bias in Higgins, M. (1997) *Looking the Part.* American Bar Association Journal p.48.

53 See Vorpagel, *op cit.* n10, p.150; Douglas, J.E., Burgess, A.W., Burgess, A.G., and Ressler, R.K., *Crime Classification Manual* (1992) Lexington: New York, p.249. See also Smith, *op cit.* n12, p.249 and Turco, *op cit.* n13, p.150.

54 See Smith, *op cit.* n12, p.250; McCann, *op cit.* n13, p.479.

55 See generally: Hodgkinson, T., *Expert Evidence: Law and Practice* (1990) Sweet and Maxwell: London; Carson, D., "Expert Evidence in the Courts" (1992) 1 Expert Evidence 13; Gudjonsson, G.H., "The Implications of Poor Psychological Evidence in Court" (1993) 2(3) Expert Evidence 120; Freckleton, I.R., *The Trial of the Expert: A Study of Expert Evidence and Forensic Experts* (1987) OUP: Melbourne, pp.18-36; Jones, C.A.G., *Expert Witnesses: Science, Medicine and the Practice of Law* (1994) Clarendon Press: Oxford; Eggleston, *op cit.* n23, Ch.10; Haward, L.R.C., "The Psychologist as Expert Witness" in Farrington, D.P., Hawkins, K., and Lloyd-Bostock, S.M.A., (eds) *Psychology, Law and Legal Process* (1979) MacMillan: London; Roberts, P.R., "Will You Stand Up In Court? On the Admissibility of Psychiatric and Psychological Evidence." [1996] J. For. Psy. 63; American Federal Rules of Evidence r.702, and Slovenka, R., "Expert Testimony: Use and Abuse" (1993) 12 Medicine and Law 627. Gudjonsson, G.H. and Copson, G. The Role of the Expert in the Criminal Investigation. in Jackson, J.L. and Bekerian, D.A. *op cit.* n11.

56 *R v Silverlock* [1894] 2 Q.B. 766: "is he *peritus*? is he skilled? Has he adequate knowledge?" *per* Lord Russell C.J. p.771.

57 [1995] 2 Cr App R 333.

58 *R v Stockwell* (2993) 97 Cr App R 260

59 Para 9.77. "It should continue to be for the courts to assess the competence of expert witnesses. The professional bodies should, however, assist the courts in this task by maintaining a special register of their members who are suitably qualified to act as expert witnesses in particular areas of expertise." See also US Federal Rules of Evidence r.706.

60 Park Elliot Dietz, Associate Professor University of Virginia School of Law and Medicine, cited by Porter *op cit.* n9, p.47.

[61] A number of the notorious miscarriages of justice in the last decade were due at least in part to the inadequacy of the expert evidence: *Maguire* (1992) 94 Cr App R 133, *McIllkenny* (1991) 93 Cr App R 287, *Ward* (1993) 96 Cr App R 1. See also Zuckerman, A.A.S., "Miscarriage of Justice: A Root Treatment" [1992] Crim. L.R. 323.

[62] Sir Fredrick Lawton wrote extra-judicially of there being "liars, damned liars and expert witnesses." Lawton, F., "The Limitations of Expert Scientific Evidence" (1980) 20 J. For. Sci. Soc. 237, p.238.

[63] See Haward, L.R.C., " A Psychologist's Contribution to Legal Procedure" (1964) 27 M.L.R. 656, at p.657; Haward, L.R.C., "The Psychologist as Expert Witness" in Farrington, Hawkins and Lloyd-Bostock, *op cit.* n55; Clapham, B., "Introducing Psychological Evidence in the Courts: Impediments and Opportunities" in Lloyd-Bostock, S.M.A., (ed) *Psychology in Legal Contexts* (1981) MacMillan: London; Mackay, R.D., and Colman, A.M., "Excluding Expert Evidence: A Tale of Ordinary Folk and Common Experience" [1991] Crim. L.R. 800; Pattenden, R., "Conflicting Approaches to Psychiatric Evidence" [1992] Crim. L.R. 92, at p.99. See also Freckleton, *op cit.* n55, p.42.

[64] *Turner* [1975] Q.B. 834 *per* Lawton L.J. The difficulty in applying this test is well reported. See generally Mackay, R.D., and Colman, A.M., "Equivocal Rulings on Expert Psychological and Psychiatric Evidence: Turning a Muddle into a Nonsense" [1996] Crim L.R. 88; Thornton, P., "The Admissibility of Expert Psychiatric and Psychological Evidence: Judicial Training" (1995) 35 Med. Sci. Law 143; Sheldon, D.H., and MacLeod, M.D., "From Normative to Positive Data: Expert Psychological Evidence Re-Examined" [1991] Crim. L.R. 881; Pattenden, R., "Conflicting Approaches to Psychiatric Evidence in Criminal Trials: England, Canada and Australia" [1986] Crim. L.R. 92; Hodgkinson, *op cit.* n55, pp.229-232.

[65] Roberts, *op cit.* n55, p.67.

[66] See Slovenko, *op cit.* n55. See also the Canadian approach in *R v Abbey* (1982) 68 CCC (2d) 394.

[67] Psychology has been noted to be likely to fall foul of the *Turner* rule "not only because psychologists lack medical training but also by reason of the fact that psychology is a science devoted in the main to the study of normal behaviour". Mackay and Coleman, *op cit.* n64, p.801.

[68] Described as "(1) A comprehensive study of the nature of the criminal act and the type of persons who have committed this offence; (2) A thorough inspection of the specific crime scene involved in the case; (3) An in-depth examination of the background and activities of the victim(s) and any known suspects; (4) A formulation of the probable motivating factors of all parties involved; 95) The development of a description of the perpetrator based upon

the overt characteristics associated with his/her probable psychological makeup. Wolbert, A., (ed) *Rape and Sexual Assault: A Research Handbook* (1985) Garland: New York, p.344.

[69] Douglas, J.E., Ressler, R.K., Burgess, A.W., and Hartman, C.R., "Criminal Profiling from Crime Scene Analysis" (1986) 4(4) Behavioural Sciences and the Law 401, p.405.

[70] Pinizzotto and Finkel, *op cit.* n30, p.227; Canter, *op cit.* n11, p.150-1.

[71] The groups were provided with hypothetical cases, with known outcomes. The results showed that the profilers produced more detailed reports than the other groups, and were more accurate in profiling sexual offenders, but that they were not more accurate in profiling homicides. See also McCann, *op cit.* n 13, p.478.

[72] Vorpagel, *op cit.* n10, notes that "psychological profiles have not yet achieved the level required for probable cause to arrest, or to attain a search warrant, we feel that in the near future sufficient expertise will have been accumulated to allow a profiler to testify as an expert witness in court" p.162.

[73] *Frye v US* (1923) 293 F 1013 (D.C. Cir). See Freckleton, *op cit.* n55, p.60-67.

[74] 113 S Ct 2786; 125 L Ed 2d 469 on which see *inter alia* [1994] 84(4) J. Crim Law and Criminology especially , Allen, R.J., "Expertise and the *Daubert* Decision" [1994] 84(4) J. Crim Law and Criminology 1157; "Confronting the New Challenges of Scientific Evidence" (1995) 108 Harv. L.R. 1481-1605; Edmond, g., and Mercer, D., "Recognising Daubert. What judges need to know about falsificationism". (1997) Expert Evidence 29. See also Bernstein, D.E., "Junk Science in the United States and the Commonwealth" 91996) 21 Yale Journal of International Law 123.

[75] *per* Sopinka J at p.25.

[76] See also Alldridge, O., "Novel Scientific Techniques: DNA as a Test Case" Crom. L.R. 687, p.692; Freckleton, *op cit.* n55, Ch.4. and pp.165-174; Bessner, R., "The Admissibility of Novel Scientific Techniques in Criminal Trials: Voice Spectroscopy" (1987-88) 30 Crim. L.Q. 294; Giannelli, P.C., "The Admissibility of Novel Scientific Evidence: *Frye v United States*, a Half Century Later" (1980) 80 Columbia Law Rev. 1197.

[77] (1991) 93 Cr App R 161. See also Alldridge, *op cit.* n76, p.694.

[78] With respect, even a soothsayer or an astrologer could give evidence as an expert, but only on matters relating to their beliefs or customs or that upon which they were qualified. The reason that astrologers and such like are not permitted to give expert evidence on the likelihood of guilt of an accused is that their evidence is irrelevant, as discussed above, in that it cannot be established to be reliable enough to support any proposition relating to guilt. Even a magician has been called to give evidence on the "fraudulent manipulation of coins". *Moore v Medley* (1955) *The Times* 3rd Feb as noted

in Smith, J.C., *Criminal Evidence* (1995) Sweet and Maxwell: London, p.113.

[79] At p.164, referring to Kenny, A., "The Expert in Court" (1983) 99 L.Q.R. 197.

[80] (1993) 97 Cr App R 260.

[81] At p.264 (emphasis added).

[82] Goldring, S.L., "Increasing the reliability, validity and relevance of psychological expert evidence: An introduction to the special issue on expert evidence" 91992) 16 Law and Human Behaviour 253 cited in Editorial Introduction, "Some Legal Issues Affecting Novel Forms of Expert Evidence" (1992) 1 Expert Evidence 79, p.79.

[83] For example, more weight attaches to finger-print evidence than to identification by facial-mapping.

[84] 88 of 192 requests led to the suspect being identified from the profile: Pinizzotto, *op cit.* n13, p.39. See further Ressler et al, *op cit.* n53, p.346. Gudjonsson, G.H. and Copson, G. The Role of the Expert in the Criminal Investigation. at p.73 in Jackson, J.L. and Bekerian, D.A. *op cit.* n11.

[85] Hazelwood, R.R., and Douglas, J.E., "The lust murderer" (1983) 49(4) FBI Law Enforcement Bulletin 18.

[86] Boon and Davies, *op cit.* n9, p.221.

[87] Grubin, D., "Offender Profiling" (1995) 6(2) Journal of Forensic Psychiatry 259, p.261; McCann *op cit.* n13, p.476. See also Editorial Introduction, *op cit.* n55, p.16.

[88] "Psychological research can seldom be of [a] strictly scientific character - 'controls' and 'subjects', with human characteristics are quite unlike chemicals, acids, atoms, electrons or neutrons." Clapham, *op cit.* n63, p.98.

[89] *Op cit.* n48.

[90] See *Aggassiz v London Tramway Company* (1872) 27 L.T. 492.

[91] Slovenko, *op cit.* n55, p.636.

[92] (1982) 88 NJ 508; 443 A 2d 1021.

[93] See Gudjonsson, G.H., "The Implications of Poor Psychological Evidence in Court" (1993) 2(3) Expert Evidence 120, p.122 listing these as key problems.

[94] *Op cit.* n87, p.260.

[95] Douglas, J.E., Burgess, A.W., Burgess, A.G., and Ressler, R.K. *Crime Classification Manual* (1992) Lexington: New York. See Jackson, J.L. and Bekerian, D.A. "Does Offender Profiling Have a Role to Play?" and Bekerian, D.A. and Jackson, J.L. "Critical Issues in Offender Profiling" in Jackson, J.L. and Bekerian, D.A. *op cit.* n11.

[96] *Diagnostic and Statistical Manual of Mental Disorder*, 4th ed, (1994) American Psychiatric Association: Washington DC; McCann *op cit.* n13, p.478. On whether psychiatry really is a science, see Kenny, *op cit.* n79.

[97] At p.38, *per* Sopinka J.

---

98 See Canter, *op cit.* n11, Ch.4. See also Davies, A. "Specific Profile Analysis: A Data-based Approach to Offender Profiling" in Jackson, J.L. and Bekerian, D.A. *op cit.* n11.

99 See Robertson, B., Vignaux, G.A., and Egerton, I. "Stylometric Evidence" [1994] Crim L.R. 645. See also Editorial Introduction, *op cit.* n82.

100 Pinizzotto, *op cit.* n13, p.35.

101 See Canter, D. and Gregory, A, "Identifying the residential location of rapists" (1994) 34(3) J. For. Sci. Soc. 169; Davies, A., and Dale, A., "Locating the Stranger Rapist" (1996) Med. Sci. Law 146.

102 Kenny, *op cit.* n79. "[C]ourts should place confidence in social science research to the extent that the research (a) has survived the critical review of the scientific community, (b) has valid research methods, (c) is generalizable to the legal question at issue, and (d) is supported by a body of other research": Monahan, J. and Walker, L., *Social Science in Law: Cases and Materials* (2nd ed 1990) Foundation Press: New York, p.468.

103 See Britton, *op cit.* n2.

104 There are numerous problems with court appointed experts: When is he to be appointed? How is he to be selected? Should the prosecution or the defence have a right to object to the proposed court expert? How would the expert inform himself as to the relevant facts? Should either party be allowed to cross-examine the court expert? Should either party be allowed to call his own expert to contradict the court expert? Smith, *op cit.* n78, p.118.

105 The advantages of court-appointed experts and the neutral expert is discussed in full in Howard, M.N., "The Neutral Expert: A Plausible Threat to Justice" [1991] Crim. L.R. 98 and Spencer, J.R., "The Neutral Expert: An Implausible Bogey" [1991] Crim. L.R. 106. See Sheldon, D.H. and MacLeod, M.D., "From Normative to Positive Data: expert psychological evidence re-examined" [1991] Crim. L.R. 811, 819. See also Freckleton, *op cit.* n55, Ch.11. See also McEwan, *op cit.* n31, p.138.

106 Gudjonsson, *op cit.* n93, p.122 notes that this 'eagerness to please' is a major problem for expert evidence in general. See Howard *op cit.* n105, p.101 and Spencer *op cit.* n105, p.107.

107 *R v Wright* (1821) Russ and Ry 456, 458.

108 (1993) 97 Cr App R 260, p.265. See generally, Jackson, J.D., "The Ultimate Issue Rule: One rule too many" [1984] Crim. L.R. 74, and May, R., *Criminal Evidence* (3rd ed 1995) Sweet and Maxwell: London, para 8-04 - 8-06; Hodgkinson, *op cit.* n55, p.150.

109 Freckleton, *op cit.* n55, p.76. "The fact that an expert witness has impressive scientific qualifications does not by that fact alone make his opinion on matters of human nature and behaviour within the limits of normality any more helpful than that of the jurors themselves; but there is a danger that the jury may think

it does." *per* Lawton L.J. in *Turner* [1975] Q.B. 834, p.840.

110 There is a historic but largely redundant exception which allows for a witness to testify as to the "general reputation for untruthfulness" of another. This is very rarely relied upon: *Toohey v M.P.C.* [1965] A.C. 595; *R v Bogie* [1982] Crim L.R. 301. See the discussion of the Royal Newfoundland Constabulary Criminal Behaviour Analysis Unit in House, J.C. "Towards a Practical Application of Offender Profiling: The RNC's Criminal Suspect Prioritization System" in Jackson, J.L. and Bekerian, D.A. *op cit.* n11.

111 Meaning simply an inference drawn from the facts: May, R., *Criminal Evidence* 3rd ed (1995) Sweet and Maxwell: London, p.157.

112 See Hodgkinson, *op cit.* n55, Part B.

113 See Carson, *op cit.* n55; Hodgkinson, *op cit.* n55.

114 Clapham, *op cit.*, n63; Carson, D., *Professionals and the Courts: A Handbook for Expert Witnesses* (1990) Venture Press: Birmingham.

115 See Balding, D.J. and Donnelly, P., "The Prosecutor's Fallacy and DNA Evidence" [1994] Crim L.R. 711. On DNA see also Gill, P., and Fedor, T., "DNA Profiling: Is It Reliable?" Sol. J 3 Dec 26; McLeod, N., "English DNA Evidence Held Inadmissible" [1991] Crim. L.R. 58. The 'DNA reliability war' which rages in the USA is discussed in: Thompson, W.C., "Evaluating the Admissibility of New Genetic Identification Tests: Lessons from the 'DNA Wars' (1993) 84 J. Crim. Law and Criminology 22; Harmon, R.P., "Legal Criticisms of DNA Typing: Where's the Beef?" (1993) 84 J. Crim. Law and Criminology 175; Neufeld, P.J., "Have You No Sense of Decency" (1993) 84 J. Crim. Law and Criminology 189; Farrington, "Unacceptable Evidence" (1993) 143 N.L.J. 806, and 857; Cellmark Diagnostics (1993) 143 N.L.J. 1596; Redmayne, M., "Doubts and Burdens: DNA Evidence, Probability and the Courts" [1995] Crim. L.R. 464; Alldridge, P., "Recognising Novel Scientific Techniques: DNA as a test case" [1992] Crim. L.R. 687; Young, S.J., "DNA Evidence - Beyond Reasonable Doubt?" [1991] Crim. L.R. 264.

116 [1997] Crim. L.R. 669. See also Redmayne, M. "The DNA Database: Civil Liberty and Evidentiary Issues" [1998] Crim. L.R. 437 and Hunter, K. "A New Direction on DNA" [1998] Crim. L.R. 478, and the Criminal Evidence (Amendment) Act 1997.

117 On the use of the hypothetical question and the expert see Jones, *op cit.* n55, pp.110-127. On hypothetical questions and the relationship to adverse trials see Carson, *op cit.* n55, p.16.

118 Balding and Donnelly, *op cit.* n115, p.713.

119 See *R v Adams* [1996] Crim L.R. 898; *R v Doheny* [1997] Crim L.R. 669. See also the discussion of the notorious US case *State v Collins* in Eggleston *op cit.* n23, p.142 and by Haward *op cit.* n55, p.49; Redmayne, M., "Doubts and

Burdens: DNA Evidence, Probability and the Courts" [1995] Crim. L.R. 464; Robertson, B., and Vignaux, G.A., "Probability - The Law of Logic" (1993) 13 O.J.L.S. 457; Robertson, B., and Vignaux, G.A., *Interpreting Evidence: Evaluating Forensic Science in the Courtroom* (1995) Wiley: Chichester; Redmayne, M., "Science Evidence and Logic" (1996) 59 M.L.R. 747.

[120] [1996] Crim. L.R. 898. See also *R v Adams* (No.2) [1998] 1 Cr App R 377. As Lord Bingham of Cornhill, the Lord Chief Justice noted, "in the light of previous rulings on this matter in this Court, and having had the opportunity of considering the [matter], we regard the reliance on evidence of this kind in such a case as a recipe for confusion, misunderstanding and misjudgement, possibly even among counsel, but very probably among judges and, as we conclude, almost certainly among jurors". p.384.

[121] *Per* Lawton L.J. *Turner* [1975] Q.B. 834, 840. See Freckleton, *op cit.* n55, Ch.6.

[122] *Turner* [1975] Q.B. 834, 840 per Lawton L.J.

[123] *Per* Lord Havers in *R v Sharp* [1987] 1 W.L.R. 7, p.11 approving Tapper, C., ed *Cross on Evidence* (6th ed 1985) Butterworths: London, p.38.

[124] Canter, D., and Kirby, S., "Prior Convictions of Child Molesters" (1995) Science and Justice 73, 75. "The data is obtained from a reliable and properly documented source which is arguably more robust than relying on an individual's account." Reliability is no exception to hearsay!

[125] *Bradshaw* (1985) 82 Cr App R 79; *Turner* [1975] Q.B. 834; *Abadom* (1983) 76 Cr App R 48.

[126] Canter and Kirby, *op cit.* n124, p.75. See also Davies and Dale, *op cit.* n101.

[127] [1996] Crim. L.R. 732.

[128] (1997) H.M.S.O.: London.

[129] [1983] 1 W.L.R. 126.

[130] See Report No.245, *Evidence in Criminal Proceedings: Hearsay and Related Topics* (1997) H.M.S.O.: London. See Tapper, C. "Hearsay in Criminal Cases: An Overview of Law Commission Report No.245" [1997] Crim. L.R. 771.

[131] It is possible that the records, because they are police records would be classified as documents created in the course of a criminal investigation. If this is the case, the statute imposes a number of other conditions before the material can be admitted, and even then it still remains at the discretion of the judge. This would also arguably apply to all self-report statistics.

[132] Boon and Davies, *op cit.* n9.

[133] FBI's NCAVC - National Centre for the Analysis of Violent Crime and VICAP - Violent Criminal Apprehension Programme both rely heavily on computer analysis of data. This is discussed at length in Douglas, et al *op cit.* n53 and Ressler, R.K., Burgess, A.W. and Douglas, J.E., *Sexual Homicide:*

Patterns and Motives (1988) Lexington: New York, pp.111-119. See Wolbert, *op cit.* n68, pp.347-9, and http://www.fbi.gov.vicap. House, J.C. "Towards a Practical Application of Offender Profiling: the RNC's Criminal Suspect Prioritization System"; Farrington, D.P. and Lambert, S. "Predicting Offender Profiles from Victims and Witness Descriptions" and Davies, A. "Specific Profile Analysis: A Data-based Approach to Offender Profiling" in Jackson, J.L. and Bekerian, D.A. *op cit.* n11.

134 Canter, *op cit.* n11, p.237.

135 See Pinizzotto, *op cit.* n13, p.38; Canter, *op cit.* n11, pp.12-14.

136 [1993] Crim L.R. 48.

137 [1997] 1 All E.R. 737.

138 [1988] R.T.R. 52.

139 [1995] Crim L.R. 232.

140 This has been heavily criticised since the computer document is being put to use by the court without being subjected to the test of reliability which s.69 provides.

141 *Smurthwaite* (1994) 98 Cr App R 437; *Christou* [1992] 2 Q.B. 979; *Bryce* (1994) 95 Cr App R 320; *Bailey and Smith* [1993] 3 All E.R. 523.

142 Ognall J described as "highly disingenuous" the prosecution's claim that the undercover operation was to afford Stagg the opportunity of eliminating himself from the enquiry. The conduct of the investigation was "thoroughly reprehensible" and displayed "not merely an excess of zeal but a substantial attempt to incriminate a suspect by positive and deceptive conduct of the grossest kind" (Transcript, p.21). In conclusion, his lordship ruled that the conduct of a fair trial demanded the exclusion of the evidence.

143 Transcript, p.9.

144 [1996] 1 W.L.R. 104.

145 *Per* Lord Steyn, p.113.

146 [1992] Crim. L.R. 735. See Farrington, D.P. and Lambert, S. "Predicting Offender Profiles from Victims and Witness Descriptions" in Jackson, J.L. and Bekerian, D.A. *op cit.* n11.

147 See also McCann, *op cit.* n13 for consideration of this in serial offences.

148 [1994] 2 S.C.R. 9, at p.19 *per* Sopinka J. (emphasis added).

149 *Per* Winncke C.J. in *R v Lavery and King* (No 3) [1992] V.R. 939, P.947.

150 [1994] 2 S.C.R. 9.

151 At p.27.

152 (1865) Le & Ca 520 (CCR).

153 See *R v Redgrave* (1981) 74 Cr App R 10. Cf Slovenko, *op cit.* n55, p.635 on the US position.

154 Cf the Canadian case of *R v Lupien* [1970] S.C.R. 263, and see Mewett, A.W., "Character as a Fact in Issue in Criminal Cases" (1984) 27 Crim. L.Q. 29.

---

[155] May, *op cit.* n108, para 7.13.

[156] See e.g.. McEwan, J., *Evidence and the Adversarial Process: The Modern Law* (1992) Blackwell: London, p.154; Tapper, C., *op cit.* n15, p.353.

[157] See e.g. *R v Redgrave* 91982) 74 Cr App R 10; *R v Kinsella, Kinsella and MacFhlionn* [1995] Crim L.R. 731 and commentary.

[158] *Toohey v M.P.C.* [1965] A.C. 595. See further text accompanying n110 above.

[159] [1974] A.C. 85. See Tapper and Cross, *op cit.* n15, pp.355-356; Hodgkinson, *op cit.* n55, p.239; Freckleton, *op cit.* n55, p.47; Eggleston, *op cit.* n23, p.134. See also Elliott, D.W., "Cut-Throat Tactics: the freedom of an accused to prejudice a co-accused" [1991] Crim. L.R. 5; *R v Mohan* [1994] 2 S.C.R. 9.

[160] *Per* Lawton L.J. in *Turner* [195] Q.B. 834, p.842. See also *Neale* (1977) 65 Cr App R 304.

[161] [1974] A.C. 85, p.101.

[162] Thornton, *op cit.* n64, 147.

[163] In this regard it is similar to *Bracewell* (1979) 68 Cr App R 44, in which B was entitled to rebut the suggestion that his co-accused, A, was a cool professional burglar unlikely to indulge in violence.

[164] [1975] Q.B. 834, 840.

[165] (1952) 36 Cr App R 169, p.172.

[166] See, for example, the recent case of *Kracher* [1995] Crim. L.R. 819. See also the strict approach taken in *R v Neale* (1978) 65 Cr App R 304; *R v Knutton and England* (1992) 97 Cr App R 115; *R v Nightingale* [1977] Crim. L.R. 744.

[167] (1977) 65 Cr App R 304.

[168] Ormerod, L.J. in *Bracewell* stated that "where the evidence is tendered by a co-accused the test of relevance must be applied, and applied strictly." (1979) 68 Cr App R 44, p.50; *Knutton* (1993) 97 Cr App R 114.

[169] See Andres, J.A. and Hirst, M., *Criminal Evidence* (2nd ed 1992) Sweet and Maxwell; London, para 15-06.

[170] [1986] A.C. 41.

[171] See Choo, *op cit.* n18, and for a further discussion see Tapper *op cit.* n15, p.356.171.

[172] There is no rule preventing a verdict on circumstantial evidence along: cf *Onufrejczyk* [1955] Q.B. 388, in which D was convicted of murder on circumstantial evidence without a body.

[173] Thornton, *op cit.* n64.

[174] Mair, *op cit.* n48, p.142.